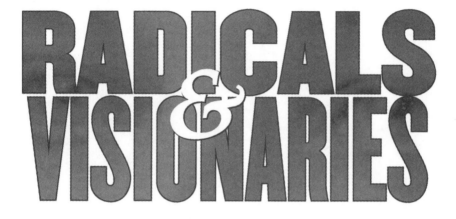

RADICALS & VISIONARIES

Thaddeus Wawro

International College
Information Resource Center
2655 Northbrooke Drive
Naples, Florida USA 34119
www.internationalcollege.edu

Entrepreneur Press
2445 McCabe Way, Irvine, CA 92614

Managing Editor: Marla Markman
Cover Design: Mark A. Kozak
Book Design: Sylvia H. Lee
Copy Editor: Alison Steiner Miller
Proofreader: Tammy Ditmore
Indexer: Ken DellaPenta
Production Assistants: William E. Gray,
Mia H. Ko, Marlene Natal

This publication is designed to provide accurate and authoritative information
in regard to the subject matter covered. It is sold with the understanding that
the publisher is not engaged in rendering legal, accounting or other
professional services. If legal advice or other expert assistance is required,
the services of a competent professional person should be sought.

Library of Congress Cataloging-in-Publication Data

Wawro, Thaddeus.
    Radicals and Visionaries: Entrepreneurs who revolutionized the 20th
century/by Thaddeus Wawro.
        p. cm.
    Includes index.
    ISBN 1-891984-13-6
    1. Businesspeople--United States--Biography. 2. Business enterprises--
United States--History. I.Title.
HC102.5.A2 W38 2000
338'.04'092273--dc21
[B]   00-020806
                            Printed in Canada
09 08 07 06 05 04 03 02 01 00   10 9 8 7 6 5 4 3 2 1

For my mother and father,
who believed in me even when I didn't.

Acknowledgments

I wish to express my deep appreciation to two special people without whom this book would not be possible. To my editor, Marla Markman, for having the trust and confidence in me to author this work. And to Sonya Shelton, whose help, support and encouragement were and always will be incalculable.

TABLE OF CONTENTS

INTRODUCTION

A greengrocer with no financial experience lays the foundation for the world's largest bank. A bright young telegraph operator proposes an idea for a "radio music box" and single-handedly paves the way for the modern mass media. A former cabaret singer thumbs her nose at the suffocating styles of the 19th century and sparks a revolution that will influence every designer who comes after her. A scrappy tinkerer drags a car frame along the dirt floor of a ramshackle garage with a rope and gives birth to mass production. A pregnant housewife starts a part-time business in her kitchen "to help make ends meet" and grows it into one of the most powerful catalog companies in the world. A computer programmer builds a simple Web page to indulge his girlfriend's passion for collecting Pez dispensers and creates a widely popular (and profitable) new form of commerce.

These are just a few of more than 70 entrepreneurs you'll meet in the following pages. They are visionaries and dreamers ... innovators and inventors ... mavericks and rebels ... trailblazers and pioneers ... men and women who, through talent, drive, ingenuity and desire, not only made their own dreams come true, but also shaped the past 100 years.

Few will argue the fact that the 20th century was an era of unprecedented progress, growth and accomplishment. This book tells the stories of the extraordinary individuals who fueled this wondrous explosion of achievement. Some, like Henry Ford, Sam Walton and Bill Gates, are legendary and their accomplishments well-documented. Others, like John Johnson, Sandra Kurtzig and Leonard Riggio, are unsung heroes whose contributions to culture, technology and business, though less obvious, have had profound and lasting effects on modern society.

The book does not attempt to rate each entrepreneur according to their importance, influence or accomplishments, but to explore the events that shaped their lives, to provide greater insight into the forces that drove them, and to define each one's role in the making of the 20th century. Although their tales of self-made success are unique, one common thread weaves throughout each entrepreneur's life story: There is no single path to success, nor a clear set of rules for getting there. In fact, you'll find that quite often it was by breaking existing rules or writing new ones that many of these empire builders attained their goals.

But while great entrepreneurs are often portrayed as heroes, and in most cases their achievements are indeed heroic, it is important to remember that they are also human. They have their faults and failings, and they face many of the same obstacles we all do in life. I believe it is that "humanness" that makes their stories so compelling. For in overcoming the obstacles of everyday life, they provide a shining example of what we can all achieve through hard work, self-determination and a willingness to venture out of the safety of convention and into the unknown.

Marc Andreessen

Co-founder of
Netscape
Communications Corp.
Founded: 1994

*"**R**ight now, today, with a little luck and brains and timing, any kid with a computer can do what Netscape has done. There are no barriers to entry anymore. Any kid can spark a revolution."*

—Marc Andreessen

INTERNET EVANGELIST

To some, Netscape Communications co-founder Marc Andreessen is a cyberspace folk hero whose programming savvy made the vast resources of the Internet's World Wide Web available to anyone with a computer and modem. To others, he's little more than a computer hacker who rode to the top on the accomplishments of others. But no matter how his supporters and detractors may feel about him, Andreessen is indeed a visionary, whose dream of creating an easy-to-use Web browser revolutionized information technology, sparked the Internet boom of the 1990s, and laid the groundwork for one of the fastest-growing companies in U.S. history.

Born in rural Cedar Falls, Iowa, in 1971, Andreessen seemed destined for a career in computers from the very beginning. Growing up in a town where football was king, Andreessen had little interest in sports. Instead, he turned his attention to computers. At age 8, while most of his friends were dreaming of scoring touchdowns for the nearby University of Illinois, Andreessen began teaching himself the BASIC programming language from a library book. By the time he'd reached the sixth grade, Andreessen had created a virtual calculator to do his math homework. By the seventh grade, he was writing his own games to play on his family's Commodore 64 computer.

Even though he seemed to be a natural computer prodigy, Andreessen had little interest in pursuing computer science as a career when he enrolled at the University of Illinois at Urbana-Champaign. "Actually, I thought I'd go into electrical engineering," he admits in a January 1996 *Nation's Business* interview. "I knew that electrical engineers got paid on average the most in the engineering field. I ended up in computer science largely because it required the least amount of work."

For most of Andreessen's college career, he was pretty much the model slacker, doing only enough work for him to get by.

("I'm a big fan of work avoidance," he reveals in a *Rolling Stone* interview.) But that changed during his senior year in 1992, when Andreessen took a $6.85-per-hour programming job at the university's high-tech think tank, the National Center for Supercomputing Applications (NCSA). It was there that he first gained access to the Internet. At that time, the Web was a crude, text-based network accessible only through primitive interfaces. And although the Web contained literally volumes of useful information, "you were still expected to be a rocket scientist to actually access anything," Andreessen recalls.

The Good, The Bad And The...Cleanly?

Marc Andreessen's phenomenal success with Netscape Communications Corp. has generated quite a bit of press...some good, some bad. Here's what a few of his supporters and detractors have had to say about him.

- "Marc's sort of a folk icon among Gen Xers and other young people turned on by the Web. It doesn't hurt that he's made a fortune. He mixes youthful idealism with the capitalism that's in now."

  —Jerry Michalski, editor, Release 1.0

- "Marc is no fun to work with. He tries very hard to make sure anything he touches he gets credit for."

  —Joseph Hardin, former National Center for Supercomputing Applications colleague

- "He has the curiosity that you see in brilliant people. When Marc doesn't know about something he thinks he needs to understand, he gets a book and talks to people and learns. The guy has a knowledge base that's just incredible."

  —Bill Gurely, Internet analyst, Deutshe Morgan Grenfell

- "[Andreessen's] true genius was taking credit for the work of others; his brilliant insight, that he could profit mightily from the ideas and achievements of a number of naive idealists in his academic field."

  —Alan Deutschman, Gentlemen's Quarterly magazine

- "He's not a typical computer nerd. He's well-dressed and bathes a lot."

  —Elizabeth Horn, Marc Andreessen's fiancee

Andreessen immediately saw a potential market for an easy-to-use browser, and in one sleepless weekend in 1993, he hacked out a crude prototype. He showed his prototype to his friend, gifted hacker Eric Bina, and in just six weeks, Andreessen, Bina and several other NCSA colleagues built it into a fully functioning browser they called Mosaic. They made the program available free of charge over the Internet, and within a year more than 2 million copies had been downloaded.

After graduation, Andreessen was offered a job with the small Silicon Valley firm Enterprise Integration Technologies. The story of Marc Andreessen may have ended right there and then, with him spending the rest of his life designing security software for Internet transactions. But fate had other plans for Andreessen.

A few miles down Highway 101 from where Andreessen worked, Jim Clark, founder of Silicon Graphics (SGI), had recently left the company and was looking to start a new business venture. He asked one of the SGI engineers if he knew any bright up-and-comers in the high-tech industry. The engineer mentioned only one name—Marc Andreessen.

Wasting no time, Clark fired off an e-mail to Andreessen proposing a meeting. It was an offer Andreessen couldn't refuse. Clark's initial idea was to produce software for interactive television. He believed a browser would be the ideal interface for interactive TV subscribers. But Andreessen had other ideas, and after explaining the World Wide Web to Clark, quickly convinced him that they should focus on making browsers and servers for the Internet instead.

Using $4 million of Clark's money, the duo founded Mosaic Communications Corp. in April 1994. (Six months later, they changed the name to Netscape after the University of Illinois claimed it owned the rights to the name Mosaic.) Andreessen's first move was to recruit some of his former colleagues from NCSA, including his old friend and Mosaic co-developer, Eric Bina. By the year's end, Andreessen's "dream team" had created a more powerful, more polished version of Mosaic, which they dubbed Mozilla—short for Mosaic Killer. Fortunately, cooler marketing heads prevailed and the browser was officially named Netscape Navigator.

In a brilliant move to generate a user base, Navigator, like

Mosaic, was launched free of charge on the Internet (although the company would eventually begin charging for the program, offering free 90-day trials instead). The browser immediately ruled the Net, claiming nearly 75 percent of the browser market.

With the success of Navigator, a few changes were needed at Netscape. From three employees in April 1994, the company had grown to 200 employees by the end of May 1995. To keep the start-up from growing out of control, Clark and Andreessen hired former FedEx senior executive Jim Barksdale to serve as CEO. With Andreessen as software guru, Clark providing the capital and Barksdale overseeing operations, Netscape expanded its product line to include high-end, high-priced software tools that companies could use to create and maintain their own Web sites, and they established virtual stores to conduct secure transactions over the Net.

By August 1995, with $16.6 million in sales but no profits, Netscape went public. Initially offered at $28 a share, Netscape's 5 million shares of stock immediately

Truth Be Told

It is a widely held belief that Marc Andreessen's Mosaic was the first Web browser. It was not. By the time Andreessen began working on Mosaic in November 1992, there were already several Web browsers designed for nontechies on the market . The initial version of Mosaic (and later, Navigator) drew on the innovations of earlier browsers, which already included many features aimed at making the Web easier to navigate, such as icon buttons (back, forward, home, for example), bookmarks (for keeping track of favorite Web sites) and a variety of fonts and typefaces.

What made Mosaic unique was that it overcame two problems that had plagued earlier Web browsers. First, Mosaic was easy to get up and running. Second, it was the first browser that could automatically display graphics along with text. It was the proliferation of pictures that transformed the Web from the insular domain of scientists and hackers to a cultural phenomenon that captured the attention of the masses and created a multimillion-dollar consumer Internet industry.

began trading at $71. When the stock market closed, Andreessen, then just 23, was worth $58 million. By December, the value of Andreessen's stock had risen to $174 million.

Netscape Navigator's success did not go unnoticed by software giant Microsoft. Since Navigator's debut in 1994, Microsoft had been working on its own browser and in December 1995 released Microsoft Internet Explorer, sparking what would become known as "the browser wars."

Initially, Navigator maintained its lead in the browser market, but Microsoft eventually usurped Netscape's dominance by bundling Internet Explorer with Microsoft Windows, effectively putting the browser directly on millions of Windows desktops. As a result, Andreessen and Netscape radically changed their strategy. Rather than focusing solely on the Internet, Netscape turned its attention to Intranets, producing software to run within corporate networks.

Andreessen's role in the company also shifted. As Netscape lost its market dominance, Andreessen faded into the background, while Netscape CEO Jim Barksdale emerged as the new face and driving force of the company. Andreessen remained with Netscape as its "principal technology visionary," but Barksdale was clearly in charge. No longer able to compete with Microsoft, Barksdale brokered a deal with AOL in December 1998 to sell Netscape for $4.2 billion. Under the terms of the buyout, Andreessen was named chief technology officer (CTO) of AOL, but his actual role within the company and his part in day-to-day operations remained vague. In fact, Andreessen seemed to be little more than a figurehead.

Wanting to play a more active role in the evolution of the Internet, Andreessen joined the board of directors of Accompany Inc.—the first Internet-based buying network to offer products and services in real time—in July 1999. He eventually stepped down as AOL's CTO in September 1999 to spend more time working with Internet start-up companies.

While Marc Andreessen's future in the world of Internet technology may be cloudy, his legacy is firmly entrenched in the annals of online history. As Netscape's technological leader and visionary, he set the standard for Internet browsers, providing an easy-to-use "on-ramp" to the information superhighway for millions of computer users and dramatically changing the way businesses access and use the Internet—paving the way for e-business and e-commerce.

Desi Arnaz & Lucille Ball

> *"**I** nstead of divorce lawyers profiting from our mistakes, we thought we'd profit from them."*
> —Lucille Ball

Co-founders of Desilu Productions
Founded: 1950

THE FIRST FAMILY OF TELEVISION

When the creators of such mega-hits as "Friends," "Seinfeld" and "ER" cash their hefty syndication residual checks, they should take a moment to pay homage to Desi Arnaz and Lucille Ball—two of the savviest and most innovative entrepreneurs ever to grace the star-studded streets of Tinseltown. In addition to laying the groundwork for the multibillion-dollar television syndication industry, they introduced many of the production techniques that would become standard television practice and almost single-handedly made Hollywood the television capital of the world.

The couple met in 1940 on the set of the RKO Studios musical "Too Many Girls." It was a classic case of love at first sight, and they married later that same year. But the first decade of their lives together would prove to be rocky. While Ball made pictures in Hollywood and gained fame as the star of the radio show "My Favorite Husband," Arnaz spent much of his time on the road touring with his band.

Arnaz's notorious womanizing, along with his excessive drinking, prompted Ball to file for divorce in 1944. But a passionate reconciliation led her to reconsider, and the lovers vowed to find more opportunities to work together. Their big chance came in 1950, when CBS approached Ball about moving "My Favorite Husband" to the fledgling medium of television. Seeing it as a chance to finally work with her real-life spouse, Ball asked the network to cast Arnaz in the role of her husband.

The network executives were reluctant, fearing viewers would have difficulty accepting the Cuban Arnaz as the husband of the all-American redhead. To prove that they could make the sitcom work, Arnaz and Ball formed Desilu Productions (the very first independent television production company) and used $5,000 of their own money to produce the pilot for "I Love Lucy." In doing so, Arnaz and Ball made themselves their own bosses, providing their product to CBS rather than working directly for the network or a sponsor, which was then the common practice in television.

This wasn't the only show biz convention the duo would shatter. In the early days of television, most production was done in New York, mainly because the Hollywood studios considered television to be a threat to their film empires. So, quite naturally, CBS expected Arnaz and Ball to move to New York. But the couple insisted on staying in Hollywood.

Again CBS protested, claiming that live production in Los Angeles was impractical. Because of the time difference between the coasts, the network would be forced to air blurry kinescopes in the East, where most television-viewing homes were located. Arnaz and Ball offered a simple solution: produce the show on film and dispense with kinescopes altogether. CBS wasn't exactly thrilled with this suggestion. Using film would double production costs. To offset the added cost, Arnaz and Ball agreed to cut their joint weekly salary from

Birth Of A Rerun

In the early days of television, shows were performed in New York and broadcast live to viewers on the East Coast. For viewers in other time zones to see the shows, they were recorded from a special television picture tube called a kinescope and rebroadcast at later times. These "kinescopes," as the recordings were called, were less clear than live broadcasts, and their quality tended to degrade as they were rebroadcast.

By insisting that "I Love Lucy" be recorded on film, which could be easily stored and broadcast over and over again without any degradation of picture quality, Desi Arnaz initiated the industry practice of airing reruns, which made summer hiatuses possible and opened up a new market for the sale of film rights.

$5,000 to $4,000 on the condition that Desilu would retain all rights to the show. CBS agreed, and in one fell swoop Arnaz and Ball invented reruns, paved the way for syndication, and pulled off what would become one of the most lucrative deals in television history.

"I Love Lucy" debuted in October 1951 and quickly became one of the top-rated shows on television. The show made production in Hollywood so acceptable that by 1961 virtually every major prime-time television show was filmed on the West Coast.

While Ball busied herself with the joys of motherhood (she gave birth to the couple's second child, Desi Jr., in 1953), Arnaz expanded the Desilu empire, producing an impressive roster of hits, including "The Ann Sothern Show," "The Untouchables" and "Sheriff of Cochise." As the growing company needed more space, Arnaz and Ball turned to the gold mine of "I Love Lucy" reruns they owned and sold the syndication rights to the first 180 episodes back to CBS for $5 million (approximately $19.5 million by today's standards).

Armed with the expansion capital they needed, the couple bought RKO Studios (Ball's former employer) in 1957. The 14-acre movie lot soon became home to such hits as "The Dick Van Dyke Show," "The Andy Griffith Show" and "My Three Sons," making Desilu a successful independent production house.

But even this tremendous success wasn't enough to keep the

star-crossed sweethearts together. The demands of running a corporation while still playing his role on "I Love Lucy" began to take their toll on Arnaz and the marriage. Arnaz's drinking became more excessive, and the couple would often break into violent arguments on the set of the show. So after 20 years together, Arnaz and Ball divorced in 1960.

By 1961, Ball had remarried and was starring in "The Lucy Show"—with ex-husband Arnaz directing. But it proved to be too much for Arnaz to handle, and in 1962, he asked Lucy to buy him out of Desilu. She paid him $2.5 million for his shares and became the first woman CEO of a major television and movie production company.

It was not the best time for such a first, however. Desilu's revenue was down, and movie studios were beginning to produce their own television shows, squeezing independent production companies out of business. Realizing she could not turn the company around on her own, Ball hired CBS executive Oskar Katz to be her executive vice president. At the time, the only show Desilu had in production was Lucy's. Katz believed the key to turning the company around was getting Desilu back into the business of production, so he produced "Star Trek" and "Mission Impossible." Based on the popularity of these now classic shows, Ball had succeeded in making Desilu profitable again by 1967. Her goal accomplished, she sold her shares of Desilu to Paramount Studios for $17 million.

By the time of their deaths in 1986 and 1989 respectively, Arnaz and Ball were firmly enshrined in the Television Hall of Fame, not merely for their talent as comedians, but for their groundbreaking contributions to the art and business of television production.

Mary Kay Ash

*Founder of
Mary Kay
Cosmetics Inc.
Founded: 1963*

*"Pretend that every single person you
meet has a sign around his or her
neck that says 'Make Me Feel Important.'
Not only will you succeed in business,
you will succeed in life."*

—Mary Kay Ash

A True Beauty Queen

Innovative, charismatic and contagiously optimistic, perhaps no woman has played a more important role in the advancement of women entrepreneurs than Mary Kay Ash. After experiencing firsthand the "glass ceiling" that kept many women from reaching top positions in the male-dominated corporate world, Ash envisioned a dream company where working mothers could determine their own levels of advancement and compensation, be their own bosses, and set work schedules that would still leave time for their children. The result of this vision was Mary Kay Cosmetics, a unique multilevel, direct-sales cosmetic firm that would provide hundreds of thousands of women with the opportunities Ash herself had been denied.

Like many business pioneers, Ash stumbled upon her entrepreneurial talents quite by accident. It happened in the latter half of the 1930s, when a door-to-door encyclopedia saleswoman struck a deal with Ash: If Ash could sell 10 sets of encyclopedias, the saleswoman would give her a set free of charge. Ash agreed and sold 10 sets in just a day and a half. This was a rather remarkable feat, considering 10 sets was the three-month quota for the company's most accomplished salespeople.

Believing she'd found her forte, Ash continued peddling encyclopedias part time and was soon earning enough money to help support her young family. Unfortunately, she also earned the wrath of many of her friends who accused her of selling them a product they didn't really need. Taking her customers' disdain to heart, Ash searched for a more useful product to sell. She turned to Stanley Home Products, a direct-sales company offering housewares and cleaning supplies.

Shortly after joining the company, Ash attended a convention at which Stanley's most successful saleswoman was crowned "Queen of Sales." Ever the competitor, Ash vowed that the next year she would be queen. To achieve her goal, she persuaded the reigning queen to hold a demonstration party, during which Ash transcribed her presentation word for word. True to her vow, the very next year Ash did indeed win the title.

A major turning point in Ash's life came when her husband returned home from World War II and ran off with another woman. With three children to support, Ash was forced to make Stanley Home Products her full-time career. But even though she quickly became a top sales producer, she watched in frustration as men who had less talent and knowledge were promoted ahead of her.

Fed up with being passed over, Ash joined the direct-sales firm World Gift Co. in 1952. Within 10 years, she had extended World Gift's distribution into 43 states and earned a position on the company's board of directors. But her suggestions were often dismissed by male members of the board with the comment, "Oh, Mary Kay, you're thinking just like woman"—a remark that never failed to enrage her. She finally quit in 1962, after a man she had trained was named her supervisor and given twice her salary.

Deciding to take an early retirement, Ash set out to write a guide to help other women avoid the pitfalls she'd faced in the male-dominated corporate world.

Pretty In Pink...And White And Red

When you mention Mary Kay Cosmetics Inc., the first thing most people think of is the pink Cadillacs rewarded to Mary Kay Ash's top consultants. The first awards were made more than 30 years ago in 1969, and today there are approximately 9,000 women driving pink Mary Kay Cadillacs and other Mary Kay career cars (including white GMC Jimmys, pink Grand Prixs and red Grand Ams). Valued at more than $140 million, the Mary Kay fleet is the largest commercial fleet of General Motors passenger cars in the world.

She composed two lists. The first outlined her negative experiences. The second detailed the qualities she thought would constitute an ideal business—a "dream company" for working women with families that would 1) treat everyone equally, 2) base promotions on merit and 3) choose products based on their sales performance and marketability, rather than profitability. Looking over the second list, Ash realized she'd created a workable direct-sales company and thought, "Why am I theorizing about a dream company? Why don't I just start one?" And that's exactly what she did.

First she needed to find a product. It had to be something women could believe in, that they could recommend with all their hearts, and, most important, a product that could be used up and re-ordered over and over. But where would she find such a product? Ironically, it was already sitting atop her bedroom dresser.

For nearly 10 years, Ash had been buying a skin softener from the daughter of a local hide tanner who had concocted the cream from tanning solutions. With her $5,000 life savings, Ash bought the recipe for the skin softener, furnished a small storefront in Dallas, and hired a local manufacturer to create a line of skin-care products based on the hide tanner's formula.

While her second husband dealt with the legal and financial matters, Ash recruited a sales force of nine of her friends. But one month before the company was scheduled to open, disaster struck. Ash's husband died of a heart attack. Convinced that she could not succeed without her husband's help, Ash's lawyer and accountant urged her to abandon her plans. But like most great entrepreneurs, Ash, who was then in her mid-40s, ignored the advice of "the experts," and Mary Kay Cosmetics opened its doors September 13, 1963.

From its inception, it was unique among direct-sales businesses. Instead of using high-pressure sales pitches, Ash instructed her salespeople (whom she christened "consultants") to show women how they could use Mary Kay products to improve their appearance. Once women saw the results, the products would sell themselves. It was a technique Ash claims no company had ever tried before.

Within three and a half months, sales of Mary Kay products totaled $34,000, and by the end of the first year, that figure had risen to an amazing $198,000. A year later, sales had quadrupled to $800,000. By that time, Mary Kay Cosmetics' sales force had grown to more than 3,000 consultants.

Keenly aware that customers became suspicious when she touted her own wares, Ash gave up direct selling and concentrated on motivating her consultants. She instilled her own infectious enthusiasm in her workers through a litany of maxims such as:

"I created this company for you."

"At Mary Kay you are in business for yourself, but not by yourself."

"God didn't have time to make a nobody. As a result, you can have, or be, anything you want."

"Fake it till you make it."

She also began rewarding her top beauty consultants with diamond jewelry, five-star vacations and, of course, the pink Cadillacs. It was a powerful success strategy that made Mary Kay Ash a millionaire when she took the company public in 1968.

By 1983, Mary Kay's sales had risen to $324 million. But as the company grew, shareholders began to question the necessity of rewarding consultants with "those frivolous pink cars." Knowing "those frivolous pink cars" were the backbone of her motivational scheme and a national symbol for her company, Ash decided she didn't need public money enough to jeopardize the very foundation of her business. Although "the experts" warned against it, Ash rebuffed their advice once again and took the company private in 1985. It proved to be a smart move: In 1993, the firm broke the $1 billion mark and

More Than Skin Deep

- In 1989, Mary Kay Cosmetics Inc. became one of the first in the cosmetics industry to cease animal testing.
- Mary Kay is the only company to be featured three times in Fortune magazine's "The 100 Best Companies to Work for in America."
- Mary Kay Ash is the only woman business leader profiled in the book Forbes Greatest Business Stories of All Time.

became the largest direct seller of skin-care products in the United States.

At present, there are more than 500,000 Mary Kay independent beauty consultants in 29 countries, generating more than $2 billion in sales per year. Even though Ash's son Richard Rogers now runs the company as chairman of the board, it is unlikely that Ash will ever retire from business completely. Today she serves as chair emeritus and is a nearly constant presence at the corporate headquarters.

When asked to name her greatest achievement, Mary Kay Ash proudly replies, "I think the biggest legacy we are going to leave is a whole community of children who believe they can do anything in this world because they watched their mamas do it."

Ian **B**allantine

"**I**an Ballantine took a chance on me when nobody else cared or dared. He was a giant."
—Bestselling author Tom Robbins

Founder of Bantam Books Inc. & Ballantine Books Inc.
Founded: 1945 (Bantam), 1952 (Ballantine)

PAPERBACK PIONEER

The founder of both Bantam Books Inc. and Ballantine Books, Ian Ballantine has been called "the father of the mass-market paperback." A literary visionary, unafraid to take chances on new writers, he has been credited with launching the careers of such bestselling authors as Arthur C. Clarke, Frederik Pohl and Tom Robbins. Ballantine's revolutionary strategy of offering affordable books to the general public made Ballantine Books one of America's largest publishers and laid the groundwork for the modern paperback industry.

The son of Scottish actor and sculptor Edward James Ballantine and theater publicist Stella (Commins) Ballantine, Ian initially had no particular interest in a business career. That changed, however, when a thesis Ballantine wrote on selling books in the United States while studying at the London School of Economics and Political Science caught the attention of Penguin Books Ltd. founder Allen Lane. In the thesis, Ballantine pointed out a loophole in the copyright law that would allow the importation of low-cost British paperbound books into the United States, something no publisher was doing at the time.

Intrigued by the tremendous moneymaking potential of this new market opportunity, Lane hired the 23-year-old Ballantine to organize and open a New York office of Penguin Books with the sole purpose of importing and distributing British books. Ballantine headed the office from 1939 to 1945. During that time, he realized there was a large potential market for paperbound reprints of books by American authors as well. Lane balked at the idea, but Ballantine was convinced it would work. So in 1945, he left Penguin and established Bantam Books Inc. to mass-market pocket-sized paperback reprints of hardcover novels. Early Bantam titles included works of great American authors such as F.

Scott Fitzgerald, John Steinbeck, Zane Grey, Mark Twain and James Thurber.

While he was president and director of Bantam, Ballantine began to study the trends in mass reading tastes and discovered a virtually untapped market for cheap paperbacks in an audience that couldn't afford the more expensive hardbacks. At the time, few publishers produced original paperbacks. Most of the paperbacks on the market were merely reprints of books originally printed in hardcover versions. To capitalize on the new market Ballantine uncovered, Bantam began producing a line of original books written solely to be published as inexpensive paperbacks. These 25-cent paperbacks were an immediate hit with middle- and working-class readers. And although most of Bantam's sales came from its line of fiction books—science fiction, western and horror titles with lurid covers that often depicted scantily clad women in suggestive poses—there were also some bestsellers among Bantam's nonfiction titles.

Determined to find out just how accurately he had predicted which books would appeal to the American reading public, Ballantine created a unique market research technique that would later become an industry standard. He sent people directly to book dealers to find out how many copies of each Bantam title were sold in key cities during a specific period of time.

Fantasy Found

One of Ballantine Books' most successful and acclaimed ventures wasn't started by Ian Ballantine, but by his wife, Betty. Published in the late 1960s and early 1970s, The Ballantine Adult Fantasy Series was the first-ever paperback fantasy series directed at the adult market rather than adolescents. This landmark set of 71 titles included novels, collections and anthologies—some reprints, others originals—and featured some of the finest fantastic literature ever written, including works by such esteemed writers as William Morris, Lord Dunsany, H.P. Lovecraft, Clark Ashton Smith, J.R.R. Tolkien, Edgar Allen Poe and even William Shakespeare.

The results of the impromptu survey proved that Ballantine did indeed have a knack for picking bestsellers. Between 1945 and 1948, his company averaged less than 1 percent of its books returned, a rate unheard of in the industry. Encouraged by the results, Ballantine announced that Bantam would begin a new marketing program for its bestsellers and would publish a monthly list of its eight leading reprint titles. This bestseller list, the first of its kind in the industry, greatly increased the sales of Bantam books as the public clamored to get its hands on the books "everyone was reading."

Ballantine's next groundbreaking innovation would come, literally, as the result of an accident. During a vacation in 1950, Ballantine broke his leg skiing. Forced to take a leave of absence from Bantam while he recovered, Ballantine used the time to formulate what David Dempsey of *The New York Times Book Review* calls "the most far-reaching development to hit Publisher's Row in a long time." Dempsey predicted that if it was successful, Ballantine's plan "could radically transform the whole conventional publishing setup."

The plan Ballantine formulated was to establish Ballantine Books, a new publishing house that would produce original fiction and nonfiction in hardbound editions starting at $1.50 while simultaneously releasing 35-cent paperbound editions. The hardbound editions, designed to appeal to the smaller "literary" market, would be offered only through bookstores, while Ballantine paperbacks would be sold from newsstands, where they could reach a larger audience and would not compete with the higher-priced hardcover editions.

It was truly a revolutionary idea. At the time, paperback versions were only published after a book had completely lost its momentum in hardcover. The controversial plan immediately caused a row among publishers who feared not only that no one would purchase the higher-priced hardbound editions, thereby driving bookstores out of business, but also that authors might lower the quality of their writing for mass production.

But Ballantine was a dedicated student of human nature, not to mention a brilliant marketer, and he had already figured out how to overcome such objections. First, he offered to co-publish with any publishers of hardbound books who wished to submit books on a single title basis. He explained to his fellow publishers that the additional capital generated by the cheaper paperbound editions would enable them to publish a greater number of hardcover books each year, thereby increasing their overall sales.

Second, to allay the fear that the quality of the books might suffer, Ballantine approached the Author's Guild Council of the Author's League of America with a unique proposal. He offered to pay authors a royalty of 10 percent on hardcover editions and 8 percent on paperbound editions, with a minimum guarantee of $5,000 in three months after publication. This represented a substantial increase in the royalty generally paid on paperback reprints, and, Ballantine claimed, would make it possible for the average author to devote full time to his or her writing instead of writing in the hours left over from a more lucrative job.

Some critics still lambasted Ballantine's plan, but they were quickly silenced when, contrary to what they'd predicted, the bottom did not fall out of the hardbound book market. Instead, sales of both paperback and hardbound books boomed.

Encouraged by the success of his plan, Ballantine set out to publish as many paperbound originals as possible. Originally, he'd planned to publish 30 titles a year, but by 1953, sales were so brisk he doubled the output to 60, or five per month. Although Ballantine initially focused on science fiction, publishing original books by such acclaimed authors as Ray Bradbury (*Fahrenheit 451*), Philip K. Dick (*Martian Time-Slip*), Theodore Sturgeon (*More Than Human*), and Anthony Burgess (*A Clockwork Orange*), he later branched out to other genres, including fantasies, westerns and mysteries.

Ballantine also broke new ground by publishing books that were ordinarily considered too literary for the paperbound market, including the favorably reviewed collections *New Poems by American Poets*, *New Short Novels* (which featured works by Jean Stafford, Elizabeth Etnier, Clyde Miller and Shelby Foote) and the bestselling *The Best American Short Stories*.

With Ballantine at the helm, Ballantine Books continued to flourish throughout the 1960s and 1970s, becoming America's largest publisher of mass-market paperback books. After selling Ballantine Books to Random House in 1973, Ballantine continued to work with selected authors at Bantam. In 1981, Ballantine and his wife, Betty, jointly founded Rufus Publications, which has published high-priced, limited-edition volumes of illustrated art and fantasy books, such as Frank McCarthy's *The Old West*, Brian Froud's *Faeries* and James Gurney's *Dinotopia*.

Nearly 43 years after Ian Ballantine uncovered a publishing pot of gold by establishing the mass-market paperback industry, he passed away in 1995 at his home in Bearsville, New York, leaving behind a living literary legacy that still bears his name. Upon Ballantine's death, bestselling author Tom Robbins commented, "Ian Ballantine took a chance on *Another Roadside Attraction* [Robbins' first published novel] when nobody else cared or dared. He was a short man. He was a giant."

Burton Baskin & Irvine Robbins

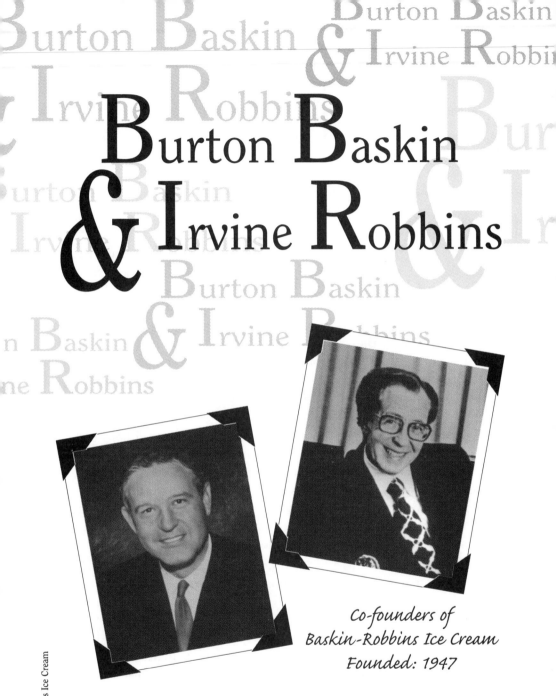

Co-founders of
Baskin-Robbins Ice Cream
Founded: 1947

"*You look at any giant corporation, and I mean the biggies, and they all started with a guy with an idea, doing it well.*"

—Irvine Robbins

ICE CREAM EMPERORS

Although Ben & Jerry may be famous for creating off-the-wall ice creams with names like Cherry Garcia, Wavy Gravy and Chunky Monkey, they weren't the first to build a business whipping up exotic frozen treats. That distinction belongs to another famous duo, Burt and Irv—better known as Baskin and Robbins. Their visionary idea of offering a different ice cream flavor for every day of the month, along with their unique franchise system, gave birth to the modern ice cream industry and paved the way for future superpremium ice cream makers such as Ben & Jerry's and Häagen-Dazs.

Born in Tacoma, Washington, Irv Robbins (pictured, left) got his early experience in the ice cream industry working in his father's ice cream and dairy store, where he noticed that people visited the store not only to buy ice cream, but also to take a break from the hustle and bustle of everyday life. "It wasn't like making a trip to the pharmacy or the grocery store," Robbins recalls. "It was a small, affordable, but very pleasurable treat."

Believing there was a market for ice cream beyond his father's ice cream parlor, Robbins toyed with the idea that he could offer his frozen delights through grocery and other retail stores. Realizing that most retail stores were interested in selling a lot of product, be it ice cream, bread or brooms, Robbins decided to give his ice cream an edge by staying up late at night preparing out-of-the-ordinary flavors and attention-grabbing signs. But he would no sooner place a sign in a grocer's store than another vendor would come by and take it down. As a result, Robbins' initial venture into the ice cream business was only moderately successful.

Robbins' ice cream dream was put on hold by a stint in the military during World War II. Upon returning home from the war, Robbins needed to find a venture to support his wife and child. While in the military, he'd come to the conclusion that offering his products through retail stores wasn't the best way to market his ice cream. Instead, he conceived the idea of opening a store where people could come in to take a break and enjoy exotic-flavored ice creams, just as they had in his father's store.

Initially, Robbins wanted to open a store in his hometown of Tacoma, but he was unable to find a suitable location. It was during a vacation to Los Angeles, while cruising the streets of Glendale, California, that he spotted a store for rent in a setting that seemed ideal for an ice cream parlor. So with $3,000 he'd saved from his military pay and another $3,000 from an insurance policy, he opened his first store—SnowBird—on December 7, 1945. People flocked to the small stand to sample Robbins' 21 different flavors, and encouraged by his success, Robbins quickly added two more stores.

While Robbins was laying the groundwork for what would become the world's most widely recognized ice cream chain, Burton Baskin was gaining his ice cream expertise half a world away as a Navy PX operator in New Hebrides (now Vanuatu). After obtaining an ice cream freezer from an aircraft carrier supply officer, the enterprising young Chicago native churned out creamy treats made from the South Pacific islands' vast array of tropical fruits for his fellow servicemen.

We All Scream For Ketchup Ice Cream?!

Not all Baskin-Robbins ice cream creations have enjoyed the sweet success of such classics as Tanganilla, Fudge Brownie and Jamoca Almond Fudge. Goody Goody Gumdrops, a flavor Irv Robbins created by mixing tiny gumdrops with vanilla ice cream, had to be pulled from the market when the company feared an unsuspecting customer might break a tooth on the gumdrops, which became rock hard when frozen in the ice cream. Other less than successful flavors include such dubious offerings as "Ketchup," "Lox and Bagels" and "Grape Britain."

During the war, Baskin married a lovely young woman named Shirley, who also happened to be Irv Robbins' sister.

When Baskin returned from the war, Robbins was about to open his fourth ice cream parlor. Instead, he offered it to his brother-in-law, saying, "You take it and do the same thing I'm doing." But the two didn't join forces right away. It wasn't necessarily that they were opposed to a partnership. They were simply heeding the advice of Irv's father, Aaron. No stranger to the pitfalls involved in the ice cream business (he'd owned his own ice cream parlor for nearly 20 years), the senior Robbins warned: "If you become partners right away, you'll compromise too many of your ideas in an effort to get along."

The advice proved sound, so after trying out their own ideas for about a year, the brothers-in-law were ready to become partners in 1947. The union was harmonious from the start because both men shared the same basic marketing philosophy—to sell nothing but ice cream, and in a multitude of flavors. The key to the strategy was offering exotic flavors. At the time, most ice cream parlors offered only a small selection of flavors: chocolate, vanilla and maybe strawberry. What would separate Baskin-Robbins from the crowd was its large flavor selection.

Initially, the duo's expectations were small, which was quite ironic considering their ultimate success. "We just wanted to make $75 a week. And we wanted to enjoy ourselves doing it," Robbins recalls. "Of course, when we reached our goal we upped it to $100, then $125 and so on."

By 1948, the partners were setting their sights on a much higher goal. They already owned nearly a dozen ice cream stores and wanted to launch more throughout Southern California. There was only one problem—they didn't have the capital needed to start those new stores. So instead of opening stores themselves, they decided to sell stores to their managers, thus becoming one of the nation's first ice cream parlor franchises. Under the franchise agreement, the company would furnish ice cream, merchandising aids and advertising, while the manager-owner would take care of the day-to-day operation of his or her store.

Fueled by the influx of capital provided by the franchising plan, the ice cream chain expanded rapidly, growing to 43 franchised stores by the end of 1949. To further spur sales and set their stores apart from other ice cream parlors, in 1953 Baskin and Robbins came up with the idea of offering 31 different flavors—one for every day of the month. To create a "buzz" for their bountiful selection, they gave their flavors offbeat names like ChaChaCha (cherry chocolate chip), Plum Nuts (plums, vanilla and walnuts) and Tanganilla (tangerine and vanilla). In addition, Baskin and Robbins rotated the mix of exotic flavors they sold to their franchisees so their selection would remain interesting to regular customers. The concept caught on, and Baskin-Robbins continues to use its "31 flavors" branding to this day.

In 1959, Baskin-Robbins made its debut outside California, when the brothers-in-law contracted with Lilly Ice Cream Co. to operate a Phoenix franchise. By 1960, the number of stores in the chain had passed the 100 mark, with new locations opening every few weeks.

In 1967, Baskin and Robbins sold their thriving ice cream empire, which by then consisted of 500 stores, to United Fruit (now United Brands) for an estimated $12 million. Less than six months after the deal was cut, 54-year-old Burton Baskin died unexpectedly. Irv Robbins remained with the company until his retirement in 1978. During that year alone, more than 20 million gallons of ice cream was sold in more than 2,000 Baskin-Robbins stores throughout the United States, Canada, Europe and Japan.

The company continued to grow after the departure of its sole surviving founder, and by 1983, Baskin-Robbins

To Top It All Off

While Ben & Jerry's and Häagen-Dazs have become major players in the ice cream market, Baskin-Robbins still reigns supreme. For 12 of the past 15 years, Baskin-Robbins has been voted "America's Favorite Sweets Chain" in the prestigious Restaurants and Institutions magazine survey, as well as receiving the highest overall rating for menu variety among all fast-service restaurant chains. In addition, Entrepreneur magazine has consistently ranked Baskin-Robbins as one of the top franchises in the United States.

could boast that during its 36 year history it had marketed close to 1,000 different flavors, many of which have become American classics.

Today, almost a half-century after Burt Baskin and Irv Robbins came up with the idea of having one flavor for every day of the month in a single ice cream store, Baskin-Robbins (now a wholly owned subsidiary of Allied Domecq PLC) is the world's largest ice cream chain, boasting more than 4,400 stores operating in more than 50 countries.

Leon L. Bean

Founder of
L.L. Bean Inc.
Founded: 1912

"Sell good merchandise at a reasonable profit, treat your customers like human beings, and they'll always come back for more."

—Leon L. Bean

COUNTRY SLICKER AND DEMON MERCHANDISER

Leon Leonwood Bean, known to his friends and loyal customers simply as "L.L.," never intended to become a mail order giant. All he really wanted to do was keep his feet dry. But there were much bigger plans in his future.

Like many entrepreneurs, Bean's early business pursuits were less than stellar. He'd achieved little success in various ventures ranging from selling soap to working in a creamery. But his unremarkable career began to change when he invented a unique product that would make him famous and become the cornerstone of one of the world's largest international mail order companies.

According to legend, in 1911, while managing his brother Ervin's store in Freeport, Maine, the avid outdoorsman decided he was tired of getting his feet soaked while hunting deer in the boggy hinterlands of Maine. In a flash of inspiration, he hit on the notion of sewing lightweight, comfortable leather uppers to the rubber bottoms of ordinary galoshes. Not much of a craftsman himself, Bean had a local cobbler make him a pair of boots based on his design. Testing them on his next hunting trip, the Maine Hunting Shoes (as he would later dub them) kept his feet so dry, Bean was convinced they were his ticket to financial success. He had 100 pairs made and set out to try selling them through the mail.

While the idea for the shoe was brilliant in itself, Bean's choice of a target market was sheer genius. From his experience working retail, Bean knew that out-of-towners who came to Maine to hunt and fish were very wary about showing up with the wrong equipment. Working out of the basement of his brother's store, Bean put together a mailing list of people who held nonresident Maine hunting licenses and sent out fliers advertising his new boots. The fliers read: "Outside of your gun, nothing is so important to your outfit as your footwear. You cannot expect success hunting deer or moose if your feet are not properly dressed. The Maine Hunting Shoe is designed by a hunter who has tramped the Maine woods for the past 18 years. They are light as a pair of moccasins with the protection of heavy hunting boots." Bean's distinctive, folksy prose, which gave the impression that he was an expert outdoorsman offering friendly advice to naive tenderfoots, became one of the company's trademarks and would later influence such catalogs as *Eddie Bauer*, *Land's End* and *J. Peterman*.

Unfortunately, Bean's claims about the quality of his shoes would prove to be somewhat exaggerated. Although all 100 pairs sold, the shoes turned out to be a flop. The stitching that held the leather tops pulled out of the soft rubber soles, and almost as quickly as the shoes had sold, 90 pairs were returned. Many would have considered this a disaster and given up. But for Bean, it turned out to be a watershed event that led him to formulate the customer-service policy his company remains famous for today.

Bean promptly refunded everyone's money. But he didn't stop there. Undaunted by this initial failure, he convinced U.S. Rubber to mold a heavier bottom that would hold the stitching, then replaced each defective pair

It's 3 a.m. . . . Do You Know Where Your Footwear Is?

In 1951, weary of being awakened at his home and asked to his store late at night by hunters and fishermen who were driving through Freeport and needed supplies, L.L. Bean announced that he was throwing away the keys and would keep his shop open and staffed 24 hours a day, 7 days a week, 365 days a year. In fact, one of the only times since then that the store actually closed was on February 5, 1967, the day of Bean's funeral.

Leon L. Bean

They Ain't Pretty, But They Get The Job Done

Although L.L. Bean's Maine Hunting Shoe won him a Coty Award in 1975 as an innovator in the fashion world, few would consider the clunky-looking hybrid boots fashionable. In fact, they've been called "footwear that Donald Duck would wear to the opera." But form follows function, and Bean's shoes do their job so well that they were the official footwear of several Arctic expeditions in the 1920s, they were parachuted to the besieged 101st Airborne Division in Bastogne during the Battle of the Bulge, and they were worn by the Israeli Army in the Golan Heights in 1974.

with the improved version,
free of charge, turning 90 angry customers into 90 potential future customers impressed with Bean's honesty.

With a new, improved product to sell, Bean sent out more fliers, and once again the orders poured in. Inspired by his success, Bean extended his product line to include other types of hunting and camping gear. A true hands-on entrepreneur, Bean personally field-tested every product he sold. (He would often sneak out of the office for an afternoon of fishing and product testing).

Bean also wrote his own advertising copy and personally replied to customer letters, giving his catalog a distinctive personality and further cultivating the image of an odd but honest Yankee merchant who truly cared about quality and customer satisfaction. When you bought from L.L. Bean, you weren't buying from some faceless company, you were ordering from a real person who had your best interest at heart. As John Skow puts it in a 1985 *Sports Illustrated* article, "It's as if Bean were family, some sort of mildly eccentric but amiable uncle who lives up in Maine and sends us packages."

Bean's sales figures increased at such a rapid rate that in 1917 he was able to move his operation from the basement of his brother's store and open a retail store of own, which still stands today. By 1924, he had 25 people working for him and yearly sales of

$135,000. Thirteen years and one Depression later, sales had passed the $1 million mark.

While the Maine Hunting Shoe remained the centerpiece of both the store and the catalog, Bean continually added new products ranging from Hudson Bay "point" blankets to zippered duffel bags. Bean is even credited with being the first cataloger to introduce a chamois shirt ("The shirt I personally use on all my hunting and fishing trips," he claimed), which has since become a clothing catalog staple.

But no matter how many new products Bean added, one thing never changed—the unconditional guarantee. At any time, for any reason, customers could return any L.L. Bean product for a replacement or full refund. And it truly was (and still is) a full refund. Unlike many catalogs, which refund the product price but not shipping and handling charges, Bean never charged for shipping. He was insistent on this. He seemed to instinctively know that what he was really selling was the absolute, unqualified reliability of L.L. Bean and his 100 percent satisfaction guarantee.

As satisfied customers shared with their friends stories about L. L. Bean fixing the tips of fishing rods broken off in car doors, resoling camp shoes, or replacing compasses smashed during rafting trips—all free of charge—the company gained priceless word-of-mouth advertising and a customer base whose loyalty bordered on fanaticism.

By the 1940s, L.L. Bean had firmly established a national reputation for quality and honesty and was visited regularly by political leaders, sports figures and other celebrities as well as thousands of satisfied customers. Bean was, and still is, so popular that his rustic Freeport store, decorated with a stuffed moose and a trout pond, is Maine's second-largest tourist attraction, drawing more than 3.5 million visitors each year.

Bean remained at the helm of the company until his death in 1967, when his grandson, Leon A. Gorman, took over as president. Today, nearly 90 years after Bean sold his first pair of Maine Hunting Shoes, L.L. Bean Inc. has grown into one of the world's leading international mail order companies, boasting sales of more than $1 billion per year and more than 4.5 million customers worldwide.

Jeff Bezos

Founder of
Amazon.com
Founded: 1995

"Our vision is to be the world's most
consumer-centric company, where
customers can come to find anything
they want to buy online."

—Jeff Bezos

The Amazin' Amazon Man

In 1994, Jeff Bezos was already what many would consider extremely successful. The youngest-ever senior vice president at Wall Street investment banker D.E. Shaw & Co., the 30-year-old Bezos was already making an estimated six-figure salary and was destined to rise even further in the company ranks. But Jeff had other plans. Fueled by a secret passion for the infant business of electronic retailing, Jeff dreamed of creating his own company in the vast, then virtually uncharted wilds of the World Wide Web. It was a risky move, but it quickly paid off. Just four years after Bezos created Amazon.com, the virtual bookstore became the template for how e-commerce businesses should be run, with sales of more than $610 million and more than 13 million customers worldwide.

Bezos first got the idea to start an Internet enterprise in 1994. While surfing the Internet in search of new ventures for D.E. Shaw & Co. to invest in, he came across the statistic that World Wide Web usage was growing by 2,300 percent a month. Bezos immediately recognized the expansive possibilities of selling online and began exploring the entrepreneurial possibilities of developing an Internet business.

He drew up a list of 20 potential products he thought might sell well via the Internet, including software, CDs and books. After reviewing the list, books were the obvious choice, primarily because of the sheer number of titles in existence. Bezos realized that while even the largest superstores could stock only a few hundred thousand books, a mere fraction of what is available, a "virtual" bookstore could offer millions of titles. The die was cast.

Bezos passed up a fat bonus, packed his wife, MacKenzie, and their dog, Kamala (named after an obscure "Star Trek" character), and headed for Seattle.

For Bezos, Seattle was the ideal city for his new business. Not only was it home to a tremendous pool of high-tech talent, it was also in close proximity to Ingram Book Group's Oregon warehouse. While MacKenzie drove, Jeff spent the trip pecking out a business plan on a laptop computer and calling prospective investors on a cell phone. With $1 million raised from family and friends, Bezos rented a house in Seattle and set up his business in the garage.

For nearly a year, Bezos and a crew of five employees worked out of the garage, learning how to source books and setting up a computer system that would make Amazon.com easy to navigate. In addition to creating a user-friendly interface that would streamline the "needle in a haystack" process bookstore shopping often entails, Bezos, a true marketing visionary, wanted to establish a "virtual community" where visitors could "hang out." To achieve this goal, he and his team created a number of innovative programs, including one that would let customers add their own book reviews to the site and a feature that recommends books based on a customer's previous purchases.

In July 1995, Amazon.com opened its virtual doors, calling itself "Earth's Biggest Book Store," with more than 1 million titles to choose from. Fueled by word of mouth, or more accurately, word of e-mail, Amazon.com rocketed off the line like a nitro-burning dragster. Enraptured by

Cadaver.com?

When Jeff Bezos first started his virtual venture, he wanted to call the company Cadabra, as in abracadabra. He phoned his Seattle lawyer to try out the name, but the attorney misheard Bezos and replied, "Cadaver! Why would you want to call your company that?" Bezos quickly reconsidered and adopted the name Amazon.com, after the world's second-largest river.

the enormous selection of books, the superior customer service and the user-friendly design of the site, Internet users ecstatically plugged Amazon.com on Internet newsgroups and mailing lists.

The orders poured in, and by September 1996, Amazon.com had grown into a company of 100 employees and had racked up more than $15.7 million in sales. Three years later, those figures would rocket to more than 3,000 employees (including some in Britain and Germany) and more than $610 million in sales.

Amazon.com's success did not go unnoticed by bookstore giant Barnes & Noble, who quickly put up its own Web site, www. barnesandnoble.com. To combat Amazon.com's claim that it was "Earth's Biggest Bookstore," Barnes & Noble embarked on an aggressive marketing campaign proclaiming that they offered twice as many books as Amazon.com. But it was a strategy doomed to failure. The forward-thinking Bezos had already expanded Amazon.com's product line to include CDs and replaced "Earth's Biggest Book Store" with the tagline "Books, Music and More," leaving Barnes & Noble, as one writer put it, "wrapping its fingers around the neck of a phantom."

Amazon.com has continued to stay ahead of its closest competitor, boasting 85 percent of the Web book market to Barnes & Noble's 11 percent. But that may soon change. In fact, in the near future, they may no longer even be considered competitors. After his successful venture into the music market, Bezos set his sights on expanding Amazon.com into other markets. Shortly before the 1998 Christmas season, Bezos added a temporary gift section to Amazon.com, where customers could buy toys and games. He also began experimenting with "Shop the Web," a program giving Amazon.com a commission for directing its customers to other, noncompeting online retailers. In late January 1999, Amazon.com went after the $150 billion U.S. pharmacy market, buying a share of Drugstore.com, a company that sells everything from breath mints to Viagra online.

To cash in on the growing popularity of online auctions such as eBay and uBID, Amazon.com joined Sotheby's Holdings Inc. in June 1999 to launch the online auction site sothebys.amazon.com. As if that weren't enough, less than a month later, Amazon.com officially added two new sections to its site that offered toys and consumer electronics.

All this begs the question, What is Bezos up to? Is he trying to make Amazon.com the Web's first superstore? Perhaps. In a March 1999 *PC Week* article, he explains, "We are trying to innovate in the e-commerce arena. That's our heritage. We are building something that can't be pigeonholed. We defy easy analogy. It's not a vision that can be communicated in a sound bite. We want to be the most customer-centric company in the world. Come and discover and buy anything online."

Clarence Birdseye

Founder of
General Seafood Corp.
Founded: 1922

"I do not consider myself a remarkable person. I am just a guy with a very large bump of curiosity and a gambling instinct."

—Clarence Birdseye

A CHILLING DISCOVERY

One of the hallmarks of a true entrepreneur is the ability to recognize a business opportunity that others overlook. It was this ability, along with a restless curiosity, a love of the outdoors and a propensity for taking risks, that enabled frozen-food pioneer Clarence Birdseye to turn a centuries-old tradition into a revolutionary process that would create a multibillion-dollar industry and make Birdseye a very wealthy man.

Born in Brooklyn, New York, in 1886, Clarence Birdseye, like many successful entrepreneurs, embarked on the path of free enterprise at an early age. When he was just 10 years old, he heard about an English lord seeking wild game for his estate, so the young Birdseye shipped off a dozen muskrats he had trapped on Long Island. His first venture netted him $9, which he used to buy a shotgun.

Fueled by a burning interest in plants and animals, Birdseye entered Amherst College to study biology. He paid his tuition through several unique ventures, including selling baby frogs to the Bronx Zoo for snake food and trapping rare black rats in a local butcher shop for a genetics professor. But the funds generated by these and other sideline businesses were insufficient to meet the increasing tuition costs, so Birdseye dropped out of Amherst College after two years to try his hand in the fur-trading business.

Grubstaked by a New York fur house, Birdseye traveled by dogsled to Labrador, Newfoundland, where he was able to turn a small profit buying and selling pelts for cash. While in the Arctic, he was introduced to the Inuit Indians' practice of "quick freezing" the fish they caught. The fisherman simply laid the fish on the ice, and the combination of ice, wind and temperature froze the fish almost instantly. Even more amazing, Birdseye noted that when the fish were cooked and eaten, they were tender and flaky, and tasted almost as good as when freshly caught. Birdseye also noticed the same was true for the frozen caribou, geese and heads of cabbage that he stored outside his cabin during the long Canadian winter.

Birdseye knew that efforts to freeze meat and vegetables commercially in the United States had failed, largely because the foods did not keep their flavor or texture. But at that time, freezing methods took 18 hours or more. Birdseye concluded that the Inuit's quick-freeze method kept large ice crystals from forming in the food, preventing damage to the cellular structure and thereby preserving the food's "fresh" quality. He also concluded that the public back home would gladly pay for such palatable frozen foods, if he could deliver them.

Armed with this knowledge, Birdseye returned to New York in September 1922. He organized his own company, Birdseye Seafood Inc., and began developing quick-freeze machinery with an eye toward retail buyers. While his early efforts were a success from a technological point of view, they were a failure commercially. Shoppers were skeptical, and Birdseye

Frozen Peas Were Just The Beginning

Clarence Birdseye did more than just create the frozen-food market. The quick-freezing process pioneered by Birdseye spawned new opportunities in both business and agriculture. It opened up a year-round market for fresh fruits and vegetables that greatly increased farm production in the United States. And in the case of frozen orange juice, it created a product where none existed before.

New industries were also created to support Birdseye's invention. In 1934, Birdseye contracted with American Radiator Corp. to manufacture the first inexpensive, low-temperature retail display cooling equipment for Birds Eye foods. Ten years later, Birds Eye leased the first insulated railroad cars designed for nationwide food distribution, giving birth to the refrigerated shipping industry.

was unable to convince grocers and housewives that his quick-frozen fish was different than the dry, tasteless food created by traditional, slow-freezing techniques. The company soon went broke.

Undaunted by this failure, Birdseye continued to work on perfecting his quick-freeze machinery. In 1924, he developed a process of packaging dressed fish or other food in cartons, then quick-freezing the contents between two flat, refrigerated surfaces under pressure. Realizing that he had discovered the basis for an entirely new type of freezing operation, Birdseye decided to form a new company to capitalize on his invention.

With the help of financial backing from several wealthy New York businessmen, Birdseye organized General Seafood Corp., and the frozen-food industry was born. Despite the revolutionary improvements Birdseye had made, he still could not overcome the public's distrust of frozen food. But even though it wasn't widely accepted, Birdseye's quick-frozen food would still make him a wealthy man. With sales lagging, General Seafood sold its assets, including Birdseye's patents, to Postum Co. in 1929 for what was then a staggering $22 million.

Postum reorganized itself as General Foods Corp. and appointed Clarence Birdseye president of its new Birds Eye Frosted Foods division. In 1930, the company launched a major campaign to win acceptance for its new lines of "frosted foods." The campaign was a success, and Birds Eye's selection of foods soon ranged from frozen peas, spinach and cherries to fish and several kinds of meat. After two false starts, Clarence Birdseye's dream of making quick-frozen food available to the general public had become a reality.

Restless as ever, Clarence Birdseye spent the next 25 years working on new inventions, including reflecting light bulbs, an electric fishing reel and a recoilless harpoon for whale hunters. Working in his kitchen with a fan, heat from an electric coffee maker, and a batch of bread cubes, he developed a process for dehydrating foods. He even wrote a book about wildflowers with his wife. At the time of his death in October 1956, he held nearly 300 patents. Shortly before his death, Birdseye offered this advice to college graduates seeking to get ahead in the world: "I would go around asking a lot of damn fool questions and taking chances."

Enid Bissett, Ida Rosenthal & William Rosenthal

Co-founders of
Maidenform Inc.
Founded: 1930

"I'd always admired my mother. She was an entrepreneur when entrepreneurial women were few and far between."

—Beatrice Coleman, on her mother Ida Rosenthal

An Uplifting Idea

Victoria wouldn't have a secret, and Hollywood wouldn't have Frederick if it weren't for the efforts of Enid Bissett (pictured, right) and Ida and William Rosenthal. These three dressmaking entrepreneurs invented the first uplift brassiere and spawned today's multibillion-dollar brassiere industry. Ironically enough, they didn't set out to become bra manufacturers and stumbled onto their fortune almost by accident.

The story of the modern brassiere begins in the early 1920s, when Bissett and Ida Rosenthal opened a custom dress shop called Enid Frocks on New York's prestigious West 57th Street. At the time, the stick-thin flapper look was all the rage, and women wore vests called "boyish forms" to make them look more flat chested. Bissett, who was proud of her curves, felt the look was extremely unflattering to women's bodies.

Both partners believed that a dress fit better over a natural bust line rather than a flat chest, so Bissett restructured the boyish form vest to have two cups separated by a center piece of elastic. The idea worked…in execution, but it was far short of attractive. So Rosenthal showed the seminal design to her husband, William, also a dressmaker, who transformed Bissett's creation into a garment shaped to support the natural contours of the bust. Because the garment uplifted and enhanced the shape of the bust, the Rosenthals dubbed it "the Maiden Form Brassiere" in 1922 and began building it into each dress they made.

Then the unexpected happened. Clients began requesting separate brassieres, prompting Bissett and Rosenthal to give away a bonus garment with every dress sold. To meet increasing demand for the revolutionary undergarment, the Rosenthals and Bissett formed Enid Manufacturing Co. in 1925 to produce the Maiden Form Brassiere exclusively.

As the demand continued to rise, the trio saw an opportunity to cash in on an untapped market. In 1930, Bissett and Rosenthal closed their dress shop, renamed the Enid Manufacturing Co. the Maiden Form Brassiere Co. to capitalize on the success of the Maiden Form brand name, and moved their manufacturing operation to Bayonne, New Jersey.

At this time, Bissett retired from the business, but Ida stayed on to manage the sales and finances, while William took care of the design and manufacturing. To create a greater demand for their product, the fledgling business became the first intimate-apparel company to advertise, with ads appearing in newspapers, magazines, on buses, billboards, local window and store-counter displays and even over the radio. The strategy worked a little too well, however, as demand for the Maiden Form brassieres soon exceeded the company's ability to manufacture them.

In the early days, each seamstress produced two or three brassieres a day. But by the 1930s, the company was forced to find a way to increase productivity. William's sister, Masha Hammer, organized an ingenious production line, the first in the women's apparel industry, where one seamstress sewed backs, another made straps, and a third sewed together the brassiere cups. This innovation worked so well that by the end of the decade, the company had sold more than a million Maiden Form brassieres.

The mom-and-pop shop became a true family business in 1938

Bound For Success

The modern uplift bra isn't the only first credited to lingerie pioneer William Rosenthal. Throughout the 1930s he continued to experiment with new and different brassiere designs, expanding Maidenform Inc.'s product line with the first nursing brassiere, the first long-line brassiere (a brassiere that extends down to cover the midriff to create a more shapely figure) and the first full-figured bra. He also introduced the Variation brassiere. Designed for the average-busted figure (rather than for larger figures, as most brassieres were back then), it became the first Maidenform style to reach $1 million in sales, with a retail price of $1 each.

Keep In Touch

Unlike many companies that got started in the early 1900s only to flounder before the end of the century, Maidenform Inc. has been able to remain one of the largest and most well-known lingerie manufacturers throughout the world by keeping in touch with its customer base.

In the early 1970s, Beatrice Rosenthal Coleman recognized that the U.S. population of people under the age of 25 was increasing. To adjust to this rapidly growing demographic, she created new brassieres designed for a young audience. This new line, called Precious Little, was produced in a variety of colors to appeal to this younger, fashion-conscious consumer.

As the 1970s turned into the 1980s, the forward-looking Coleman set her sights on a larger market by introducing color-coordinated intimate apparel under the name Sweet Nothings. Sold through in-store boutiques called Sweet Shoppes, the collection quickly became the most popular and profitable in Maidenform history.

when the Rosenthal's daughter, Beatrice Rosenthal Coleman, joined the company. In a 1987 *Working Woman* interview, Coleman recalled her entrance into the family business. "I was studying to be a teacher at the time, but deep down I knew I really didn't want to teach. So when my mother asked me to come into the business, I was overjoyed. I'd always admired my mother. She was an entrepreneur at a time when entrepreneurial women were few and far between."

Coleman's first job at Maiden Form was on the production line. "My mother wanted me to learn the business from the ground up," Coleman explained. Though not necessarily a raging success with a needle—she often had to rip the stitches out of the bra cups she was sewing and start over—Coleman did exhibit management potential and quickly moved from production to the sorting department, and finally into advertising.

Maiden Form experienced its first sales slump just as the United States entered World War II. Nylon was requisitioned for the war, so the company was forced to substitute other fabrics. To ride out the slump, Maiden Form turned its facilities over to the war effort, producing brassieres for members of the Women's Army Corps, parachutes for the U.S. Army Air Forces and vests for messenger pigeons. Despite the limited wartime brassiere production, Coleman continued pushing the products through various media to "safeguard the value and goodwill of Maiden Form's name."

The effort paid off, and at the end of the war Maiden Form soon regained its place at the head of the intimate-apparel market. It was also at this time that Beatrice's husband, Dr. Joseph Coleman, decided to give up his medical practice and join his wife's family's company. Beatrice told him that if he joined, she would quit. Her decision wasn't made out of malice. "That was the way things were then," she explains. "When the boys came home, the girls went home." But Joseph refused to join if his wife left, so she agreed to stay. A few years later, Joseph was directing the company's advertising while Beatrice, by then the mother of two daughters, worked part time in the design department.

By the late 1950s, Ida Rosenthal had taken over as company president after the death of her husband, and Maiden Form was experiencing its most successful sales years ever, thanks to the introduction of Chansonette. The most popular brassiere ever produced by Maiden Form, this broadcloth basic sold more than 90 million units in more than 100 countries from its introduction in 1949 through 1978.

Ida Rosenthal remained at the helm of the company she'd founded until 1959, when she became CEO and handed over the presidency to Joseph Coleman. In 1960, the company changed its name to Maidenform Inc. Joseph Coleman remained president until his death in 1968, at which time Beatrice succeeded him. A feisty entrepreneur, Ida went to her office every day until she suffered a stroke in 1966. In March 1973, at the age of 87, Ida passed away. Beatrice would remain president of Maidenform for the next 22 years. After her death in 1990, her son-in-law, Robert A. Brawer, was named president and CEO. Maidenform remained a family-run business until 1998 when Paul Mischinski was named CEO and Maurice Reznik was named president.

Citing herself as living proof that one good idea can start a family business and fund a family fortune, shortly before her death Beatrice Coleman counseled women to start their own business-es, saying: "If you really want to make it, become an entrepreneur. If you're an entrepreneur, you're in charge of your own destiny."

S. Duncan Black & Alonzo Decker Sr.

*Co-founders of
Black & Decker Corp.
Founded: 1910*

*"**B**lack and Decker's innovations literally
brought power tools to the people and
laid the foundation for the modern
power tool indusstry."*

Power Tool
Potentates

Black and Decker—the names are revered by craftsmen and tool users the world over, from professional construction workers to weekend do-it-yourselfers. And with good reason. Before S. Duncan Black (pictured, left) and Alonzo Decker, electric power tools were large, cumbersome pieces of machinery that required the user to come to them. Black and Decker's innovations literally brought power tools to the people and laid the foundation for the modern power tool industry.

Although both were born in the Baltimore area, Black and Decker had very different upbringings. Decker, whose father died when he was 13, was forced to quit school and seek employment to support his struggling family. His first job was in a foundry, where he was assigned the arduous task of ladling molten brass. It was backbreaking work, and Decker sought a way out. With help from his girlfriend, who later became his wife, Decker landed a less taxing job with Boyden Air Brake.

Displaying a natural aptitude for engineering, Decker was transferred to the engineering department of Boyden's parent company, National Cosmotype, where he joined a team of workers that produced an automatic type-casting machine. A born salesman, Decker soon found himself being sent across the country to demonstrate and install the machines. He was even sent to England, where he negotiated a $1 million distribution deal with Lord Northcliffe. Flush with his success, Decker promptly returned to America and got married. Unfortunately, National Cosmotype didn't act quickly enough on Northcliffe's offer, and the English businessman lost interest. The resulting fiasco so discouraged Decker that he quit National Cosmotype and accepted an $18-per-week position as an engineer at Rowland Telegraph Co., where in 1906 he would meet and befriend his future partner.

S. Duncan Black had a much easier childhood. The son of middle-class parents, he attended high school and was hired by Rowland upon graduation. He began as a testing engineer and designer and later moved into sales. His early training at Rowland would come in handy when he and Decker eventually set out on their own.

Both men were exemplary employees, but there was little room for advancement. When Rowland refused to meet a $25 offer from another company, Decker quit. A loyal customer encouraged Decker to start his own company, offering to steer as much business as possible his way. Encouraged by the support, Decker opened his own shop and attempted to persuade Black to join. With a wife and three children to support, Black was hesitant to give up his secure income. But when Rowland cut his sales commission, Black knew it was time to move on.

In the fall of 1910, the partners decided to start their own company. Only a lack of funds stood in their way. To raise the capital needed, Black sold his prized Maxwell-Briscoe runabout to Decker's father-in-law, and Decker mortgaged his home. Putting up a combined investment of $1,200

Have Tools, Will Travel

One of the main reasons behind the tremendous success of Black & Decker Manufacturing Co. is a unique marketing technique pioneered by its founders, Alonzo Decker Sr. and S. Duncan Black. Firm believers in the power of customer-centric selling, in the 1920s the partners converted two buses into schoolrooms on wheels, which were manned by company salespeople who toured the United States offering product demonstrations to salespeople and plant operators.

To boost lagging sales during the Depression, the company bought a six-passenger airplane and transformed it into a flying showroom that took tools for reconditioning aircraft engines directly to end users.

S. Duncan Black & Alonzo Decker Sr.

Like Father, Like Son

After graduating from college in 1929, Alonzo Decker Sr.'s son, Alonzo Decker Jr., joined Black & Decker as an electrical engineer, focusing on engineering, research and manufacturing. During the 1940s, when Black & Decker did a brisk business selling electric drills to defense contractors, the younger Decker was perplexed by the large number of reorders Black & Decker was receiving. Believing that the drills were failing, he looked into the situation and discovered that workers were taking the tools home.

Realizing that he had stumbled onto a virtually untapped market, Alonzo Jr. convinced his father that Black & Decker should begin making tools for the home. As a result, after the war, Black & Decker became the first large power tool company to focus on the do-it-yourself market. An obvious inheritor of his father's vision, in the 1960s, Alonzo Jr. was also directly responsible for creating the first cordless drill, creating a new and very lucrative market for the power tool juggernaut.

and backed by $3,000 from other investors, the partners formed the Black & Decker Manufacturing Co.

Initially, the company manufactured an array of products made to order, including a milk bottle cap machine, a vest-pocket adding machine, a candy-dipping machine and machinery for the U.S. Mint. But despite their early success, Black and Decker wanted to develop their own products—tools and machinery that would appeal to a broad market. In 1917 the duo released their first official Black & Decker tool—a portable air compressor called the Lectroflater. It sold well but not enough to keep the company afloat. Their second product, however, would start a power tool revolution and become something of a signature product that would define the company: a portable half-inch electric drill with a patented pistol grip and a trigger instead of a switch. (The original drill is now on display at the Smithsonian in Washington, DC.)

Fueled by Decker's expert engineering and Black's uncanny

sales ability, the company took off like a rocket. By 1918, Black & Decker had a factory in Washington, DC, and offices in Boston and New York City. The brand was also represented overseas in England, Canada, Russia, Australia and Japan. Worldwide growth was phenomenal, and by the end of the decade, Black and Decker's original investment of $1,200 had mushroomed into annual sales of more than $1 million.

After surviving the rigors of the Depression and the turbulence of World War II, Black & Decker expanded beyond the industrial and professional power tool markets to become the world's largest manufacturer of consumer power tools.

Black served as president of the company from 1910 until his death in 1951, when Decker replaced him. Decker in turn passed the torch to his son, Alonzo Decker Jr., upon his death in 1956.

Today, Black & Decker Corp. is one of the world's largest producer of power tools. Boasting more than $4 billion in annual sales, the company has manufacturing operations in 10 countries, and its products and services are marketed in more than 100 countries. In addition to portable electric power tools, its product line has expanded to include electric lawn and garden products, home products such as the Dustbuster, security hardware, plumbing supplies and fastening systems.

Arthur Blank & Bernie Marcus

*Co-founders of
The Home Depot
Founded: 1978*

*"We believed from the start that if
we brought the customer quality
merchandise at the right price and offered
excellent service, we could change retailing
in the United States. Today, we are the
model of what retailing should be."*

—Bernie Marcus

THE DO-IT-YOURSELFER'S BEST FRIENDS

In 1978, when co-founders Bernie Marcus and Arthur Blank (pictured, left) stated that they wanted to make The Home Depot the Sears Roebuck of the home-improvement industry, a lot of people laughed at them. But no one's laughing anymore. By combining the convenience and service of mom-and-pop hardware stores with the low prices and huge product selection of warehouse outlets, this dynamic do-it-yourself duo transformed a few ragtag stores into the largest home-improvement retailer in the United States.

The tale of how Marcus and Blank created their hardware empire ranks as one of the greatest entrepreneurial comeback stories of all time. In the late 1970s, they were both officers in a Southern California home-center chain called Handy Dan when turnaround artist Sanford S. Sigoloff took over Handy Dan's ailing parent company, Daylin Inc. The corporate raider was notorious for gutting senior management, but as Marcus writes in the duo's autobiography, *Built From Scratch*, "Handy Dan made so much money that we thought Sigoloff would be stupid to get rid of us."

They thought wrong. In 1978, citing trumped-up charges that they had allowed an underling to create a fund that was improperly used to fight a union at Handy Dan stores in San Jose, California, Sigoloff did indeed fire Marcus and Blank.

Before they were let go, Marcus and Blank had begun experimenting with discounting in one Handy Dan outlet. They observed that when they marked down items, volume increased and costs as a percentage of sales decreased. They had planned to expand the experiment to other Handy Dan stores. But now they decided to use that plan to strike out on their own. Envisioning a nationwide chain of warehouse stores filled with a wide assortment of products at the lowest possible prices and staffed with trained associates giving absolutely the best customer service in the industry, Blank and Marcus set up shop in two defunct Treasure Island discount stores in suburban Atlanta. With an infusion of cash from a New York City investment firm, they stocked the shelves with 18,000 different items—from paint to plumbing fixtures—slashed prices to the bone, and personally hired and trained the staff.

On opening day, they gave their kids a wad of $1 bills and stationed them by the entrance to hand out the money as a thank-you gift for the shoppers. They expected the money to run out before noon. "But by 5 or 6 in the evening, our kids were out in the parking lot stopping people and giving them money to come in the store," Blank recalls. "It was a crushing disappointment."

When Marcus and Blank met for lunch the next day, "We just sat there in stunned silence," Marcus remembers. "It looked like curtains for us. My wife wouldn't let me shave for days. She didn't want me to have a razor in my hands."

Fortunately, day three brought a glimmer of hope, when a satisfied customer returned to the store with a bag of okra for Marcus—her way of saying thank you for the positive shopping experience she'd had at The Home Depot.

On The Road Again

While The Home Depot may be huge, Bernie Marcus and Arthur Blank still do their best work where the little things count—out on the store floors. On a regular basis, they embark on "road shows," during which they make unscheduled visits to Home Depot stores across the country. "Over the years, these road shows have changed the way we merchandise products, because Bernie and I re-learn our business first-hand from the people on the store floor," Blank writes in the partners' autobiography, Built From Scratch. "Associates know more about the products and what the customers are looking for than we do. It is a learning experience and an opportunity to change."

Arthur Blank & Bernie Marcus

Tools For Success

In their book, Built From Scratch, Bernie Marcus and Arthur Blank outline the universal core values they believe apply to every business:

- Give excellent customer service.
- Take care of your people.
- Develop entrepreneurial spirit.
- Respect all people.
- Do the right thing; don't just do things right.
- Give back to the community as an integral part of doing business.
- Take care of your shareholders.
- Build strong relationships with associates, customers, vendors and communities.

While the transplanted New Yorker admits he really didn't appreciate the okra on a culinary level, he did see it as a sign that the fledgling enterprise was on the right track. And it was. Word of mouth began to pull more and more first-time customers into the stores, and before long, the days of paying suppliers straight from the cash register drawer were over.

Inspired by the success of their first two stores, Marcus and Blank decided to open two more stores. Cash was still a little short in those early days, so they had employees stack empty cardboard boxes and paint cans on top shelves to make the stores look more full.

The partners' next venture was into the Miami market, where they opened two stores in September and two more in November 1981. On November 22, they took the company public, and both investments and profits soared. Originally projecting sales of $9 million per store, the founders and investors were delighted to see average sales exceed $17 million. Over the next few years, the company exploded with growth, and in less than a decade, there were 118 Home Depot outlets ringing up $2.7 billion in sales.

One of the main reasons for Home Depot's phenomenal success, and what has separated it from other discounters, is the company's mission to make a Mr. or Ms. Fixit out of someone who thinks about calling the plumber to change the bath water. From the very beginning, Marcus and Blank's aim was to demystify the mechanics of plumbing, electrical wiring and construction. To this end, the founders staffed their stores with knowledgeable salespeople who could answer shoppers' questions and guide them to the proper equipment. They also began offering free clinics on all aspects of home remodeling and repair.

Another secret of Marcus and Blank's success is their "running scared" management philosophy. "If you attend any of our meetings, you would never believe that this company is the size it is or doing as well as it is," Blank explains. "We spend very little time talking about the things we are doing well. We spend 80 to 90 percent of our time focusing on the issues and problems, what the competition is doing, what our customers are looking for, what they are not finding in our stores, which stores are having problems. The whole focus of the company is to take today's standards and accept them for what they are but to say we have to improve upon them for the future."

The strategy seems to work. By 1999, only two decades after the less-than-spectacular grand opening of its first two stores in Atlanta, The Home Depot has grown to become the world's largest home-improvement retailer, with more than 800 stores operating in 44 states, five Canadian provinces, Chile and Puerto Rico. What's more, Home Depot plans to open an additional 800 stores by 2002.

Even though The Home Depot has grown into an international chain, Arthur Blank insists that the basic guiding principles of the company "were cemented in those early years and have never changed. Our prices were low then, and they are still low today. And our service was excellent then and still is today."

Richard Branson

*Founder of
The Virgin Group
Founded: 1970*

*"**I** don't go into ventures to make a fortune.
I do it because I'm not satisfied with the
way others are doing business."*

—Richard Branson

THE P.T. BARNUM OF
BRITISH BUSINESS

He appeared in public dressed in a $10,000 white silk bridal gown. Drove a tank into New York City's Times Square and fired a cannon at the Coca-Cola sign. Rented a boat and sailed the Sex Pistols down the Thames River so they could serenade the House of Commons with "God Save the Queen"—a song the British government had banned from the airwaves. And he's even buzzed Big Ben in an Airbus A340 jet.

Much like P.T. Barnum, the flamboyant 19th century showman he's often compared to, it seems that there's little self-proclaimed "adventure capitalist" and Virgin Group CEO Richard Branson won't do in the name of promotion. But if his over-the-top publicity stunts strike some as eccentric, then the way he runs his multibillion-dollar business must appear completely insane.

Branson has no centralized headquarters—preferring to operate out of his Holland Park home in west London—refuses to hold board meetings, can't operate a computer, keeps his appointments in a paper diary and scribbles ideas on his hand.

Still, this maverick entrepreneur's outrageous escapades have made Virgin one of the best-known and most popular brand names in the world. And his unusual business and management practices have created a $5 billion empire that embraces everything from an international airline to a bridal-wear shop.

Branson began his diverse entrepreneurial career in 1967 when he quit school at the age of 16 to start a magazine. Branson hoped his magazine, simply titled *Student*, would become a voice for young activists. When the first issue debuted in 1968, the headmaster of Stowe, where Branson had been a student, wrote Branson a rather prophetic note that said: "Congratulations,

Branson. I predict you will either go to prison or become a millionaire." Branson would eventually do both.

Even though he filled his publication with articles and interviews from such luminaries as existentialist Jean-Paul Sartre, novelists James Baldwin and Alice Walker, and poet Robert Graves, the magazine never made money, and Branson seemed doomed for failure. Then he hit upon the idea of selling records through the mail at discounted prices. Branson ran ads in *Student*, and his mail order record business soon became more lucrative than the magazine. To take full advantage of this newfound market, Branson rented an empty shop above a shoe store, put up a few shelves, recruited the staff of *Student* as employees, and opened a discount record store. They dubbed the store Virgin, because everyone involved was a complete virgin at business.

The Gospel According To Richard

- **On management:** "If you take care of your employees, your employees will take care of your customers and your customers will take care of your shareholders."
- **On his flamboyant publicity stunts:** "If you are willing to make a fool of yourself and make people smile—as long as you do it with a sense of fun—you can get away with it."
- **On risk-taking:** "You fail if you don't try. If you try and you fail, yes, you'll have a few articles saying you've failed at something. But if you look at the history of American entrepreneurs, one thing I do know about them: An awful lot of them have tried and failed in the past and gone on to great things."
- **On his ability to succeed at so many different businesses:** "I immerse myself in getting the businesses set up and am very involved the first three or four months, get good people to run them, give them a stake in the company and a lot of freedom, and then step back and move on to the next."
- **On the future of Virgin:** "We're a company that likes to take on the giants. In too many businesses these giants have had things their own way. We're going to have a lot of fun competing with them."

Richard Branson

With the opening of the Virgin record store, Branson seemed to be on his way. But he hit a major roadblock when, strapped for cash, he concocted a scheme to avoid paying the British sales tax. The scam was quickly uncovered, and Branson was arrested and jailed. He negotiated an out-of-court settlement, agreeing to pay back the taxes over the next three years. Left a little wiser by the experience, Branson set out to turn his loosely run business into a company focused on and ruled by balance sheets.

Branson's next entrepreneurial adventure began in 1973 when he formed Virgin Records and released Mike Oldfield's "Tubular Bells." The haunting instrumental became a worldwide hit and put Virgin Records on the map. But the company really took off in 1977, when, even though he was advised against it, Branson signed the Sex Pistols, who had already been dropped from two other record labels because of their scandalous antics on and off the stage. The Pistols self-destructed shortly afterward, but the fledgling Virgin Records flourished, becoming the world's largest independent record label with a stable of stars that included artists such as the Rolling Stones, Peter Gabriel, UB40, Steve Winwood and Paula Abdul.

By 1983 Branson's empire encompassed more than 50 companies involved in everything from filmmaking to air conditioner cleaning and generating combined sales of more than $17 million. But according to Branson, money is not the driving force behind his varied business endeavors. Instead, his principal motive for expanding into new ventures is that he enjoys the challenge of trying to do something better than other people. And in 1984, Branson embarked on what would prove to be the biggest challenge of his life—Virgin Atlantic airlines.

Branson's colleagues thought he was crazy. Starting a transatlantic airline would mean going up against the behemoth British Airways, which had already thoroughly trounced Freddy Laker when he attempted to enter this highly lucrative market. But Branson was undaunted. He felt the major airlines, especially British Airways, were no longer responsive to their customers' needs, and he became convinced that if he started an airline that made traveling an affordable and enjoyable experience, he could beat British Airways at its own game.

The initial response to Virgin Atlantic was tremendous. The

airline became famous for its superior service and lavish amenities, which included in-flight massages, hydrotherapy baths, free ice cream during movies and seat-back video screens in every class. But the early 1990s would prove to be a turbulent era for the upstart airline. Economies were floundering worldwide. The price of airline fuel had more than doubled. And fewer people were traveling abroad due to fear of terrorist attacks. To make matters worse, in 1991, British Airways launched a secret campaign to drive Branson out of business.

By 1992, Virgin Atlantic's financial situation was so shaky that Branson's bankers forced him to sell Virgin Records to Thorn-EMI to raise enough cash to keep the airline flying. The sale generated nearly $1 billion, enough for Branson to pay off the bank and own Virgin Atlantic outright. But Branson was crushed at being forced to sell the music company he loved and vowed never to put himself at the mercy of bank lenders again.

Just Call Him "Evel"

Richard Branson thrives on challenges. A true adventurer in every sense of the word, he hasn't limited his risk-taking to business ventures only. More than once he's embarked on death-defying personal challenges that have nearly cost him his life. In 1985, he had to be rescued from a roiling ocean after his racing boat, the Virgin Challenger, was swamped. Undaunted, the very next year he crossed the Atlantic in a similar boat, the Virgin Challenger II, in the fastest-ever recorded time.

For his next challenge, Branson took to the air and in 1987 became the first man to cross the Atlantic in a hot air balloon. As if that weren't enough, at the time, his balloon, the Virgin Atlantic Flyer, was the largest ever flown (2.3 million cubic feet) and reached record-setting speeds in excess of 130 mph. Both those records stood until 1991, when Branson flew another Virgin Atlantic Flyer 6,700 miles across the Pacific from Japan to Arctic Canada, again breaking all existing records, hitting speeds up to 245 mph, in a balloon of 2.6 million cubic feet. Since then he has made three unsuccessful attempts to become the first man to fly around the world in a balloon.

To this end, he developed a new business approach, which he calls "branded venture capital." This remarkable strategy has enabled Branson to launch a patchwork of businesses with minimal investment. The key to this strategy lies in licensing the highly regarded Virgin name. Basically, Branson manages the business and supplies the Virgin name, usually in exchange for a controlling interest, while his wealthy partners put up most of the cash.

As a result of this strategy, Branson now owns or holds interests in more than 200 different companies, including two airlines, Virgin Interactive Entertainment, Virgin Radio, Virgin Studios, Virgin Hotels, Virgin Bridal, Virgin Clubs, Virgin Cola, Virgin Publishing, Virgin Vodka, Virgin Net, the Virgin Megastore chain, V2 (a global record company), a financial planning network, a blimp business, a modeling agency, a life insurance company and the high-speed European railway Eurostar.

And he's not about to stop expanding his empire. Branson's future plans include a shuttle service into space. Why not? As Branson states in a 1997 interview in *Forbes* magazine, "It's virgin territory."

Samuel Bronfman

Samuel Bronfman Samuel Bronfman Samuel Bronfman Samuel Bronfman Samuel Bronfman Bronfman Bronfman Bronfman Bronfman Bronfman

"I don't want my sons going to school with holes in their pants."

—Samuel Bronfman

Founder of Joseph E. Seagram & Sons Inc.
Founded: 1933

"Mr. Sam," The Whiskey Man

The driving forces behind successful entrepreneurs are as varied as the entrepreneurs themselves. For some, it's the pursuit of money. For others, it's a craving for power. For still others, it's the challenge itself. But the force that drove Samuel Bronfman to build a small-town distillery into an international liquor empire was the burning desire to be socially accepted. Although he seemed to have it all—wealth, prestige and a loving family—Bronfman (whose name in Yiddish literally means "whiskey man") always felt he was an outsider, whom upper-class society looked down upon because he was born poor and Jewish and because booze and bootleggers were the foundation of his fortune. This hunger to "be somebody," along with his unwavering determination that his children would never suffer the humiliation of being poor as he did, became the fire that fueled Bronfman to turn a family-owned business into a multibillion-dollar dynasty.

Bronfman's entry into the liquor business came indirectly, as a hotelkeeper. In the early 1900s, using the money they'd earned as horse traders, Bronfman and his brothers, Abe, Harry and Alan, purchased several hotels throughout the prairie lands of Manitoba, Canada. Each hotel had its own bar, and the brothers quickly discovered that selling liquor was the most lucrative aspect of the hotel business. But that changed in 1915 when, prompted by the temperance movement that was spreading across Canada, bars in the prairies were banned. The Bronfman brothers almost went out of business—their hotels simply couldn't survive without bars.

But there were gaping loopholes in the new law, including one that allowed the sale of liquor from one province of Canada to another. So the versatile Bronfman and his brothers went into the mail order business, shipping whiskey by rail. When the government banned the mail order business but said it was legal to sell alcohol as medicine, the Bronfmans just slapped on new labels, such as "Rock-A-Bye Cough Cure" and "Liver & Kidney Cure."

With the passage of the Volstead Act in 1919, making and drinking liquor became illegal in the United States, opening up a lucrative new market for the Bronfmans. Rather than reduce alcohol consumption, Prohibition seemed to stimulate it, as more and more Americans succumbed to the temptation of this newly forbidden fruit. The liquor kept flowing, now controlled by gangsters. The gangsters were constantly looking for more alcohol, and the Bronfmans had it.

Risky Business

In the process of building his empire, Samuel Bronfman had to deal with some of America's most notorious mobsters, including the likes of Charles "Lucky" Luciano, Meyer Lansky and Dutch Shulz. Although Bronfman's business dealings with these and other infamous gangsters were completely legal, thanks to loopholes in both Canadian and American law, Bronfman was never really comfortable walking the thin line between the two sides of the law. And his connections with organized crime would place him in an uncomfortable position on more than one occasion.

In 1935, Sam and his brothers were charged with smuggling whiskey back into Canada. In the end, thanks to what some said were "suspiciously missing" shipping records, the charges were thrown out of court. Bronfman's Prohibition-era dealings would again return to haunt him in the 1950s, this time in the United States, during a congressional investigation into organized crime led by Senator Estes Kefauver. On the stand, Bronfman's name was mentioned by a number of America's biggest gangsters. A lawyer for one of them referred to Bronfman as "a plain, ordinary bootlegger." There's no doubt Bronfman met with mobsters. Meyer Lansky's widow even talked about the lavish dinners Bronfman threw for her husband. But while there were certainly connections, no crimes were ever proven.

Although the sale of liquor for use within Canada was prohibited, Canadian authorities did not ban its export to the United States. In fact, the government almost encouraged it because of the tremendous tax revenue it generated.

As the demand for alcohol in the United States grew, the Bronfmans found themselves running short. So Sam and his brother Harry decided to make their own. Their first attempt was a disaster: The batch turned blue.

Putting the debacle behind them, the Bronfmans expanded their business by opening up export houses along the Saskatchewan-North Dakota border. They continued to experience tremendous success, but that success would not come without a price. While it was legal for the Bronfmans to sell their liquor to their American partners, the booze had to be illegally smuggled across the border, a situation that forced the Bronfmans to cut deals with gangsters. The brothers knew they were in business with a dangerous lot, but in 1922 they discovered just how dangerous when their brother-in-law, Paul Matoff, was killed, allegedly by bootleggers. The murder smeared the family name in the press, prompting Bronfman to decide it was time to move on ... to get respectable.

In 1924, Bronfman arrived in Montreal, the liquor supply capital of Canada. His brothers followed, and they built a distillery just outside Montreal. Though it was a joint venture, it was Sam, now the dominant figure in the business, who ran it. But Sam wasn't satisfied with just one distillery. He wanted the means to make the best whiskey in the world. To gain capital and a source of Scottish malt whiskies to blend with his own grain alcohol, Sam formed a partnership with Scotland's Distillers Company Ltd., the world's largest whiskey conglomerate.

Back in Canada, Bronfman continued to expand. He purchased the prestigious Seagram & Sons distillery in 1928 and, using the new name, founded Joseph E. Seagram & Sons Inc. With two distilleries, a new name and the aid of his Scottish partners, Bronfman had laid the groundwork for what would become the Seagram empire of today.

Despite the fact that he had built Seagram with the help of his brothers, Sam decided that the business was his and his alone. Through a series of shrewd, some say ruthless maneuvers, Sam forced his brothers out of the company and declared that only his two sons, Edgar and Charles, would ever work for Seagram.

The end of Prohibition in 1933 would create a new era of prosperity for Bronfman and Seagram. But unlike other whiskey makers, who were frantically selling any drop of booze they could get their hands on, Bronfman didn't immediately jump into the fray—a move that shocked his competitors. Bronfman believed that Americans, who were used to heavy whiskies, would switch to lighter brands that were more refined. That meant aging his whiskey for better quality, and that took time. So while his competitors were making millions, Bronfman held back, quietly building up his stock. The strategy worked. By 1934, Bronfman's aged, blended whiskies had become America's bestsellers. And by the 1940s, Seagram was the largest distiller in both the United States and Canada.

Sam's next venture was in construction. In 1955, he commissioned Ludwig Mies van der Rohe to build his company a New York headquarters. The Seagram Building quickly became a New York landmark.

Above And Beyond

An ardent fighter of anti-Semitism, Samuel Bronfman gave generously to Zionist causes throughout his lifetime. But perhaps his greatest contribution to Zionism was when he came to the aid of future Israeli prime minister Shimon Peres, shortly after the founding of Israel. In 1951, Peres approached Bronfman seeking assistance for his fledgling country. Peres explained that Israel had no arms and would be unable to defend itself if attacked.

Bronfman immediately took Peres to Ottawa to try to buy guns from the Canadian government. He succeeded in getting Peres $2 million worth of guns at half price. But after the deal was cut, Peres sheepishly explained that Israel did not have the money to pay for the guns. Bronfman immediately called his wife, Sadie, and asked her to arrange a fund-raising dinner for that evening, and, true to form, Bronfman raised the $1 million.

Over the next decade and a half, Bronfman would gradually turn over the running of the business to his sons. But as long as he was alive, it was understood that Seagram was his company. In his later years, Bronfman would finally gain some of the acclaim and acceptance he'd longed for, including winning the Order of Canada—that country's highest honor for lifetime achievement. But he still felt he deserved more. As longtime friend Sol Kanee reveals in an "A&E Biography" on Bronfman, "He was king of the heap in the whiskey business. He had more money than he knew what to do with. But he didn't have the status that he wanted. He wanted to be a senator. He wanted to be a governor of a big university. That's what drove him on."

But Bronfman wouldn't live to see those dreams come true. In 1971, at the age of 81, he died of prostate cancer. It was perhaps in death that Samuel Bronfman finally achieved the acceptance he so craved. On the day of his funeral, Montreal's airport had to be temporarily closed to regular traffic due to the arrival of so many private jets shuttling in dignitaries from around the world to pay their respects.

Today, under the guidance of Bronfman's grandson, Edgar Bronfman Jr., Seagram has expanded beyond the liquor business to become an entertainment giant, owning movie studios, music labels and theme parks around the world. But no matter how much the company has changed, it still bears the indelible imprint of the visionary trailblazer affectionately and respectfully referred to as "Mr. Sam."

Joseph R. "Rod" Canion

"*The world is moving so fast that it's become change or die. Nobody knows that better than me.*"

—Joseph R. "Rod" Canion

Co-founder of Compaq Computer Corp.
Founded: 1982

CLONING AROUND

In 1981, when soon-to-be Compaq Computer Corp. co-founder Joseph R. "Rod" Canion sketched out a plan for a portable IBM-compatible PC clone on a napkin in a Houston pie shop, he knew he was onto something big. But he never imagined that he was laying the groundwork for what would become the first start-up company ever to reach more than $100 million in its first year of sales and firing the opening salvo in a PC clone war that would last well into the next decade and beyond.

A soft-spoken Texan whose boyhood spent tinkering with hot rods led him to study engineering, Canion received his master's degree in electrical engineering with an emphasis in computer science in 1968, and he immediately began working for Dallas-based electronics titan Texas Instruments (TI). During his 13-year tenure at TI, Canion became close friends with two other company engineers, Jim Harris and Bill Mutro.

Although both Mutro and Harris aided Canion in creating his groundbreaking design, none of the three initially intended to become computer manufacturers. They had actually planned to build a computer disk drive and peripherals company. But they were dissuaded by Wall Street analyst-turned-venture capitalist Benjamin J. Rosen, who offered instead to help the trio raise $1.5 million in venture capital to build the industry's first MS-DOS transportable computer—a 28-pound "luggable" PC.

Rosen came through with the capital he promised, and in 1982, with Rosen as chairman, Canion, Harris and Mutro started Compaq Computer Corp. Under Canion's direction, Compaq's initial game plan was to build PC clones that offered complete compatibility with IBM personal computers, but with more power and more features.

Canion knew that if he was to compete against the Big Blue juggernaut and the hundreds of other PC-clone makers who had popped up after the enormous success of IBM's personal computer, he would have to find a way to make Compaq stand out from the crowd. So he developed a plan that would rocket Compaq to the head of the pack, not through technology, but through keen financial planning and superior marketing.

Canion's first step was to acquire the monetary resources Compaq would need to survive what he knew would be a war of attrition. While long-since-vanished cloners like Victor, Vector and Hyperion were building nearly identical machines, Compaq was building a colossal war chest. In just a few months, Canion had gathered the largest pool of venture capital ever concentrated on a single venture—nearly $25 million. This strong capital base enabled Compaq to offer potential computer dealers solid reassurance about Compaq's future

Management 101

Joseph R. "Rod" Canion pushed the computer technology envelope further and faster than any before him. He built one of the world's most successful businesses, brought the first IBM-compatible portable PC to market, introduced the first computer based on Intel's 386 chip, and was the driving force behind the first PC-based superservers. But perhaps his greatest accomplishment lies not in developing new hardware or technology, but in the visionary management policies he pioneered as CEO of Compaq Computer Corp.

A positive and encouraging manager who listened as he led, Canion's style was to empower people, get them working together, then challenge them to be the best they could be. The "can-do" corporate culture Canion created made him a talent magnet. He attracted the best and brightest in the industry and built them into teams and management structures that fostered incredible innovation and made Compaq the undisputed champ in the PC market for nearly a decade. A tribute to the loyalty and passion Canion inspired in his workers, about 150 employees staged an impromptu protest after news of his dismissal in 1991, many carrying signs that read "We love you Rod." Several weeks later, the same group took out a newspaper ad saying "Rod, you are the wind beneath our wings. We love you."

Joseph R. "Rod" Canion

stability as a manufacturer, which was vital if the second phase of Canion's plan was to work.

Unlike IBM and many of the other cloners of the time, Canion saw the hazards of offering computers both directly from the company as well as through dealers. He decided the path to success lay in selling only through dealers, thereby avoiding the headaches of competing with his own channel market.

"There was nobody going exclusively through dealers," Canion explains in a 1985 *Computerworld* magazine interview. "That was our own invention. But as to how to deal with the dealers—what they expected and what they needed—we hadn't a clue. We had to get that from the dealers themselves and from observing what other people had tried."

Canion's strategy made a point of keeping a wide spread between the wholesale price and the "suggested retail price" that Compaq published. The spread was handsome enough to secure a highly visible place for Compaq's machines on dealers' shelves next to the IBM PC. Canion allowed the dealers to use the spread to either offer deals to their customers or to fatten their own margins. And dealers had an added incentive to push Compaq computers— Compaq backed its dealers with a flood of TV advertising.

Canion's plan was a huge success. During the company's first year in business, Compaq shipped more than 53,000 PCs and set its first of many U.S. business records with revenue topping $111 million. Compaq was off and running—at a dead sprint.

In 1983, Compaq made its first public stock offering, which raised $67 million. Canion used a portion of the profits to develop Compaq's first desktop computers. Released in 1984, the DeskPro line was a family of modular desktop systems based on Intel's new 8086 chip. The new chip offered more power than IBM chips, but without sacrificing IBM compatibility.

Compaq's next groundbreaking computer hit the streets in April of that same year, when it rolled out the first systems based on Intel's 80286 processor. By the end of 1984, Compaq had shipped nearly 150,000 PCs and set another revenue record of $329 million.

Based on Canion's philosophy of advancing existing technology while offering more power and more features, Compaq continued to grow and prosper, becoming the youngest company ever to join the Fortune 500—just five years after it was founded.

In 1987, the 42-year-old Canion and Compaq faced their first major potential roadblock when IBM introduced its new line of PS/2 computers. Abandoning the industry standard MS-DOS, the PS/2s ran on IBM's newly created OS/2 operating system, which IBM promised would deliver faster speeds, expanded versatility and more features. Many industry pundits claimed the PS/2 was a "clone crusher" that would run Compaq and all other clone makers out of business.

Is There Life After Compaq?

It may be cliché, but in Joseph R. "Rod" Canion's case it is true—you really can't keep a good man down. Just months after his dismissal as CEO of Compaq Computer Corp., Canion joined fellow Compaq co-founder Jim Harris in a new business venture. Renting space in the same Houston office where they started Compaq, the two old friends started Insource Management Group (IMG) in 1992, a computer consulting firm dedicated to helping customers evaluate their business processes and then design information systems to help them improve those processes.

Canion has remained chairman of IMG since its inception, but that hasn't stopped him from exploring other avenues of business. In 1998, he became chairman of GK Intelligent Systems, a software company that was experimenting with artificial intelligence to help children learn more quickly and easily. But that relationship didn't last long. Within four months of accepting the position, Canion left GK, citing "basic philosophical differences" as the reason for his departure.

Canion's latest venture began in 1999, when he was appointed co-CEO of Tricord Systems Inc., a former maker of Intel superservers. Tricord Chairman and CEO John Mitcham tapped Canion to help him re-launch Tricord as a storage company. When asked in an interview in the May 24, 1999, issue of Computerworld magazine if he expects his relationship with Tricord to be a long-term one, Canion replied, "No. When we get through this launch phase and we're up and running as a company, I will step back. But I like working with start-ups, and I'm likely to be doing that again in the future."

Joseph R. "Rod" Canion

But the pundits were wrong, at least in Compaq's case. Having firmly established its reputation for providing superior quality, speed and features at competitive prices, Compaq continued to outsell the competition and became the first 6-year-old company in U.S. history to break the $1 billion sales mark.

Under Canion's firm hand, Compaq would became the industry's technological leader. Over the next three years, Compaq would pioneer every new class of personal computer, introducing the first 386 machine, the first 20MHz, 25MHz, and 386SX-based systems.

Then in late 1991, the unthinkable happened. Compaq announced its first-ever quarterly loss—nearly $70 million. Canion suddenly found his company confronting an entirely new market from the one it had entered nine years before. As a new generation of clone builders, such as Dell, Zeos and ALR, discovered they could bypass the dealers and sell direct through the mail, PC prices plummeted and Compaq was left stranded with an obsolete philosophy based on pampering dealers. No longer could it win premium prices by being first with the best and brightest technology. Buyers now wanted discounts, not premiums.

In reaction to the loss, Canion laid off 1,400 workers and developed an 18-month plan to create a new line of low-priced computers to counter the cut-rate clones. Worried about further losses, without Canion's knowledge, Compaq chairman Benjamin Rosen commissioned a team to discover just how quickly and cheaply a low-priced computer could be made. The answer, which turned out to be half Canion's allotted time, meant Canion's days as Compaq's CEO were numbered. On October 25, 1991, Compaq's board of directors, led by Rosen, announced that Canion was being replaced as CEO by Compaq executive vice president and COO Eckhard Pfeiffer. Two weeks later, Compaq accepted the resignation of co-founder Jim Harris, who was then vice president of engineering.

Some claim Canion was the cause of Compaq's downturn. Others claim he was merely a scapegoat. Regardless of which theory is correct, one thing remains true: Rod Canion changed the way the world computes. By pushing the technological envelope, Canion created many of today's computer industry standards and inspired the computer industry to keep developing better PCs.

Steve Case

"*We want to be the Coca-Cola of the online world.*"

—Steve Case

Founder of America Online Inc.
Founded: 1985

THE MAN WHO PUT AMERICA ON THE INTERNET

If anyone ever earned the right to say "I told you so," it's America Online (AOL) founder Steve Case. Almost from the very day it was launched, industry pundits, business experts and market analysts have been predicting the demise of AOL. True, the company and Case have experienced roller coaster ups and downs (at one point, Case's own board members considered firing him). But Case has ridden them out with the grace and style you might expect from a Hawaiian-born body surfer. By faithfully following his conviction that easier is better, Case has out-maneuvered his competitors, silenced his critics, and made AOL the number-one online service provider in the world.

Case's entrepreneurial talents developed early. As a child growing up in Honolulu, he and his brother, Dan, embarked on a series of business ventures. Through these early business experiences, Case developed a fascination with marketing. Unfortunately, his college of choice, Williams College (his father's alma mater) in Williamstown, Massachusetts, didn't offer a marketing degree, so Case majored in political science because, he said, "it was the closest thing to marketing." After graduation, the future online tycoon landed a marketing position at Procter & Gamble (P&G). Although Case admits he learned much of what he knows about marketing during his stint at P&G, he chafed under the constraints of mainstream corporate America.

Deciding that managing a mature business was not for him, Case left P&G and accepted a position with Pizza Hut. As manager of new development, his job entailed traveling around the country in search of new ideas for pizza toppings. While he chewed his way through several pies a day, Case spent his evenings exploring the then infant Internet on a clunky Kaypro computer and 300-baud modem. Though the computer was difficult to use and the modem snail-slow, Case was awed by the wonders he discovered through early online services such as The Source. "I remember it being frustrating," Case told *Time* in a 1997 interview, "but there was something magical about the notion of sitting in Wichita and talking to people from all over the world."

Enraptured by the Internet, Case began looking for ways to turn his hobby into a lucrative business. In 1982, he hit upon the idea of starting an Atari video game subscription club, similar to the Book-of-the-Month Club. According to a 1997 article in *Gentlemen's Quarterly*, when Case turned to his brother, Dan, for his input, the elder Case bluntly replied, "It's a bad idea. You're going to get your ass kicked." It wouldn't be the first time someone would tell Case that,

Natural-Born Entrepreneur

Steve Case claims he was always meant to be an entrepreneur. In fact, he's been involved in one moneymaking scheme or another since the age of 6. Steve opened his first business with his brother, Dan—a roadside stand where they sold lemonade made from lemons they'd picked in their backyard. They charged two cents a cup, but many of their customers gave them a nickel and let them keep the change. "We learned early the value of high margins," Dan later told Businessweek.

A few year later, the two boys formed Case Enterprises, an international mail order business that sold everything from seeds to greeting cards by mail and door to door. Somehow, Case Enterprises won the exclusive local rights to sell a brand of Swiss watch. They didn't sell a single watch. But that didn't faze them. They kept moving ahead, creating an affiliate, Aloha Sales Co., which sold ad circulars. They even shared a newspaper route. The duo never made much money. But then, according to Steve, that wasn't why they were doing it. "It was the challenge," he later told Businessweek, "the pursuit of the idea."

but this was one of the few times he would listen. A year later the brothers came across the business plan for Control Video—a start-up that planned to charge Atari owners $1 to download a video game over the phone. After one play, the software would no longer work. Dan suggested his firm, venture capitalists Hambrecht & Quist, invest in the company. Steve wanted in on the deal as well. But it wasn't the video game angle that intrigued him. It was the idea that once computers were hooked up to phone lines, they could be used for other things, such as e-mail.

Steve wrangled an introduction with the founder of Control Video and was immediately offered a position in the company. Once again, Dan told his brother he was making a mistake. Dan argued that even though the start-up's founder was brilliant, he wasn't good with money. This time, Steve chose to ignore his brother's advice, and he packed up and headed to northern Virginia to join Control Video. Two weeks after he arrived, the firm's capital dried up.

But Case wasn't about to give up. From the rubble of Control Video, he created Quantum Computer Services, an online bulletin board for owners of Commodore 64 computers, the most popular home computer at the time. It was a small market, but he felt it might have potential. He was right. Over the next six years, Quantum membership grew from 24 members on its first night to more than 100,000.

In 1991, Case made a decision that would forever change the online world. He renamed his company America Online, and with 110,000 members, launched an attack on the two largest online service providers—CompuServe, whose membership was around 800,000, and the IBM-Sears joint venture Prodigy, which boasted a membership of 1.1 million. Everyone, including his mother, thought Case was insane. Critics said AOL would never last. How could Case possibly hope to compete with IBM and Sears?

But Case had a plan...several, actually. First, he had spotted a flaw in IBM and CompuServe's online strategies that he felt he could use to his advantage. Both online giants believed that the best way to lure in customers was with lots of fancy, high-tech features. But based on his experience at Pizza Hut, where he'd seen dozens of complex pizzas fail miserably, Case concluded that what America really wanted in an online service was, as one writer put it, "cheese, tomato sauce and occasionally some pepperoni." With this in mind, Case set out to make AOL as simple and easy-to-use as possible. In fact, it was Case who introduced the first graphical interface to the online world, allowing users to point-and-click their way to wherever they wanted to go on the Internet.

Second, Case knew that if he was going to beat IBM and CompuServe at their own game, he would have to gain subscribers and market share—and fast. To accomplish this, he drew on his P&G marketing training and began giving away free samples—bundling AOL floppy disks with popular computer magazines and offering 10 hours of free use. It worked so well that Case was soon flooding the mail with free diskettes, a practice that still remains at the core of AOL's marketing strategy.

With literally tens of millions of AOL disks floating around, membership grew at light speed. From 200,000 members in 1992, AOL surged to 4.7 million by 1995 and to more than 10.7 million by 1997. As AOL soared to the top, it passed CompuServe and Prodigy on the way down. (In fact, AOL bought CompuServe in 1997.) But the news wasn't all good. By 1997, AOL had so many members that it couldn't keep up with subscriber demand. Its network was often overloaded, users regularly experienced busy signals for hours at a time, and when they were able to log on, their connections were frequently cut off for no apparent reason. Infuriated subscribers began canceling their memberships at an alarming rate, causing AOL to suffer a $350 million loss.

Once again, the soothsayers of the online world predicted AOL's demise. And once again, Case proved them wrong. To silence the busy signals and keep customers online, Case paid $35 million for his own data network, erected a $50 million network facility next to AOL's Dulles, Virginia, headquarters, and spent $300 million to add

Blast-Off!

Between 1992 and 1999, AOL added more than 13 million new subscribers. That's more new subscribers than The New York Times and The Washington Post together have added in the past 50 years.

modems from Florida to Alaska. The result? At the end of 1998, AOL hauled in $98.1 million in net income from revenue of $2.6 billion.

By mid-1999, AOL—which two years earlier had been declared by Internet insiders "an idea whose time had come and gone"— was boasting more than 17.6 million subscribers and had become the undisputed champ of the online world. But as his company looks to the new millennium, Case realizes he cannot rest on his laurels. "Even though we've been at it for over a decade, this is like the second inning in terms of the development of this medium," Case says in a 1999 *Time* magazine interview. "The online business is about to become the most competitive market in the world."

Indeed, it is his burning desire to remain competitive that led Case to make the biggest deal of his already legendary career. Fearing that millions of customers might dump AOL in favor of the faster connections offered by cable companies, in October 1999 Case began secretly working on a deal to merge AOL, the world's largest Internet provider, with Time Warner, the world's largest media company. Time Warner had spent billions of dollars to buy cable systems in the early 1990s, and Case felt that a marriage between Time Warner and AOL would not only provide AOL with access to cable systems but also to a virtually limitless supply of online content, ranging from magazines to music to movies.

Working with Time Warner chairman and CEO, Gerald M. Levin, Case crafted a $183 billion deal to purchase Time Warner. Under the aegis of AOL Time Warner, Case and his partners hope to define the future of the Internet. By assembling more assets, audiences and advertisers for the new digital marketplace than anyone has previously even thought of, Case sees a chance to move so far ahead that others won't catch up for years.

"We're kicking off the new Internet century with a unique company with unparalleled assets and unprecedented ability to accelerate the next Internet revolution," Case told Inter@active Week. And he's convinced he has the game plan to make it work. "We plan to offer the most magical service possible. Our strength is to use the latest technology while hiding its complexity. We'll use the technology as a means to an end, but we've gotten here because we figure out what the customers want, not what the technologists think."

Gabrielle "Coco" Chanel

> *"Success is often achieved by those who don't know that failure is inevitable."*
>
> — Gabrielle "Coco" Chanel

Founder of Chanel Inc.
Founded: 1913

HAUTE COUTURE ANARCHIST

Her first customers were princesses and duchesses, but she dressed them like secretaries and stenographers in faux pearls, trench coats, simple knits, turtleneck sweaters and "little black dresses." By thumbing her nose at the haute couture styles of the 19th century, Coco Chanel freed women from the suffocating clutches of corsets and bustles and created a fashion revolution that would influence every designer that came after her. In fact, her signature suit—a collarless cardigan jacket trimmed in braid with an elegantly straight skirt—is the single most copied fashion of all time.

But perhaps this entrepreneurial dilettante's true genius lay in her shrewd recognition of the value of spinning off her name—a name that would remain one of the most famous and revered in the fashion world, even 30 years after her death.

Chanel's rags-to-riches story reads like a Harlequin romance novel. The illegitimate daughter of a poor French peddler and a shop girl, Gabrielle "Coco" Chanel was born in 1883 in the Auvergne region of France. After her mother died and her father ran off, Chanel spent much of her early life in a convent. When she was 17, the nuns who ran the convent helped Chanel get a job as a seamstress. But the beautiful young woman yearned to escape the humdrum life of provincial France and ran off to the garrison town of Moulins to become a cabaret singer.

While she never found stardom as a chanteuse, she did find Etienne Balsan, a rich young playboy who took her in as his "back-up" mistress and moved her to Paris. Always the rebel, Chanel refused to dress her part. Instead of the extravagant satin dresses that were de rigueur for coquettes of the day, Chanel wore plain, dark-colored dresses that marked the beginning of the fashion trend that would make her name famous throughout Europe.

To keep her busy while he attended to his other mistress, Balsan helped Chanel open her own hat and dress shop in Paris. That arrangement led to bigger and better things when Chanel left Balsan for his friend Arthur "Boy" Chapel in 1913. A wealthy English businessman, Chapel, who is claimed to have been the true love of her life, provided the capital for Chanel to open two additional boutiques in the coastal towns of Deauville and Biarritz.

Chanel had always loved wearing men's clothing, which she borrowed freely from her lovers' closets, so it's no surprise that the inspiration for her early designs came from menswear. She even made many of her creations out of traditionally masculine materials, such as wool jersey, which had never before been employed for women's clothing. Almost at once, her simple, yet elegant designs began to alter the way women of style

The Mata Hari Of The Fashion World?

Alternately the toast and scourge of Paris, Coco Chanel's reputation never fully recovered from her affair with a Nazi intelligence officer during World War II. But according to one historian, Chanel may have been more of a war hero than a war criminal. Edmonde Charles-Roux, considered the most reliable of Chanel's biographers, has offered circumstantial but credible evidence that Chanel was sent by Walter Schellenberg, a ranking officer in German intelligence, on a peace mission to British prime minister Winston Churchill. Schellenberg was reportedly acting on behalf of Gestapo leader Heinrich Himmler, who attempted to offer secret peace initiatives to the Allies toward the end of the war.

After the liberation of France, French resistance forces arrested Chanel for her wartime activities. But Churchill, a close friend of one of Chanel's former lovers, the Duke of Westminster, is said to have intervened on her behalf. Chanel was released just 24 hours after her arrest and immediately left France for Switzerland.

Gabrielle "Coco" Chanel

looked and dressed. Urged by Chanel, women the world over cut their hair and discarded their corsets in favor of loose-fitting sweaters, blazers, simple knit skirts, trenchcoats and Chanel's trademark "little black dress." Chanel was so successful that she was able to pay back Chapel in full, just four years after he set her up in business. Their affair continued, even after he married another woman, and did not end until Chapel died in a car crash on his way to join Chanel for New Year's Eve in 1919.

Throughout the 1920s, Chanel's social, sexual and professional progress continued, and her eminence as a fashion designer grew to the status of legend. Her growing fame made her one of the "in crowd." She befriended Stravinsky, Picasso and other members of Paris' exclusive art clique, and she designed costumes for Russian ballet impresario Sergei Diaghilev and French filmmaker Jean Cocteau. (Known for her generosity to her friends, Chanel paid for Diaghilev's funeral when he died penniless in Venice.)

During this time, Chanel experimented with many different styles, including gypsy skirts, over-the-top faux jewelry and glittering eveningwear made of crystal and jet beads. It was also during the '20s that Chanel introduced the product that would ensure her immortality. After the death of Chapel, Chanel became the mistress of Russian Grand Duke Dmitri. Through him, she met Ernest Beaux, a perfumer whose father had worked for the czar. Beaux was working on an essence for French perfume maker Francois Coty. According to legend, after sampling the scent, Chanel made a few suggestions, then convinced Beaux to give it to her. In 1924, she released it as Chanel No. 5—the first perfume ever to bear a designer's name. Boldly advertised as "A very improper perfume for nicely brought-up ladies," the dark, leathery, distinctly masculine blend in its Art Deco bottle proved to be liquid gold.

Chanel's fame continued to grow throughout the 1930s, as Hollywood courted her services and she nearly married one of the richest men in Europe, the Duke of Westminster. (In later years, explaining why she chose not to marry the duke, Chanel replied, "There have been several Duchesses of Westminster. There is only one Chanel.") Chanel's confidence, some say arrogance, was hard won. She'd worked her way up from literally nothing to become one of the most popular designers in the history of fashion. But with the coming of World War II, her fame would turn into infamy.

During the war, Chanel became mired in controversy. When the Nazis marched on Paris, Chanel responded by shutting down her business and becoming involved with Hans Gunther von Dincklage, a Nazi officer 13 years her junior. In return, von Dincklage allowed Chanel to continue to reside in her beloved Ritz Hotel.

Believing her career as a designer was over, Chanel stayed out of the public eye for the next decade and a half, relying on the sales of her perfume as her main source of income. Then in 1954, at the ago of 71, Chanel announced she was making a comeback.

Depending on the source, Chanel's return to the fashion world has been attributed to falling perfume sales, disgust at what she was seeing in the fashion world of the day or simple boredom. Some say she became jealous of Christian Dior's growing fame and returned to fight for her fashion crown.

Regardless of why she returned, reactions to her return were decidedly mixed. In Europe, her comeback was initially deemed an utter failure. Fashion critics were less than impressed with her new line, which merely reiterated her message of casual chic. But in the United States, Americans couldn't buy her suits fast enough. Both Europe and the critics soon relented to Chanel's success in America.

Rumor Has It

One of the enduring mysteries surrounding Coco Chanel is exactly how she got her nickname. Some of her biographers go along with the story that her father nicknamed her "Coco." Others contend that Chanel came by the name during her brief stint as a cabaret singer because her repertoire consisted of only two songs: "Ko ko ri Ko" and "Quiqu`a vu Coco?" But according to one source, Chanel herself once explained that the name was nothing more than a shortened version of "coquette," the French word for "kept woman."

Gabrielle "Coco" Chanel

Like a Phoenix rising from the ashes, Chanel once again found herself at the forefront of fashion by following the same simple yet radical philosophy with which she started: It is possible to be comfortable and chic at the same time. While it did not destroy Dior, by the time of her death in 1971, Chanel's remarkable comeback had earned her the title of "the best designer of her time."

Today, under the guidance of designer Karl Lagerfeld, Chanel remains not only one of the oldest, but also one of the world's most prestigious active fashion houses. A tribute to her unique vision, the designs of the woman who carried fashion into the 20th century promise to remain just as popular well into the 21st century.

Ben Cohen & Jerry Greenfield

"**B**usiness has a responsibility to give back to the community."

—Ben Cohen

Co-founders of Ben & Jerry's Homemade Inc.
Founded: 1978

CARING CAPITALISTS

Whoever coined the phrase "nice guys finish last" obviously never met Ben Cohen (pictured, left) and Jerry Greenfield. By making humanitarianism and philanthropy integral parts of their business ethic, they found a way to combine profitability with social responsibility, created a progressive new approach to employee management, and built one of the largest ice cream empires in the world.

Bored with their lives and wanting to do something that would be "fun," boyhood friends Cohen and Greenfield decided to start a food business in 1977. At first they considered making bagels. But when the necessary equipment turned out to cost more than they could afford, they settled for ice cream instead. There was only one problem—neither of them knew anything about the business. So they signed up for a $5 correspondence course in ice cream making offered by the Pennsylvania State University. Both got A's.

In May 1978, using $8,000 of their own money and $4,000 they had borrowed, Cohen and Greenfield opened their first Ben & Jerry's Homemade Inc. ice cream scoop shop in a renovated gas station in Burlington, Vermont. True entrepreneurs in every sense of the word, they ran all aspects of the business themselves. While Greenfield was the principal ice cream maker, Cohen served as taste-tester, scooper, truck driver, director of marketing and salesman.

With its 12 eclectic flavors of ice cream, including Dastardly Mash (with nuts, chocolate chips and raisins), Heath Bar Crunch, Chunky Monkey (with bananas), Tuskegee Chunk (with peanut butter) and Cherry Garcia (named in honor of Grateful Dead lead singer Jerry Garcia), the store quickly became a rousing success.

Unfortunately, neither of the young entrepreneurs was very good with money, and they would later admit they had no idea what was going on financially. They actually closed the store one day to pay bills, putting up a sign that read: "We're closed because we're trying to figure out what's going on."

Realizing they needed an experienced businessperson to handle their accounts, Cohen and Greenfield hired local nightclub owner Fred "Chico" Lager as their first COO. With Lager watching the books, both sales and profits rose steadily.

In 1980, Cohen and Greenfield rented packing and storage space in a former spool-and-bobbin mill and began packaging their ice cream in pints, which they distributed to local grocery stores and restaurants in Cohen's station wagon.

The popularity of their "superpremium" ice cream spread rapidly, and the pint-packing operation quickly outgrew the spool-and-bobbin mill, so Cohen and Greenfield moved it to a larger location in South Burlington in 1981. In July of that same year, Ben & Jerry's first franchise opened in Shelburne, Vermont. Ten days later, *Time* magazine published a

Rebels With A Cause

What makes Ben Cohen and Jerry Greenfield so unique as entrepreneurs is that they redefined corporate philanthropy. While many companies only go as far as to set aside a portion of their profits for charity, Cohen and Greenfield have actually created products that have in turn created jobs in economically depressed regions both in the United States and overseas.

In their quest to initiate innovative ways to improve the quality of life for a broad community, they have launched flavors such as Chocolate Fudge Brownie, which contains brownies made by homeless and unemployed workers in Yonkers, New York; Wild Maine Blueberry, made with blueberries harvested by Passamaquoddy Indians; and Rainforest Crunch, for which the company buys Brazil nuts collected in the Amazon rain forest by indigenous peoples, thereby providing an economically viable alternative to deforestation. In addition, 60 percent of the profits from that flavor go to environmental groups dedicated to preserving the Amazon rain forest.

cover story about ice cream that opened with the sentence, "Ben & Jerry's, in Burlington, Vermont, makes the best ice cream in the world." The article went on to praise other local ice cream operations in equally laudatory terms, even saying another made the best ice cream in the universe. But Cohen realized that the first sentence, taken out of context, was as effective as it was misleading and played it for all it was worth. Even more customers flocked to the stores.

As Ben & Jerry's reputation grew, so did their company's profits. By 1984, their gross receipts increased 120 percent over the previous year, with sales of more than $4 million. But as the company soared, both men began to suffer a crisis of conscience. Greenfield went into "retirement." Cohen, realizing that he was no longer an ice cream man but a businessman, contemplated selling the business. Instead, he decided to adapt the company so that he and his friend could be proud to say they were the businessmen behind Ben & Jerry's.

At first they simply returned some of their profits to the Vermont community by sponsoring local concerts and film festivals and giving away tons of free ice cream at charity events. Then in 1985, Greenfield came out of retirement to oversee the newly established Ben & Jerry's Foundation, which donates 7.5 percent of the company's pre-tax profits to nonprofit charities nationwide.

Cohen also took it upon himself to be caring within the company. Believing that the company's success came from the support of its workers, he wanted to return that support. Besides being entitled to three free pints of ice cream a day, Ben & Jerry's began rewarding their employees with profit-sharing programs, free health club memberships, day-care service and college tuition aid.

To help foster a sense of community and further empower their workers, Cohen instituted the practice of having supervisors evaluated by their subordinates and encouraged the free exchange of ideas and opinions. He also established a pay scale in which the highest-paid employee could not earn more than five times the salary of an entry-level worker. (That ratio was later adjusted to 7 to 1 in 1990.) These and other worker-focused policies garnered praise from industry experts and prompted other companies to follow suit.

As the company grew, it became necessary to hire more senior-level employees, many of whom came from traditional business backgrounds, and, unlike Cohen and Greenfield, were more interested in profits than philanthropy. As he watched the company's "one big happy family" culture begin to erode under this new breed of manager, Cohen was heard to lament, "Growing is dying." Cohen's hands-on management style also annoyed many of the new top executives, adding to the tension between him and the company's senior managers.

To correct this problem, Ben & Jerry's brought in an outside consultant who advised that the company temporarily slow down its expansion in order to gain time to reconcile their economic and philanthropic aims. The managers eventually accepted the fact that the company would not discard such policies as the salary caps, and those who disagreed left. For his part, Cohen came to the conclusion that expansion was not inherently a bad thing, providing it was accompanied by efforts to use the resulting profits for public good.

Following this new policy, which Cohen dubbed "Caring Capitalism," Ben & Jerry's continued

Ice Cream Exploits

- The very first Ben & Jerry's Homemade Inc. ice cream flavor was a variation of vanilla.
- Not all Ben & Jerry's ice cream experiments have been successful. Jerry Greenfield admits he once made a batch of rum raisin that stretched and bounced.
- In 1983, Ben & Jerry's donated 27,201 pounds of ice cream to help create the "world's largest sundae" for The Guinness Book of World Records.
- It's a little-known fact, but Ben Cohen has always wanted to create a flavor called "Rose."
- In 1986, Cohen and Greenfield set out across the country in a "cowmobile" to promote their company by giving away free ice cream. Just outside Cleveland, the cowmobile caught fire. Fortunately, neither man was injured.

to grow and expand, soaring to an incredible $132 million in sales by the end of 1992. In June 1994, Cohen announced that he was stepping down as the company's CEO. "We've never had an experienced CEO," he explains in an interview in *The New York Times*, "and we have reached the point when we need one." Although he retired as CEO, Cohen remains active in the company. As the company chairman, he concentrates on what he calls "the fun stuff," such as searching for new ways to promote worker morale and developing new ice cream flavors.

Greenfield's official titles at the company include vice chair of the board and director of mobile promotions. He often joins Cohen at speaking engagements, and both are very active in Businesses For Social Responsibility, a group that works to promote an alternative business model based on socially responsible business practices.

Ben & Jerry's has come a long way from 12 flavors and a renovated gas station. With annual sales topping $200 million, the company reigns as the world's second-largest producer of super-premium ice cream, and both of its founders are multi-millionaires. It just goes to show you, good guys don't always finish last.

Michael Dell

"You don't have to be a genius or a visionary or even a college graduate to be successful. You just need a framework and a dream."

—Michael Dell

Founder of Dell Computer Corp.
Founded: 1984

Taking The Direct Approach

Michael Dell wasn't the only young entrepreneur to ride the computer boom of the late 1980s and early 1990s from rags to riches. Like Rod Canion of Compaq and Steve Jobs of Apple, Dell turned a fledging start-up into a multibillion-dollar computer empire. But unlike the ill-fated Canion and Jobs, who lost control of their creations as they grew, Dell has managed to hold on to the reins of his maverick venture and achieve the unique distinction of being the computer industry's longest-tenured CEO.

Following the simple idea that by selling customized personal computer systems directly to customers he could best understand their needs and provide the most effective computing solutions to meet those needs, Dell has made Dell Computer Corp. the world's leading direct computer systems company.

Dell's parents wanted him to be a doctor. But by the time he was in junior high, Dell was hooked on computers. While most of his classmates were tinkering under the hoods of old cars, Dell loved to tinker with his Apple IIe.

To please his parents, Dell enrolled as a premed student at the University of Texas in 1983, but by then his only real interest was in computers. During his first semester, Dell spent his spare time buying up remaindered, outmoded PCs from local retailers, then upgrading and selling them from his dorm room. He was so successful that one day his roommate piled his ever-growing inventory up against the door of their dorm room.

Dell took this as a sign it was time to move his burgeoning business off campus. His parents were furious when he told them he wanted to drop out of college, so to appease them, Dell agreed to go back to school if the summer's sales proved disappointing. In his first month in business, Dell sold some $180,000 worth of PCs. He never returned for his sophomore year.

While looking for ways to expand his fledgling start-up, Dell concluded computers would soon become a commodity, and with commodities, what matters most is price and delivery. Dell saw that the quickest way to achieve both goals was to cut out the middleman. He realized that he could buy components and assemble the whole PC himself more cheaply. Then he could sell each machine over the phone directly to customers at a 15 percent discount to established brands. This technique, which came to be known as "the direct model of selling," would revolutionize the industry and make Dell a multibillionaire in the process.

The 19-year-old Dell dubbed his venture PCs Ltd., and the Austin-based company soon became one of the fastest-growing enterprises in the country. Rather than flooding the market with hundreds of thousands of "plain brown wrapper" computers, the company would focus on what it did best—creating customized machines to order.

The strategy worked. During its first year in operation, PCs Ltd. pulled in more than $6 million in

If It Ain't Broke...Fix It Anyway

One of the reasons Dell Computer Corp. has remained so successful is Michael Dell's firm belief in constantly rethinking his company's operations. Case in point: Although the company's computers have always boasted some of the highest quality ratings in the PC industry, in 1997 Dell became obsessed with finding a way to reduce his machines' failure rate. Convinced that the key to achieving this goal lay in reducing the frequency hard drives were handled during assembly, Dell insisted that the number of "touches" be dramatically cut down from the existing level of more than 30. After extensively revamping the company's production lines, the number of touches was trimmed to fewer than 15. The result? The rate of rejected hard drives fell by 40 percent, and the overall failure rate for Dell PCs dropped by 20 percent.

sales, and Dell quickly gained a reputation as a "boy wonder." To cash in on his growing fame, he changed the company's name to Dell Computer Corp. in 1987. Sales continued to soar, topping $159 million by the end of 1988. That same year, Dell made an initial public offering which raised $30 million, about $18 million of which went directly into Dell's pocket.

For many start-up entrepreneurs, that would have been a pinnacle signaling it was time to move on to the next promising adventure. But in Dell's mind he was just getting started. He now set his sights on overtaking industry leader IBM, rallying his employees by telling them his newborn daughter's first words were "Daddy, kill IBM." The technique got a response, and Dell's sales leapt to more than $800 million by 1991. In 1992, Dell set a goal of passing the $1.5 billion mark by the end of the year. Always the overachiever, Dell met his goal and then some, as sales rocketed to $2 billion. But in the midst of this success, there were storm clouds gathering on the horizon.

The company was growing at a pace that was too fast for the young entrepreneur to handle. By mid-1993, Dell Computer Corp. seemed to be spiraling out of control. Stock prices had plummeted from $49 in January of 1993 to a mere $16 by July. Dell's CFO resigned, leaving a management void. And worst of all, Dell had scrapped all its new lines of notebook computers because of poor production and was forced to sit on the sidelines of the fastest-growing segment of the PC market for more than 12 months.

Dell realized he needed to do something—and do it quickly. His solution was to seek out older, more experienced managers to help him regain control of his 9-year-old juggernaut. First he brought in Mort Topfer, a seasoned executive from Motorola, to handle day-to-day operations. Next he tapped the talents of Kevin Rollins, an organizational expert from Bain and Co., to run the American operations. And, perhaps his most important coup, Dell stole Apple Powerbook designer John Medica.

Within 12 months the listing company was righted, and the following year profits climbed to $149 million. But even with this amazing turnaround, Dell knew his company's place in the increasingly competitive PC industry was in no way guaranteed. To ensure continued success, Dell and his top executives made a pair of controversial strategic decisions that ran counter to prevailing industry trends. First, instead of initiating a price war in pursuit of greater sales units, Dell chose to focus on high-margin business customers. Second, the company opted to rely exclusively on direct marketing rather than retail.

Industry pundits questioned the second move, pointing out that by selling direct Dell was slighting the then sizzling home PC market. But Dell knew better. In an earlier brief foray into retail stores, Dell discovered he could not compete with Compaq's strong brand name and Packard Bell's cutthroat pricing. Selling through retail stores was definitely out. But Dell wasn't about to give up the lucrative consumer market. Instead, he decided to sell fully customized PCs via phone, fax and direct sales to more sophisticated, second-time home computer buyers.

Once again, Dell proved his critics wrong. The company's new approach had sales topping $5.5 billion by the end of 1996. But Dell had yet another ace up his sleeve. In July 1996, Dell launched one of the first direct-sale computer Web sites, and in just two months, was averaging Internet sales in excess of $2 million a day (a number that would rise to

Business In His Blood

Michael Dell has often been quoted as saying, "I always knew I wanted to run a business someday." Indeed, it does appear that Dell was born a businessman. At the age of 12, he was making thousands of dollars in mail order sales to stamp collectors. During his senior year in high school, he made $18,000 selling newspaper subscriptions for the now defunct Houston Post and bought his first BMW—paying in cash, no less. Obviously no ordinary paperboy, Dell had figured out that the most likely subscribers were newlyweds or families who had just moved in. So using sources such as the city marriage license bureau, he put together a targeted mailing list on his first computer—an Apple IIe—and sent out personalized mailings offering special subscription deals. By age 18, Dell was telling people his life's ambition was to compete with IBM. Ironically, today a lot of folks at IBM have the ambition of competing with Dell.

$6 million a day by 1998). The combination of selling direct via phone and Internet pushed Dell's sales to $7.7 billion by February 1997.

Until this time, industry experts and Dell's three main rivals, Compaq, IBM and Hewlett-Packard, were convinced that direct sales would only gain Dell a niche market. But as Dell's direct onslaught began to increasingly cut into their market share, all three competitors adopted the direct model of selling, but unlike Dell, continued to offer their machines through retail stores as well.

Whether or not Compaq, IBM and Hewlett-Packard's revamped strategy will eventually recapture the market share lost to Dell remains to be seen. But by being first, Dell definitely has the advantage, as the numbers clearly show. While the PC industry grew by a paltry 5 percent in 1998, Dell grew at an incredible pace of more than 50 percent, achieving sales of $12.3 billion. By January 1999, Dell was outselling both IBM and Hewlett-Packard and was poised to overtake the number-one computer maker, archrival Compaq.

While he has yet to completely silence his critics, Michael Dell has proven that he has the flexibility, the stamina and the vision to remain at the top of the country's most competitive business, even through the bumpiest of times. As Internet sales rocket skyward ($30 million a day in July 1999), Dell continues to baffle his competitors, astound analysts and enthrall stockholders.

Walter Elias Disney

"*If you can dream it, you can do it.*"
—Walter Elias Disney

Founder of Walt Disney Co.
Founded: 1923

Uncle Walt

Few individuals have had a greater impact on both the entertainment industry and the popular culture of the 20th century than Walter Elias Disney. His many innovations include the first cartoons with synchronized sound, the first full-length animated feature film and, of course, the theme park. His most famous creation, Mickey Mouse, is a universally recognized cultural icon. And his numerous films celebrating the triumph of the little guy and the simple charms of small-town life captured the imaginations and fueled the dreams of six generations. But while wholesomeness and nostalgic sentimentality were Disney's trademarks, the forces that shaped this maverick movie mogul and his empire were much darker and more complex.

Walt Disney's childhood was anything but idyllic. His father was a strict disciplinarian who thought nothing of taking a switch to Walt and his brother Roy to administer the "corrective" beatings that became a part of their daily routine. Young Walt found an escape from his father's brutality through drawing. With pen and ink, he created his own little fantasy world where life was always beautiful, people were always happy, and, most important, he was always in control. World War I provided Disney with yet another means of escape. At the age of 16, he joined the Red Cross Ambulance Corps and was sent to France.

After the war, Disney moved to Kansas City, Missouri, where he took a job with Film Ad Co. The firm's principal products were animated advertisements that were shown before feature films. Disney had found his calling. He loved bringing his drawings to life through the magic of animation. Advertising was less than fulfilling, though, so he converted his garage into a studio and, with borrowed equipment, began producing his own shorts, called Laugh-O-Grams. But he found it difficult to persuade local theater owners to show them. Strapped for cash, Disney gave up his apartment and started living out of his office, surviving on cold beans. But it was to no avail.

It wasn't until he moved to Los Angeles in 1923 and teamed up with his shrewd and kindly older brother, Roy, who took care of business for him, that Walt began to modestly prosper. Even so, his first commercially successful creation, Oswald the Lucky Rabbit, was stolen from him. Disney had carelessly allowed the character to be copyrighted not under his name, but under his distributor's name. It was a mistake Disney would not repeat. In subsequent years, he would gain a reputation for keeping close tabs on his creations and insisting on complete control.

Searching for a replacement for Oswald, Disney hit upon the idea of creating a new cartoon character based on a mouse that had lived in his office in Kansas City. As Disney liked to tell it, "Mice gathered in my wastebasket when I worked late at night. One of them was my particular friend."

With the help of Roy and Ub Iwerks, an illustrator from his Film Ad days, Disney fleshed out his new character—and Mickey Mouse was born. Disney released two Mickey Mouse cartoons, which met with moderate success. But the real breakthrough came in 1928 with the release of "Steamboat Willie." The first cartoon to include a synchronized soundtrack, "Steamboat Willie" was an instant hit. The day after its debut in Manhattan, *Variety* gave the cartoon a rave review, and *The New York Times* called it ingenious.

Disney hired a team of artists and animators, and Mickey Mouse films rolled out of the studio. Disney continued to embrace the latest techniques, adopting the new medium of Technicolor just as readily as

Mortimer Mouse?

Originally, Walter Elias Disney wanted to name his famous mouse Mortimer. But his wife, Lillian, thought it sounded "too sissy" and suggested the name Mickey instead. In what was probably one of the smartest decisions of his life, Disney chose to take his wife's advice.

he had sound. While the Depression gripped the rest of the country, the Disney studio flourished. Disney's cartoons offered escape at a time when Americans needed it most. Meanwhile, as his short features raked in cash, Disney was planning a bigger project—a movie-length cartoon in full color, with music.

Given the time-consuming nature of animation, the project was costly and risky. But when "Snow White and the Seven Dwarfs" was released in 1937, it proved to be no risk at all. Three years in the making, it was Hollywood's first full-length animated film. Previously, Disney's work had been the sideshow; now it was the main event. Critics raved at this artistic breakthrough and audiences crowded the theaters. Disney even received a special Academy Award for his work.

"Snow White" was followed by other animated features: "Pinocchio," "Fantasia," "Dumbo" and "Bambi." Each became a classic and contributed to the legend that was growing around its creator. In addition, Disney began making nature documentaries and live-action films such as "Treasure Island" and "20,000 Leagues Under the Sea." He was also the first Hollywood studio head to embrace the new medium of television, with "The Mickey Mouse Club" and "Walt Disney Presents." The latter, hosted by Disney himself, became not just a profit center for the company, but also a promotional engine for all its works, including Disney's greatest achievement, which was still yet to come.

Disney had long dreamed of creating an amusement park

based on his characters, but had difficulty getting financing for the project. Finally, in the early 1950s, he mortgaged his life insurance, stock holdings, house and furniture to purchase an orange grove near Anaheim, California, and finance the construction of a 185-acre amusement park. Opened in 1955, Disneyland quickly became one of the world's most popular tourist attractions. Dubbed "The Happiest Place on Earth," Disneyland became the real-life version of the fantasy world Disney had escaped to in his youth.

By the early 1960s, Disney presided over a sprawling family entertainment empire, but, unsatisfied, he bought 27,000 acres near Orlando, and soon a second magic kingdom, Walt Disney World, began to rise above the Florida swamps. But Disney never saw his dream completed. He died of lung cancer in 1966, at the age of 65.

Shortly before his death, Disney said, "I hate to see downbeat pictures…I know life isn't that way, and I don't want anyone telling me it is." Clearly millions of his fans agreed, and their adulation made him one of the most popular and influential figures in postwar American culture. And as the studio he founded continues to churn out films that bear his personal signature, Disney's magic is sure to touch the lives of many more generations to come.

David Filo & Jerry Yang

"This company is not really about technology; it's about solving people's basic needs for efficiency, effectiveness and simplicity."

—Jerry Yang

Founders of Yahoo! Inc.
Founded: 1995

THE CHIEF YAHOOS

"Don't put off until tomorrow what you can postpone to the day after." This parody of the old proverb could very well be the motto of Yahoo! Inc. co-founders David Filo and Jerry Yang (pictured, left). By following such a philosophy of procrastination, they not only created the world's most popular (and most profitable) World Wide Web search engine, they also made themselves multimillionaires in the process. Well, sort of.

The story of Filo and Yang's success begins at Stanford University, where the two doctoral candidates were involved in a project to create computer chips using computer-aided design. Both found the work less than exciting, and when their faculty supervisor took a sabbatical to Italy, the duo decided to take a little sabbatical of their own. Forsaking their academic work, they began spending most of their time surfing the Web.

This proved to be a delightful diversion from their engineering studies as they surfed the Net in search of new and exciting sites to explore. There was only one problem: There were plenty of interesting sites, but due to the Internet's lack of formal organization, finding them was akin to searching for a book in a library without the aid of a card catalog.

Time and again, Filo and Yang would find a site that interested them, then would be unable to locate it the next time they logged on. Frustrated at their inability to keep track of the good places they'd visited, Filo and Yang came up with the idea to provide a kind of road map for online users. They put together a list of their favorite sites, organized them into topics, then designed a search engine that made finding the right site as simple as typing in the right keywords.

In early 1994, they began posting their list online as "David and Jerry's Guide to the Web" so their friends could access the informal guide to "cool" sites. As the list of sites grew, Filo and Yang began dividing them into categories, then subcategories to provide more structure and easier searching. Later that summer they re-dubbed the system Yahoo!

As Yahoo!'s list of sites expanded, so did its number of users. By November 1994, 170,000 people a day were visiting the site. By 1998, Web surfers were dropping into Yahoo! at the rate of more than a million a day. Internet access service giant AOL offered a buyout. Microsoft and Prodigy approached them with partnership deals. But Filo and Yang refused them all. They weren't in it for the money. They were doing it for the sheer enjoyment of it.

Stanford, however, was not enjoying Yahoo!'s tremendous success. Claiming that Yahoo! was tying up their network with all the traffic and regularly crashing their system, the university suggested Filo and Yang move Yahoo! off campus. Given the bum's rush, Filo and Yang began considering turning their hobby into a business. "It was a really gradual thing, but we'd find ourselves spending more and more time on it," Yang told the *San Jose Metro*. "It was getting to be a burden." In fact, Filo and Yang were putting up to 20 hours a day into their labor of love and not making a dime.

At the end of 1994, Yang recruited Tim Brady, a college friend who was then attending Harvard Business School, to devise a

Say What?

How David Filo and Jerry Yang came up with the name Yahoo! is one of the Web's enduring "urban legends." As the story goes, Yahoo! is an acronym for Yet Another Hierarchic Officious Oracle, which believers say is partly a hacker's pun on a UNIX program called YACC—Yet Another Compiler Compiler. But Yang says he and Filo picked the name out of a dictionary. "We thought it fit well with what we were doing. It was irreverent. It was reflective of the Wild West nature of the Internet. A lot of people found it easy to remember, and besides, it's exactly what me and Jerry are...a couple of yahoos."

The Netscape-Yahoo! Connection

Yahoo! Inc. and Netscape Communications Corp. are two of the biggest names on the Internet, and each a Web legend in its own right. So it's not too surprising that these two Silicon Valley start-ups have a long history together. In 1995, in return for a graphical link on Yahoo!'s homepage, Netscape co-founder Marc Andreessen lent David Filo and Jerry Yang the computer equipment and phone lines they needed to get Yahoo! up and running. Andreessen also added a "Directory" button on Netscape's Navigator Web browser, which linked users directly to Yahoo!

Both companies profited from this synergy until late 1995, when Netscape ditched Yahoo! for a competitor who paid them a handsome sum to direct users to their search engine instead. Industry experts predicted that Yahoo! would soon drown in the sea of other directories, many of which had corporate backing. Though Netscape's back-out did result in a temporary drop in Yahoo!'s Web traffic, Yahoo! survived—perhaps because of its unique appeal—and continues to reign as the Internet's number-one search engine.

prospectus for Yahoo! that he and Filo could use to lure in potential venture capitalists. It didn't take long for someone to take the bait. That someone was Mike Moritz of Sequoia Capital, the same venture capital fund that financed several other Silicon Valley start-ups, including Apple, Oracle and Cisco Systems. Despite his reservations about the venture—among them his doubts that the grungy young cofounders could manage a company, and the fact that Yahoo! had yet to make any money, not to mention its goofy name—Moritz staked $1 million on the fledgling Web directory.

Armed with Moritz's money, Filo and Yang took a leave of absence from Stanford, printed business cards identifying themselves as Chief Yahoos, and hired a staff of graduate school friends and interns. Realizing that neither of them had any real business experience, the Chief Yahoos hired former Motorola Inc. executive Tim Koogle as company president and CEO.

By the summer of 1995, thanks to a series of shrewd business moves and timely events, Yahoo! had become one of the hottest high-tech properties around. Filo and Yang began selling advertising on their page. Initially, the move prompted a hail of criticism from Web purists who accused Filo and Yang of "selling out." But the criticism quickly died down as advertising became a regular feature on the Web. In a second groundbreaking move, Yahoo! teamed up with London-based Reuters news service so users could access news wire stories online with the click of a mouse.

Over the next two years, Filo and Yang added new enhancements that further increased Yahoo!'s popularity. Their innovations included links to weather, stock quotes, phone listings, sports scores, interactive maps, flight schedules, "My Yahoo " (a feature which enables users to create their own customized Yahoo! page with the particular information and links that interest them), and "Yahooligans"—a special version of the directory tailored to children ages 8 through 14.

Yahoo!'s popularity was not lost on investors looking for ways to turn a profit from the booming interest in the World Wide Web. When Yahoo! made its first public offering on April 12, 1996, shares originally priced at $13 rose as high as $43 before closing at $33, making it the second-largest first-day gain ever recorded on the NASDAQ exchange. At the end of the day, Yahoo! was valued at $850 million. Although its stock prices fluctuated, Yahoo! remained the only search engine company to post a profit until March 1998, when its closest competitor, Lycos, boasted its first profits.

By 1999, Yahoo! was making money not only by charging for ad space on its pages, but also through special co-op deals with online retailers. The arrangement entitled Yahoo! to a flat fee and a commission on any sale made to a customer Yahoo! directed to their site. Yahoo! also established a partnership with MCI and became an Internet service provider as well as an information provider.

Even though they are now the owners of a controlling interest in a multimillion-dollar business concern, Yang says little has changed in his and Filo's lives. Yang has bought himself a nice home in Los Altos, California, and a new Isuzu Rodeo, while Filo still drives a beat-up, junk-filled Datsun to the company's headquarters in Santa Clara, California, where his office is littered with empty cans, Rollerblades and assorted CDs.

As for the dynamic duo's future with Yahoo!, Yang says, "Both Dave and I realize that we want to be contributors to Yahoo! The inevitable fact is that we want the company to get to the point where it perhaps doesn't need us…where it's on its own. At that point, it will have grown enough for us to say we're successful."

Eileen Ford

Co-founder of
Ford Modeling Agency
Founded: 1946

"I create a look and I create a style.
American women mean a great deal
to me. I help them understand how they can
look better; how to do this, do that, get a job."

—Eileen Ford

THE VERY MODEL OF A MODERN MODEL AGENT

What do Kim Basinger, Rachel Hunter, Christie Brinkley and Lauren Hutton all have in common (besides being beautiful supermodels)? They were all "discovered" by Eileen Ford. Since founding the Ford Modeling Agency more than half a century ago, superagent Eileen Ford has been responsible for launching and managing the careers of some of the world's top models. Known for being blunt, tough, difficult, protective, maternal, and very, very good at what she does, Ford's notion of the ideal height, the properly wide-spaced eyes, the correct protuberance of cheekbones, breasts and hips set the standard for models for much of the latter half of the 20th century. Through a combination of this image of beauty and hardheaded business sense, Ford revolutionized the industry and created the template for the modern multimillion-dollar modeling agency.

The pampered only daughter of Loretta and Nathaniel Otte, Ford had an idyllic childhood growing up in the affluent neighborhood of Great Neck, New York. "My family believed I could do no wrong," she reveals in a *People Weekly* interview. "That's probably why I have utter confidence in myself—even when I shouldn't."

She developed a love for fashion, clothes and etiquette early in life but never imagined these could be the foundations of a career. Instead, she followed her mother's advice and entered Bernard College to pursue other studies. It was around that time she met her future husband, Jerry Ford (pictured), a varsity football player at Notre Dame. Three months later, on November 20, 1944, the couple eloped to San Francisco. But their honeymoon was cut short when Jerry was sent off to fight in World War II.

Ford returned to New York City, where she worked as a stylist for Sears Roebuck catalogs and at a Fifth Avenue specialty store. It was during this time that Ford began to develop the distinct sense of style and beauty that would become a hallmark of the Ford agency.

Two years after Jerry returned from the war, the less-than-docile Eileen, now pregnant with her first child, decided she and Jerry could use some extra cash. She began working as a secretary for two of her model friends who had become frustrated with their agencies. At that time, models were responsible for setting and collecting their own fees. Getting paid was often difficult.

The 25-year-old Ford took the job for $65 per month, and the Ford Modeling Agency was born. Ford, who had modeled briefly herself, knew better than anyone the difficulties models faced. She quickly moved from being a secretary to a full-fledged agent. When their baby arrived, Jerry stepped in and became Ford's partner and co-founder.

Ford worked hard for her models out of her small walk-up office on Second Avenue in New York City, offering services that no other agency had before. In addition to handling bookings and ensuring that her models got paid,

A Talent For Talent

Eileen Ford was once quoted as saying, "I can't add above 10, I can't draw a stick figure, and I'm tone deaf. So I had to be able to do something...I found that something was picking successful models." Indeed, Ford does seem to have a keen eye when it comes to picking the cream of the crop. Today her top clients include Veronica Webb, Naomi Cambell and Stephanie Seymore. In addition to becoming supermodels, many of Ford's former clients have used modeling as a springboard to TV and movie stardom, including Peggy Lipton, Ali McGraw, Lauren Hutton, Kim Basinger, Sharon Stone and Rene Russo.

The One That Got Away

After more than 50 years in the modeling industry, Eileen Ford has few regrets. But she does admit one gaffe that haunts her to this very day—her decision not to represent Grace Kelly. "Somebody asked me if I wanted to represent her and I said no," Ford reveals in a 1997 interview in The Columbian. "That was really stupid because she was one of the most beautiful women ever born. But I was in my 20s and very, very opinionated. Grace Kelly was a very commercial model; she had no interest in being a fashion model. None at all."

she also gave them advice on clothes, hair and makeup. She rallied for models to receive payments for fittings, residuals for print work, and fees for bookings that were canceled for bad weather. And she even helped her models with career planning. As Ford's name and fame spread through the fashion world, models began seeking her out. By 1948, the agency was grossing $250,000 a year.

A stern but loving taskmaster, Ford set strict rules for her clients. To maintain an aura of glamour and high standards, she refused to let her models accept deodorant or bra ads, pose in bathtubs or display "excessive amounts of bosom." Unlike most agents of the time, Ford became intimately involved with her models, running their personal as well as professional lives, expecting them to conform precisely to her standards of behavior.

To one weary young model who had stayed up all night with her boyfriend, Ford once gave this adamant advice: "Look, dear, you're a mess. If you want to model, fine. If you want to fool around, that's fine too. But you can't do both, so make up your mind and that's that."

Her no-nonsense manner has riled both rivals and models alike, prompting one of her protégés to call her "a sour, nasty old lady with a lot of enemies." And to John Casablancas, Ford's chief competitor, "Eileen is simply a mean person." But others are more understanding. According to Cheryl Tiegs, who was with the Ford agency in the mid-'70s and '80s, "Eileen is hard where her standards of discipline are concerned. But she has to be. There are too many beauties around to put up with girls acting up."

Even Ford herself admits that she can be difficult to work with but explains that in a ferociously competitive business where top models can earn $15,000 or more per day and an agency collects 10 percent to 15 percent, the high stakes vindicate her methods. And considering that when she first started out her models got $25 an hour, and now they get million-dollar contracts, her methods do indeed seem justified.

Regardless of what her detractors may think, Ford has proved that her policy of stringent standards works. In 1997, the Ford Modeling Agency celebrated its 50th anniversary. The small walk-up office has long since been replaced with a fashionable redbrick building, and Ford's original $65-per-month job has blossomed into a multimillion-dollar operation. But Ford girls continue to be assured of the close personal attention Ford pioneered more than half a century ago.

Although she handed over the day-to-day operations of the agency to her daughter, Katie, and her son, Bill, in the late 1980s, Ford has not retired. In fact, at age 77, the co-chair of the agency spends much of her time traveling the United States and Europe on the lookout for new talent. She has also found time to write five beauty books and is frequently sought out for her fashion and beauty advice.

"The last 50 years in a business like ours has been absolutely astonishing, and Eileen is one of the main reasons why," says former agent Nina Blanchard, summing up Ford's contributions to the industry. "She was the first to start everything that was helpful to models and their agents. She is truly the godmother of the modern modeling industry."

Henry Ford

"*I will build a motor car for the great multitude. . . it will be so low in price that no man will be unable to own one.*"

—Henry Ford

Founder of Ford Motor Co.
Founded: 1903

Photo Courtesy: Ford Motor Co.

The Man Who Taught America To Drive

Henry Ford was nearly 40 when he founded Ford Motor Co. in 1903. At the time, "horseless carriages" were expensive toys available only to a wealthy few. Yet in just four decades, Ford's innovative vision of mass production would not only produce the first reliable, affordable "automobile for the masses," but would also spark a modern industrial revolution.

Ford's fascination with gasoline-powered automobiles began in Detroit, where he worked as chief engineer for the Edison Illuminating Co. The automobile offered the promise of a bright new future…a future Ford wanted to part of. So in 1891, Ford began devoting his spare time to building what he called the "Quadricycle"—a crude contraption that consisted of two bicycles placed side by side, powered by a gasoline engine. After working on the Quadricycle for nearly a decade, Ford took Detroit lumber tycoon William H. Murphy for a ride in his hand-built automobile. By the time the ride was over, they were in business.

The Detroit Automobile Company opened in 1899 with Ford as superintendent in charge of production. But the venture only lasted a year. Ford could build a car, but he couldn't build them fast enough to keep the company afloat. Undaunted, Ford hatched a new plan—to build a racer. Ford saw racing as a way to spread the word about his cars and his name. Through the notoriety generated by his racing success, Ford attracted the attention of the backers he needed to start Ford Motor Co. in June 1903.

Ford set up shop in a converted wagon factory, hired workers, then designed and produced the Model A, the first of which he sold to a Chicago dentist in July 1903. By 1904, more than 500 Model A's had been sold.

While most other automakers were building luxury-laden automobiles for the wealthy, Ford had a different vision. His

Strike!

Ford Motor Co. was the last major automaker to unionize. Initially, Henry Ford kept his workers from organizing by paying nearly twice the going rate, cutting the workday from 10 hours to eight hours and introducing the five-day workweek. But Ford couldn't keep the United Autoworkers Union (UAW) out forever. When generosity failed, he turned to intimidation.

Ford formed the Service Department to ensure workers did their jobs and to keep the union out of his factory. Under the direction of Henry Bennett, a notorious figure with underworld connections, this group of ruthless thugs brutally repressed any attempt by UAW to organize Ford workers. In 1937, the Service Department mercilessly beat a group of union organizers attempting to pass out leaflets at the Ford factory. The beating left the union leaders battered but undaunted. It took another four years of pushing before something broke.

On April 1, 1941, Andy Dewar, a worker in the Rouge River plant's rolling mill, changed labor history at Ford. After an argument with a foreman over working conditions, Dewar began yelling "Strike! Strike!" The call echoed through the plant, and the entire rolling line walked out.

Ford was preparing to do whatever it took to keep the UAW out of his factory until his wife, Clara, demanded he settle with the union. Clara rarely interfered in Ford's business dealings, but she was genuinely afraid that the situation would explode into real violence. She threatened to leave Henry if he didn't end the strike. In May 1941, Ford Motor Co. became a union shop. The agreement led to a new era of labor relations in the automobile industry, as workers turned away from their dependence on Ford's paternalism and fear of Bennett's Service Department and toward the union shop steward and the skills of UAW negotiators.

dream was to create an automobile that everyone could afford. The Model T made this dream a reality. Simpler, more reliable and cheaper to build than the Model A, the Model T—nicknamed the "Tin Lizzie"—went on sale in 1908 and was so successful within just a few months that Ford had to announce that the company couldn't accept any more orders—the factory was already swamped. Ford had succeeded in making an automobile for the masses, but only to create a new challenge...how to build up production to satisfy demand. His solution? The moving assembly line.

Ford reasoned that if each worker remained in one assigned place and performed one specific task, they could build automobiles more quickly and efficiently. To test his theory, in August 1913, he dragged a chassis by rope and windlass across the floor of his Highland Park plant—and modern mass production was born. At peak efficiency, the old system had spit out a finished Model T in 12 $\frac{1}{2}$ working hours. The new system cut that time by more than half. Ford refined and perfected the system, and within a year it took just 93 minutes to make a car.

Because of the more efficient production, Ford was able to cut hundreds of dollars off the price of his car. Cutting the price enabled Ford to achieve his two aims in life—to bring the pleasures of the automobile to as many people as possible and to provide a large number of high-paying jobs.

But there was one problem Ford hadn't foreseen. Doing the same task hour after hour, day after day quickly burned out his work force. The turnover rate became such a problem that the company had to hire close to 1,000 workers for every 100 jobs it hoped to fill. To solve the problem, Ford decided to pay his employees $5 per day—nearly twice the going rate. Workers flocked to Ford's gates.

His labor problems solved, Ford turned his attention to another matter—the issue of who really controlled Ford Motor Co. Believing they were parasites who continually interfered with his plans, Ford bought out all his stockholders in 1919. Free to lead the company as he chose, Ford explored a number of different ventures. In addition to building tractors and single-passenger planes, Ford also operated an early mail route and the first regularly scheduled passenger flights. Undoubtedly the grandest of

Ford's ventures was The Rouge—a factory that was in itself one giant machine. Built on the Rouge River, the 1,096-acre plant was the largest industry complex of its time.

Throughout the 1920s, workers at The Rouge pumped out hundreds of thousands of Model T's, but the marketplace was changing and Ford began to fall behind the times. Ford had met its first serious competitor—Chevrolet. While Ford had dedicated the past 20 years to producing only one model, Chevrolet had developed a counterstrategy of releasing a new, improved model every year. The counterstrategy worked, and Chevrolet soon surpassed Ford in sales. Chevrolet's success proved that people wanted style, not just utility.

In this new era, Ford's "Tin Lizzie" was hopelessly outdated. A change was needed, but it wouldn't come without cost. In May 1927, Ford laid off thousands of workers while he figured out a way to get back into the market-

The Getaway Car Of Choice

When Ford Motor Co.'s new V-8 hit the streets in 1932, it was an immediate hit with an American public who craved greater luxury and more power. With a top speed of more than 80 miles per hour, it was the fastest thing on four wheels. Not surprisingly, the speedy roadster quickly became a favorite of Depression-era bank robbers and gangsters.

John Dillinger was so impressed with the V-8's power that he sent Henry Ford a letter which read, "Hello, old pal. You have a wonderful car. It's a treat to drive one. Your slogan should be 'Drive a Ford and watch the other cars fall behind you.' I can make any other car take a Ford's dust."

Clyde Barrow of Bonnie and Clyde fame also felt compelled to compliment Ford on his achievement. "Even if my business hasn't been strictly legal," he wrote, "it don't hurt anything to tell you what a fine car you got in the V-8." Barrow remained loyal to Ford for the rest of his life. When he and Bonnie were shot to death in 1934, they were riding in a Ford V-8. In 1973, the bullet-riddled car sold at auction for $175,000—more than Hitler's Mercedes Benz.

place. At the age of 64 he was starting over. With the release of a brand new Model A, Ford came roaring back to life. When the stock market crashed in October 1929, Ford Motor Co. was better off than most of its competitors. Thanks to the success of the new Model A, the company rode out the first two years of the Depression relatively untouched. Henry Ford even raised his workers' wages while dropping the price of his automobile. But he could only hold out for so long.

In 1931, the Depression caught up with Ford. After three years on the market, Model A sales fell dramatically. Chevrolet, with its new six-cylinder engine, and a new model from Plymouth cut into Ford's market share. Once again Ford was forced to shut down production and send workers home. What brought the workers back was yet another of Henry Ford's inspirations—the Ford V-8. This innovative eight-cylinder engine put Ford back on top.

But those who went back to work for Ford found that working conditions had changed. The young, humanistic idealist had become a hardened industrialist who believed the average worker wouldn't do a day's work unless he or she was trapped and couldn't get out of it. To ensure his workers put in a full day's work, Ford created the Service Department, a foreman and a group of supervisors, many of whom were ex-cons and boxers, who ruled the plant through fear and coercion.

When World War II erupted, the government asked Ford to build the B-24 Liberator Bomber. Ford had suffered a stroke in 1941, and due to his rapidly deteriorating physical and mental health, supervision of the project fell largely to Ford's only son, Edsel. Optimistic Ford spokespeople predicted that B-24s would roll out of the factory at the rate of one per hour. But by the end of 1942, only 56 planes had been built. Plagued by medical problems of his own, the project and the pressure proved to be too much for Edsel. In May 1943, 50-year-old Edsel Ford died. So at the age of 80, in spite of his clearly diminished capacities, Henry Ford once again took up the reigns of Ford Motor Co.

The news alarmed President Franklin D. Roosevelt. As the nation's third-largest defense contractor, Ford was a major part of the war effort. Aware of Ford's increasing mental incompetence, Roosevelt toyed with the idea of bringing in outside managers, or even nationalizing the plant. Instead, in August 1943, the Navy sent Ford's 26-year-old grandson home in hopes that Henry Ford II could bring order to the chaos that Ford had become. For months Clara Ford tried to convince Henry to step down and let their grandson take over. But Ford held out. Finally, Edsel's widow, Eleanor, threatened to sell her considerable holdings in the company if her son wasn't immediately named president. Henry Ford relented, and in September 1945 the crown was passed to Henry Ford II.

After stepping down as president, Ford went into seclusion, appearing only occasionally at company events. The raging fire that had driven him for more than eight decades had died out. On an April evening in 1947, Ford laid his head on his wife's shoulder and died of a cerebral hemorrhage at the age of 84. Tens of thousands of people lined up to view Henry Ford's body as it lay in state. Some factories closed, while others shut down for a moment of silence. In all, it's estimated that several million workers were involved in some kind of demonstration of sympathy for the man who had irrevocably changed their lives and taught America to drive.

Bill Gates

"*Ultimately, the PC will be a window to everything people are interested in—and everything we need to know.*"

—Bill Gates

Co-founder of Microsoft Corp.
Founded: 1975

DIGITAL DEMAGOGUE

Some see him as an innovative visionary who sparked a computer revolution. Others see him as a modern-day robber baron whose predatory practices have stifled competition in the software industry. Regardless of what his supporters and detractors may think, few can argue that Bill Gates is one of, if not the most successful entrepreneur of the 20th century. In just 25 years, he built a two-man operation into a multibillion-dollar colossus and made himself the richest man in the world somewhere along the way. Yet he accomplished this feat not by inventing new technology, but by taking existing technology, adapting it to a specific market, and then dominating that market through innovative promotion and cunning business savvy.

Gates' first exposure to computers came while he was attending the prestigious Lakeside School in Seattle. A local company offered the use of its computer to the school through a Teletype link, and young Gates became entranced by the possibilities of the primitive machine. Along with fellow student Paul Allen, he began ditching class to work in the school's computer room. Their work would soon pay off. When Gates was 15, he and Allen went into business together. The two teens netted $20,000 with Traf-O-Data, a program they developed to measure traffic flow in the Seattle area.

Despite his love and obvious aptitude for computer programming, and perhaps because of his father's influence, Gates entered Harvard in the fall of 1973. By his own admission, he was there in body but not in spirit, preferring to spend his time playing poker and video games rather than attending class.

All that changed in December 1974, when Allen showed Gates a magazine article about the world's first microcomputer, the Altair 8800. Seeing an opportunity, Gates and Allen called the manufacturer, MITS, in Albuquerque, New Mexico, and told the president they had written a version of the popular computer language BASIC for the Altair. When he said he'd like to see it, Gates and Allen, who actually hadn't written anything, started working day and night in Harvard's computer lab. Because they did not have an Altair to work on, they were forced to simulate it on other computers. When Allen flew to Albuquerque to test the program on the Altair, neither he nor Gates was sure it would run. But run it did. Gates dropped out of Harvard and moved with Allen to Albuquerque, where they officially established Microsoft. MITS collapsed shortly thereafter, but Gates and Allen were already writing software for other computer start-ups including Commodore, Apple and Tandy Corp.

The duo moved the company to Seattle in 1979, and that's when Microsoft hit the big time. When Gates learned IBM was having trouble obtaining an operating system for its new PC, he bought an existing operating system from a small Seattle company for $50,000, developed it into MS-DOS (Microsoft Disk Operating System), then licensed it to IBM. The genius of the IBM deal, masterminded by Gates, was that while IBM got MS-DOS, Microsoft retained the right to license it to other computer makers.

Much as Gates had anticipated, after the first IBM PCs were released, cloners such as Compaq began producing compatible PCs, and the market was soon flooded with clones. Like IBM, rather than produce their own operating systems, the cloners decided it was cheaper to purchase MS-DOS off the shelf. As a result, MS-DOS became the standard operating system for the industry, and Microsoft's sales soared from $7 million in 1980 to $16 million in 1981.

Microsoft expanded into applications software and continued to grow unchecked until 1984,

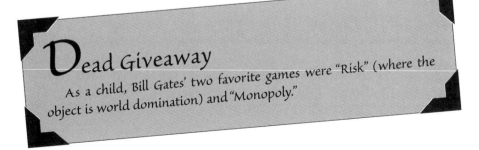

Dead Giveaway

As a child, Bill Gates' two favorite games were "Risk" (where the object is world domination) and "Monopoly."

when Apple introduced the first Macintosh computer. The Macintosh's sleek graphical user interface (GUI) was far easier to use than MS-DOS and threatened to make the Microsoft program obsolete. In response to this threat, Gates announced that Microsoft was developing its own GUI-based operating system called Windows. Gates then took Microsoft public in 1986 to generate capital. The IPO was a roaring success, making Gates one of the wealthiest people in the country overnight.

When Windows was finally released in 1985, it wasn't exactly the breakthrough Gates had predicted. Critics claimed it was slow and cumbersome. Apple wasn't exactly pleased either. They saw Windows as a rip-off of the Macintosh operating system and sued. The case would drag on until the mid-1990s, when the courts finally decided that Apple's suit had no merit.

Meanwhile, Gates worked on improving Windows. Subsequent versions of the program ran faster and froze less frequently. Third-party programmers began developing Windows-based programs, and Microsoft's own applications became hot sellers. By 1993, Windows was selling at a rate of 1 million copies per month and was estimated to be running on nearly 85 percent of the world's computers.

Microsoft solidified its industry dominance in the mid-1990s by combining Windows with its other applications into "suites" and persuading leading computer makers to preload their software on every computer they sold. The strategy worked so well that by 1999 Microsoft was posting sales of $19.7 billion, and Gates' personal wealth had grown to a phenomenal $90 billion.

But with success has come scrutiny. Microsoft's competitors have complained that the company uses its operating system monopoly to retard the development of new technology—a claim Gates soundly refutes. Nevertheless, the U.S. Justice Department filed an antitrust lawsuit against the company in 1998 over its practice of bundling software with Windows.

In November 1999, a U.S. District Court ruled that Microsoft indeed had a monopoly in the market for desktop-computer operating systems. The court also found that Microsoft engaged in tactics aimed at snuffing out any innovation that threatened its dominance of the multibillion-dollar computer industry. A federal mediator was appointed to oversee "voluntary" settlement talks between the government and the software giant. (As of press time, a settlement had not yet been reached.)

Attempting to explain his tremendous success, industry experts have pointed out that there are really two Bill Gateses. One is a consummate computer geek who can "hack code" with the best of them. The other is a hard-driven businessman who, unlike most of his fellow Silicon Valley superstars, took readily to commerce and has an innate instinct for the marketplace. This combination enabled Gates to see what his competitors could not. While they were focusing on selling software, Gates was focusing on setting standards, first with MS-DOS and later with Windows. The standards he helped set shaped the modern computer industry and will continue to influence its growth well into the next century.

Charles Geschke & John Warnock

Co-founders of
Adobe Systems Inc.
Founded: 1982

"*Our only cleverness was in the perception of what was happening, and in being quick enough to take advantage of it.*"

—Charles Geschke

THE FATHERS OF DESKTOP PUBLISHING

Mention the names Bill Gates and Steve Jobs, and most people immediately know whom you're talking about. But mention the names Charles Geschke (pictured, left) and John Warnock, and chances are you'll be met with blank stares. Ironically, these two publicity-shy high-tech trailblazers played major roles in the success of both Microsoft and Apple. In fact, without the PostScript language created by the company Geschke and Warnock co-founded, Adobe Systems Inc., desktop publishing as we know it wouldn't exist.

Like many Silicon Valley firms, Adobe was a spin-off of a bigger company—in this case, Xerox Corp. Geschke and Warnock first met and began working together at Xerox's Palo Alto Research Center (PARC), where they helped develop Xerox's page-description language, Interpress. The language won accolades within the corporation, but to Geschke and Warnock's dismay, Xerox decided to keep the technology proprietary rather that release it to public domain. Geschke and Warnock were flabbergasted by the decision. As Geschke explains in a 1987 *PC Week* interview, "We didn't see how you could make an industrywide standard with something that was proprietary."

Deciding that they could "get old and gray and frustrated somewhere else and have more fun," Geschke and Warnock left PARC to found Adobe Systems Inc. in late 1982. Originally, they planned to build a copy-service business, but quickly abandoned the idea. Next, they considered offering a complete turnkey system for office printing but dismissed that idea as well when they realized that the industry would probably head in a different direction.

Finally, they decided to concentrate on what they did best—developing specialized printing software. The result of this decision was the Adobe PostScript page-description language. A revolutionary breakthrough in printing technology, PostScript was the first printing software that enabled users to print pages that included text, line art and digitized photos.

Realizing that their best chance for success lay in making PostScript an industry standard, Adobe quickly made the PostScript language public domain. But if the product was public domain, and therefore free, how could Adobe make money from its new software? Simple: Without the PostScript program that interprets the PostScript language, the language itself is useless. In a unique twist on the classic "sell them the razor cheap then make your profits on supplying the blades," Adobe would make its money from selling the PostScript interpreter, which executes page descriptions generated by other software packages, such as desktop publishing and word processing programs. In addition, the company would also provide original equipment manufacturers (OEMs) with designs for interpreter boards to be used in their printers.

The strategy worked. By the end of their first year in business, Geschke and Warnock had licensed PostScript to Apple Computer Inc., which in turn introduced the first PostScript-based laser printer, the Apple

Five Days Of Terror

On May 25, 1992, an event occurred that would rock Silicon Valley. On his way to Adobe's headquarters in Mountain View, California, Charles Geschke was abducted by two kidnappers who demanded $650,000 in ransom for his return. Geschke's family was instructed to put the ransom in a knapsack and drop it off at an isolated beach. FBI agents hiding nearby lost one of the kidnappers in the fog as he was picking up the ransom but captured him several hours later. During questioning, the kidnapper revealed the location where Geschke was being held, and Geschke was returned to his family after five days in captivity.

LaserWriter, in January 1985. And thus, the PostScript laser printer industry was born.

Thanks to what Geschke has described as a unique combination of forward thinking, marketing savvy, timing and luck, Adobe was a success almost from the very start. By the end of 1984, it was posting revenue of $2.2 million, which grew to $16 million by the beginning of 1986. Based on their rapidly increasing revenue, Geschke and Warnock made an initial public offering in August 1986, and Adobe stock immediately became one of Wall Street's darlings. It rocketed from $11 to a peak of $56 in May 1987 (which in reality was a $112 peak, considering an earlier 2-for-1 stock split).

But more important, by 1987, Adobe's PostScript had become the industry-standard printer language. More than 400 third-party software programs supported PostScript, and Adobe boasted licensing agreements with 19 printer companies (including IBM, Digital, AST and Texas Instruments). Even Hewlett-Packard, which had initially refused to endorse the language in any way, was forced to adopt PostScript. To further increase PostScript's popularity, Adobe began building what would eventually become the world's largest typeface library.

With PostScript firmly entrenched as the industry standard, Geschke and Warnock branched out into the end-user software market with the release of Adobe Illustrator in March 1987. This high-end graphic package for professional artists and illustrators was an instant hit with both users and critics.

By 1993, Illustrator had also become an industry standard; Adobe's second software program, PhotoShop (another professional graphics package that enables users to manipulate both black-and-white and color photographs), was generating impressive reviews and even more impressive sales; and Adobe's typeface library had grown to include 1,800 fonts.

Flush with this success, Geschke and Warnock set their sights on a new goal: creating a "paperless office." To this end, they developed Adobe Acrobat, an innovative program that enables users to create documents that others can view regardless of their application software. In a brilliant marketing move, Adobe decided to offer Acrobat Reader, the program needed to view Acrobat documents, free of charge. Instead, they would charge for Acrobat

Distiller, the program that creates Acrobat documents. Although it's not the raging success PostScript or Illustrator were, Acrobat is widely used for transferring, sharing and viewing documents electronically.

The duo's next big move was to join forces with Aldus Corp., the creator of the popular desktop publishing program PageMaker, in 1994. The merger handed Adobe unquestioned leadership of the publishing-software market, creating one vendor with a broad array of products that covers both Windows and Macintosh users.

Adobe's position as "king of the hill" would not go unchallenged, however. By 1996, the once undisputed ruler of desktop publishing was losing market share to Quark Corp.—whose Quark Xpress desktop publishing program had muscled PageMaker out of the top spot in the Macintosh market—and Corel Corp., whose CorelDraw was gaining ground on Illustrator in the Windows market.

Rather than go toe-to-toe with these two up-and-coming contenders, Geschke and Warnock decided to change the rules on their competitors. They attempted to reposition Adobe as a high-profile World Wide Web publisher with the release of two Web-page authoring tools: PageMill and SiteMill. They also retooled Illustrator, PageMaker and PhotoShop to include Web-content creation tools. The gambit proved worthwhile, as Adobe once again became the kingpin of the professional graphics market, averaging nearly $900 million in sales in 1998.

By 1999, Adobe found itself competing with a new, more powerful challenger—software titan Microsoft.

Bookworm

In what very well may be one of the computer industry's greatest ironies, "paperless office" prophet and Adobe Acrobat apostle John Warnock has a passion for old books. His extensive collection of rare first editions includes literary treasures ranging from a 16th century Euclid tome to all of Charles Darwin's books.

Before Microsoft's emergence in the image-editing market, many industry analysts had noticed a change in Adobe. While it was still producing innovative products, sales were down, mostly because its marketing and PR efforts seemed to stall. *PC Magazine* columnist John C. Dvorak suggests that was partially due to the continually increasing isolation of both Geschke and Warnock, which Dvorak proposes was caused by Geschke's abduction by terrorists in 1992.

Whatever the future may hold for Geschke and Warnock, one thing is certain—Adobe's influence on the computer industry and image editing will be apparent for decades to come. Whether you browse the World Wide Web, flip through a magazine or newspaper, pick up a product box, or look up at a billboard, chances are the images and text were created with one or more Adobe products.

Amadeo Peter "A.P." Giannini

Founder of
Bank of America
Founded: 1904

"I have worked without thinking of myself. This is the largest factor in whatever success I have attained."

—Amadeo Peter "A.P." Giannini

THE "LITTLE FELLOW'S" BANKER

It may seem strange today, when there are banks on just about every corner and lenders incessantly hawk low-interest loans on TV and radio, but at the turn of the century, banks were only interested in lending money to the wealthy. In fact, many things today's bank customers take for granted, such as checking accounts, saving accounts, home mortgages, auto loans and other installment credit simply didn't exist... at least not for the working man. They had to hide their savings under mattresses and borrow from loan sharks at astronomical interest rates. But Amadeo Peter "A.P." Giannini changed all that. Through his dogged determination and unusual focus on "the little people," Giannini built what was at his death the largest bank in the country and created the model for modern international banking.

The son of poor Italian immigrants, Giannini was born in San Jose, California, in 1870. At age 14, he quit school to assist in his stepfather's produce business. By 19, the amiable young charmer was a partner in the thriving enterprise, built largely on his reputation for fairness and integrity.

In 1892, Giannini married Clorinda Cuneo, the daughter of an Italian immigrant who had made a fortune in real estate. At the time, Giannini had income from investments of about $250 a month, plus his half-interest in his stepfather's firm. He decided that was enough. "I don't want to be rich," he said. "No man actually owns a fortune; it owns him." So he sold his interest in the family business to his employees for $100,000 and "retired" at the ripe old age of 31. But fate had other plans, and unbeknownst to Giannini, his real career was about to begin.

Less than a year after Giannini went into retirement, his father-in-law died, and Giannini took over his seat on the board of the Columbus Savings and Loan Society, a small bank in San Francisco's "Little Italy" section of North Beach. But Giannini soon found himself at odds with the other directors, who had little interest in lending money to hard-working immigrants. Like most banks of the day, the Columbus S&L dealt only with businesspeople and the wealthy. Giannini tried desperately to convince the board it would be immensely profitable to lend to the working class, which he knew from personal experience to be hard-working and very credit-worthy. But the board turned a deaf ear, so the determined entrepreneur decided to strike out on his own.

In 1904, Giannini raised $150,000 from his stepfather and 10 friends and opened the Bank of Italy in a converted saloon directly across from the street from the Columbus S&L. It was the first of what is known today as a full-service bank, providing both savings and commercial checking accounts while also offering small loans. From the very beginning, Giannini intended his bank to be

Putting The Gold In Golden Gate

In the 1920s, the only way to get from Marin County to San Francisco was to take a ferry across the San Francisco Bay. As the population of Marin grew, the ferries quickly become overcrowded, creating a commuting nightmare. To solve this problem, a visionary engineer named Joseph Strauss proposed a plan for building a suspension bridge across the mouth of the San Francisco Bay that would link Marin and the city. Unfortunately, to raise the money needed to make his dream a reality, he had to fight through more than 2,000 lawsuits filed by skeptics and special interests groups.

In 1932, he approached Amadeo Peter "A.P." Giannini and said, "If Bank of America does not buy these bonds, this bridge will not be built." Giannini asked Strauss only one question: "How long will this bridge last?" "Forever!" Strauss replied. Giannini shook his head and said, "California needs that bridge. We'll buy the bonds." Thanks to Giannini's investment, the Golden Gate Bridge was begun in 1933.

Amadeo Peter "A.P." Giannini

To The Rescue

Without Amadeo Peter "A.P." Giannini, the movie industry as we know it might never have existed. In the early days of Hollywood, motion pictures were still a gamble. Many lenders felt the fledgling medium was at best merely a fad and at worst a sure money-loser. But not Giannini. In 1923, he created a motion-picture loan division, which backed such luminaries as Charlie Chaplin, Cecil B. DeMille, Douglas Fairbanks and Frank Capra and financed hundreds of films, including such classics as "West Side Story," "Lawrence of Arabia," "It's a Wonderful Life" and "Gone With the Wind."

When Walt Disney couldn't get a loan to complete the first full-length animated film, Bank of America stepped in and lent Disney the $1.7 million he needed to finish "Snow White and the Seven Dwarfs." Bank of America would go on to finance many of Disney's later films, "Fantasia," "Pinocchio," "Peter Pan," "Cinderella," "Bambi," as well as Disney's very special dream...Disneyland.

for "the little fellow,"
and he routinely lent money to farmers, merchants and laborers, most of whom were immigrants. He also encouraged recent immigrants to move their small savings from their mattresses to his bank.

The Bank of Italy continued to grow and prosper until the morning of April 18, 1906, when, like a lot of folks in the Bay Area, Giannini was thrown from his bed as the great San Francisco earthquake turned much of the city to rubble. After ensuring the safety of his family, Giannini raced to North Beach in a vegetable wagon, arriving at his bank just ahead of the fire that was sweeping through the downtown area. Sifting through the ruined building, he discreetly loaded $80,000 in gold, coins and securities into the wagon and, wary of looters, covered it all with a layer of fruits and vegetables.

In the days after the disaster, most San Francisco bankers wanted area banks to remain shut until the damage could be sorted out. But Giannini had a different plan. He set up shop on the docks near North Beach. With a wooden plank straddling two barrels for a desk, he extended credit "on a man's face and a signature" to small businesses and individuals desperately in need of money to help rebuild their lives. Giannini became a hero, and his actions spurred the city's redevelopment.

Giannini's experience in 1906 left him a changed man. "At the time of the fire, I was trying to make money for myself. But the fire cured me of that," he recalls. He saw how the power of banking could improve people's lives and made that his life's mission. He came up with the idea for a statewide system of branch banks that could bring monetary resources to far-flung communities. "By opening branches, I foresaw that we could give better service to everybody," he explains.

At the time, no other bank in America had such a system, prompting many in the business to deride Giannini's dream as mere folly. But in 1909, Giannini opened his first out-of-town branch in San Jose, and in 1913, he expanded into Southern California. In less than 10 years, Bank of Italy had 24 branches throughout California and was the fourth-largest bank in the state. Then in 1928, Giannini established the TransAmerica Corp. to act as a management company for his extensive businesses, which now included industries other than banking. The following year, he combined Bank of Italy with other banks he had acquired, under the name Bank of America. By the end of the 1920s, Bank of America had become one of the largest banks in the country.

Giannini retired a second time in 1930, convinced that his successors would carry on in his spirit. But during the Great Depression, TransAmerica management shifted focus and tried to sell off some of Bank of America's branches. Feeling betrayed, Giannini waged a successful proxy fight to regain control. Once more running the show, Giannini successfully nurtured his beloved bank through the banking crisis of March 1933 and doubled its assets in the next six years. By the time Giannini retired as active head in 1945, Bank of America had become the largest bank in the United States.

Surprisingly, when Giannini died in 1949, he left behind a relatively meager estate of just $500,000. But it was purely by choice. He could have been a billionaire, but he disdained great wealth, fearing it would cause him to lose touch with the people he wanted to serve. In the final analysis, Giannini's greatness lay not in the money he left behind, but in the bank he created—a bank that had grown to prominence on the once-radical notion of serving ordinary citizens.

Berry Gordy

Berry Gordy (decorative background text)

"*I didn't want to be a big record mogul and all that stuff. I just wanted to write songs and make people laugh.*"
—Berry Gordy

Founder of Motown Records
Founded: 1959

SWEET SOUL MUSIC

When Berry Gordy launched a small independent record label in 1959 in a two-story frame house on West Grand Boulevard in Detroit, he had no idea his dream of writing and producing his own music would spark a musical revolution. Throughout the 1950s and the early 1960s, the music industry was sharply divided along racial lines. Jazz, blues, R&B, soul and other so-called "black music" was played solely on "black" radio stations. But Gordy would change all that. His unique style of music, which he dubbed "the Sound of Young America," was the first to break the race barrier. In addition to gaining the national acceptance of black music and the well-deserved recognition of the singers and musicians behind it, Gordy's "Motown sound" gave birth to the largest and most successful black-owned business in America.

Growing up on Detroit's Lower East Side, Gordy's two greatest loves were boxing and jazz. By the time he graduated from Northeastern High School in 1948, Gordy was ready to put boxing first. But after winning 15 Golden Gloves matches, his career as a pugilist was cut short when he was drafted to fight in the Korean conflict. After the war, Gordy was too old to continue in boxing, so he turned to his other love, opening a record store specializing in jazz. Unfortunately, Gordy had failed to notice that blacks in Detroit were not especially interested in jazz. They wanted to hear rock 'n' roll. Gordy's 3-D Record Mart went bankrupt after only two years.

After this initial failure, Gordy reluctantly accepted a job at Ford Motor Co., nailing upholstery in Lincoln automobiles. But he wasn't about to give up his dream of a career in music. He began listening to rock 'n' roll and wrote several songs in this style, which he tried to sell to local singers and music labels. He had some success, but his big break came when he attracted the attention of singer Jackie Wilson, who recorded Gordy's "Reet Petite" and the now legendary "Lonely Teardrops." Both songs became instant hits, and based on their success, Gordy quit his $85-per-week job at Ford and struck out on his own as an independent producer.

But even with two hit songs under his belt, Gordy was far from a financial success. "As a writer, I had problems getting money at the time that I needed it," he explains. "I was broke even with hit records in certain cases." In one case, a New York publisher refused to pay Gordy. Advised that the cost of suing the publisher would be more than the royalties owed him, Gordy chose to cut his losses. But the incident taught him an important lesson about the music industry: If you have no control, you have no power.

To gain the control he needed, Gordy decided to start his own record company. Borrowing $800 from

Spit And Polish

One of the main reasons for Motown Record's tremendous success was the personal attention Berry Gordy paid to each Motown artist. At Gordy's insistence, every Motown performer attended an in-house finishing school, where they learned how to comport themselves both onstage and in social situations.

Gordy also instituted an internal program of "quality control," including weekly product-evaluation meetings, which he modeled after his experiences working for Ford Motor Co. At the same time, Gordy promoted a work environment that was sufficiently loose and freewheeling to foster creativity. As Gordy once explained, "Hitsville had to be an atmosphere that allowed people to experiment creatively and gave them the courage not to be afraid to make mistakes."

Thanks to this unique management approach, Motown generated hundreds of hit singles. In 1966 alone, Motown's "hit ratio"—the percentage of records released that made the national charts—was an unprecedented 65 percent.

his family, he founded Hitsville USA in 1959. The first major hit for the fledgling label was "Way Over There" by William "Smokey" Robinson—a teenage singer Gordy had found performing on street corners. Under Gordy's guidance, Robinson and his group, the Miracles, quickly became a sensation, attracting other young black performers to the fledgling record company. Within three years, Gordy's stable of performers would grow to include a number of chart-toppers, including Mary Wells, the Marvelettes, Marvin Gaye, the Contours, the Prime (whose name Gordy changed to the Temptations), and a 9-year-old blind boy named Stevie Morris—better known as Stevie Wonder. By 1960 Gordy had produced no fewer than five hit records and changed the name of his company to Motown, a contraction of Detroit's nickname, Motor Town.

Scouring the nightclubs and street corners of Detroit, Gordy found a virtually limitless supply of talented, young black performers, including The Four Tops, Diana Ross and the Supremes, and Martha Vandella and the Spinners, all of whom he quickly signed to Motown Records. By 1966, three out of four Motown releases were chart-topping hit singles. The company was so successful that Gordy opened Tamla-Motown Records in London in 1965. The hits continued to pile up, and Motown would go on to dominate the pop charts throughout the 1960s.

The 1970s brought a series of changes to Motown, and not all of them for the better. Gordy moved his operations from Detroit to the heart of the entertainment industry—Hollywood. Gordy branched out, establishing a motion picture division whose first film, "Lady Sings the Blues," a biography of blues legend Billie Holliday starring Diana Ross, was both a commercial and critical success. Gordy also made plans to produce Broadway shows, television specials and television movies. In 1973, Gordy resigned as president of Motown Records to head Motown Industries, a huge umbrella corporation overseeing all his enterprises. But as Gordy achieved success in his other ventures, Motown Records began to lose its grip on the pop charts. Most of the label's big stars left for other companies, and new talent seemed to lack that "certain something" Motown was famous for. The hits were not coming nearly as fast or as plentifully as they once did.

In 1988, Gordy sold Motown to MCA and investment group Boston Ventures for $61 million. That same year, he was inducted into the Rock and Roll Hall of Fame. Today, Gordy remains active in the entertainment industry, writing songs, producing records and working with the newly established Motown Historical Museum in Detroit.

Although Motown no longer dominates the charts as it once did, Gordy's impact on the music industry cannot be overstated. Motown's sound influenced everyone from the Beatles and the Rolling Stones to more recent chart-toppers such as Janet Jackson and Paula Abdul. A true pioneer, Gordy assembled nothing less than the rock 'n' roll era's most remarkable roster of artists, musicians, songwriters and producers; and in pursuing his dream, he brought two races together through music.

Andrew Grove & Gordon Moore

Co-founders of Intel Corp.
Founded: 1968

"*Only the paranoid survive.*"

—Andrew Grove

SILICON MAGICIANS

The history of the modern computer industry is rife with pioneering duos: William Hewlett and David Packard, Steve Jobs and Steve Wozniak, Bill Gates and Paul Allen. But the duo that is most responsible for making personal computers as common a consumer durable as television sets is Andrew S. Grove (pictured, left) and Gordon E. Moore. Through the combination of Moore's inventive engineering and Grove's hard-driving, sometimes ruthless management style, these innovative entrepreneurs provided the "ammunition" for the personal computer revolution and built one of the most profitable businesses in the annals of industry.

Born in Pescadero, California, a tiny coastal town about 50 miles north of San Francisco, Gordon Moore never dreamed he'd become an entrepreneur. He wanted to pursue the quiet, contemplative life of academia. But after graduating from the California Institute of Technology with a Ph.D. in chemistry and physics, he found that teaching jobs were scarce and accepted a position with Shockley Semiconductor, a research lab founded by Nobel Prize winner and co-inventor of the transistor, William Shockley. At Shockley, Moore met and became friends with another engineer, Robert Noyce.

William Shockley may have been a brilliant scientist, but he proved to be a merciless manager and virtually impossible to work for. After a year of frustration, Moore, Noyce and six other engineers left Shockley and started Fairchild Semiconductor, a West Coast subsidiary of Fairchild Camera & Instrument. Together, this close-knit group developed the first integrated circuits, which combined several electronic components onto a single chip rather than devoting a separate chip to each function. As Moore would later recall, "We had no idea that we had turned the first stone on something that was going to be a $1 billion business."

During his time at Fairchild, Moore interviewed and hired his future partner, Andrew Grove. A Holocaust survivor, Grove had immigrated to the United States in 1957 when the Soviet Union invaded his homeland of Hungary. Grove arrived in New York City with $20 in his pocket and little knowledge of the English language. He enrolled in the City College of New York—a free school that had become kind of an immigrant's Oxford—to study engineering.

Overcoming the language barrier, Grove received his bachelor's degree, graduating near the top of his class. From there he headed to California, where he entered the Ph.D. program at University of California, Berkeley. Again he was an academic star, and upon graduation in 1963, he had his pick of American research corporations. He narrowed his choices down to Bell Laboratories or Fairchild Semiconductors, and finally chose to cast his lot with Fairchild. For the next five years, Grove would work side by side with Moore, who became his mentor and friend. At Fairchild, Grove was a

Tech Prophet

Gordon Moore is a true visionary in every sense of the word. Like Jules Verne and H.G. Wells, Moore seems to have the uncanny ability to very accurately predict the future of technology. In a little-known article published in Electronics magazine in 1965, Moore formulated what would become known as "Moore's Law." It states that the density of transistors in an integrated circuit would double every year with proportionate decreases in cost. Moore was only off by a couple of months. In the more than three decades since he made his prediction, not only transistor density, but also microprocessor performance, has doubled every 18 months.

"Integrated electronics," Moore writes, "will make electronic techniques more generally available throughout all of society." He then went on to predict the coming of such things that have since become commonplace consumer items, including home computers, portable telephones and cars made smarter by use of dozens of relatively cheap computer chips.

member of the team that perfected the use of silicon in transistors, which set the stage for the semiconductor revolution.

But while Grove and his team were revolutionizing the semi-conductor industry, Fairchild was falling apart. Engineers were leaving, top executives didn't understand the business, and science was being replaced by politics. Sensing Fairchild was doomed, Robert Noyce and Gordon Moore decided to start their own company. Knowing Grove's excellent organizational, communica-tion and leadership skills, they asked him to join them.

Backed with money provided by San Francisco venture capi-talist Arthur Rock, the trio founded Intel (short for Integrated Electronics) Corp. in 1968. With Noyce as CEO, Moore as exec-utive vice president and Grove as director of operations, Intel produced its first product—a bipolar memory chip—in 1969. From the beginning, Intel adopted what Moore calls the "Goldilocks Strategy." Intel's execs knew they had a choice of three technologies: an easy one that could be quickly copied by the competition, a complicated one that might easily bankrupt them, or a moderately complicated one. Like Goldilocks, they chose the middle course—a decision that would eventually enable Intel to dominate the microchip market.

Intel's first big product, the 1101 Static RAM chip, gave the company a strong lead on its competitors, a lead it maintained for nearly 10 years. In the early 1970s, Intel reached beyond the memory chip market and began experimenting with "multipur-pose" chips—using software to make one chip perform multiple functions. It was this research that led Intel to produce the world's first microprocessor—a single chip powerful enough to run a small computer—in 1971. Ironically, Grove and most other Intel execs did not think of it as part of the company's core business. Nevertheless, Intel continued to refine its microprocessors.

Intel experienced tremendous growth throughout the 1970s, dominating the memory chip market and increasing its earnings with each fiscal year. Moore succeeded Noyce as CEO in 1979, and Grove became the company's president. Two years later, IBM chose Intel's 8086 microprocessor for its fledgling personal com-puter. It couldn't have happened at a better time. Japanese semi-conductor companies had begun dumping cheap memory chips into the U.S. market and were rapidly eating away at Intel's profits.

The crisis forced Grove to reassess the value of the micro-processor. In 1984 he and Moore suggested that Intel shift its focus from memory chips to microprocessors. This proposal would change the course of Intel history. IBM's decision to use only Intel chips in its computers had already given Intel a tremendous lead in the microprocessor market. In addition, IBM had purchased $400 million of Intel stock, which provided Intel with the capital it needed to design and construct new micro-processor plants.

By 1985, personal computer sales were booming as IBM clones poured into the market at record pace. But while cloners such as Compaq Computers were rapidly swiping market share from IBM, nearly all of them had to use Intel's chips, which had become the industry standard. With the huge and growing market assured by IBM as well as the cloners, Intel quickly became the world's largest producer of microprocessors.

Crisis Turned Caveat

If nothing else, Andrew Grove is a survivor. Although he made few missteps as head of Intel, his one major gaffe actually turned into a boon for the company. In 1994, Intel released millions of flawed Pentium computer chips. Consumers demanded replacements. But Grove refused, insisting the glitch was so small that conventional PC users would not be affected unless they were working on "some advanced astrophysics problems."

Dissatisfied with this response, Pentium users turned to the press, and Grove had a public relations nightmare on his hands. Within a few days, he reversed his decision and agreed to spend $475 million to replace the chips, going so far as to offer home delivery. Grove would later admit that the incident was "a difficult education" in customer relations. Ironically, Grove's decision turned a PR disaster into an adver-tising bonanza. The extensive press coverage made Intel's name better known than ever. And once the firm agreed to replace the chips, cus-tomers saw Intel as a company that was determined to get things right, regardless of the cost.

In 1987, Moore retired, handing the title of CEO over to Grove. Under Grove's guidance, Intel produced increasingly powerful microprocessors throughout the 1990s, achieving near-monopoly conditions in supplying chips for PCs. In fact, Intel experienced little or no competition until the close of the decade.

As the popularity of PCs grew, competition in the market became fierce. A number of computer companies began using cheaper chips from other manufacturers in order to offer consumers PCs priced under $1,000. Unwilling to walk away from a market whose size Grove predicted "is going to be measured in tens of millions of units per year, maybe bigger," Intel began producing chips for "value PCs" in 1997. Once again, Grove was able to keep Intel on top. By the end of 1997, Intel held nearly 90 percent of the microprocessor market, with sales exceeding $25 billion.

In May 1998, three decades after he helped found Intel, Andrew Grove relinquished his CEO title to company COO Craig Barret. In an interview for CNNfn.com, Grove explained his reason for stepping down: "I have been CEO for 11 years. Intel has been around 30. I'm the third CEO, so I've had more than the average share of tenure."

Joyce Clyde Hall

*"**G**ood taste is good business."*
—Joyce Clyde Hall

Founder of Hallmark Cards Inc.
Founded: 1910

A SHOEBOX
FULL OF DREAMS

When 18-year-old Joyce Clyde Hall stepped off a train in Kansas City, Missouri, in 1910, he didn't have much—just a battered suitcase and two shoeboxes of picture postcards. Full of youthful enthusiasm, J.C. (as he preferred to be called) was determined to make his mark on the business world. He had big plans and the energy to make them happen. And happen they would— over the next 56 years, Hall would create a new industry and build the world's largest greeting-card company.

Hall's early life was marked by a nearly constant struggle to overcome abject poverty. His father, an itinerant preacher, abandoned his family, leaving Hall and his two older brothers to provide for their semi-invalid mother. He took his first job as a farm hand at age 8, and a year later he was selling cosmetics and soap door to door for the California Perfume Company (which later became Avon).

In 1902, Hall's older brothers moved to Norfolk, Nebraska, and opened a bookstore. Not long after, the rest of the family joined them, and Hall went to work in the store for $18 per month. Believing there was a large local market for postcards imported from Europe, Hall and his brothers established Norfolk Post Card Co. when he was 16. Unfortunately, there wasn't enough local demand to keep the company in business. Realizing there might be a larger market for postcards outside Norfolk, Hall quit school, packed two shoeboxes full of postcards and headed for Kansas City.

When Hall arrived in Kansas City, he had only enough money to rent a small room at the YMCA, which served as his home, office and stockroom for the next year. He sent out packets of 100 postcards to dealers throughout the Midwest in hopes of starting a successful mail order business. Some of the dealers kept the cards without paying. Others returned the unsolicited merchandise with angry notes. But about one-third of the dealers sent the young entrepreneur a check. In just a few months he had earned $200.

Despite his initial success, Hall believed illustrated postcards were a passing fad, so he added a line of imported Christmas and Valentine's Day cards. Within a year his brother Rollie joined him in the business, and by 1912 the Hall Brothers logo started appearing on greeting cards. J.C. and Rollie further expanded their line and opened retail stores in Kansas City and Chicago.

Just when success seemed to be within the brothers' grasp, disaster struck. In 1915, just a few weeks before Valentine's Day, fire swept through their warehouse, destroying their entire inventory of Valentine's Day cards and leaving the brothers $17,000 in debt. "If you want to quit, that's a good time to quit," Hall says of the calamity. "But if you're not a quitter, you begin to think fast." And that's exactly what he did.

Rising to the challenge, Hall borrowed enough money to purchase a local engraving firm so he and Rollie could replenish their stock quickly and cheaply by printing their own cards. They produced their first two cards in time for Christmas 1915. The hand-painted yuletide greetings quickly became a success with holiday shoppers, providing the brothers with a badly needed influx of cash.

Now that he had his own printing press and some capital to work with, Hall began experimenting with other card concepts. At the time, most of the greeting cards sold in the United States were elaborately engraved imports from England and Germany, made only for Christmas and Valentine's Day. But Hall believed Americans, who were much more casual than

Card Shark

In 1998, Americans spent more than $7.5 billion on greeting cards; Hallmark Cards Inc. leads the industry with more than 41 percent of the market share.

Joyce Clyde Hall

It's A Wrap

In addition to creating the modern greeting-card industry, Hallmark Cards Inc. is also credited with introducing decorated gift wrap as a replacement for the plain brown wrapping paper and standard white, red and green tissue that had been used for years. The innovation was somewhat of a fluke, however. During one Christmas season, the Hall brothers ran out of colored tissue, and quick-thinking Rollie substituted the fancy French paper that was used to line envelopes. The shoppers loved it, so Hallmark began producing a complete line of colored wrapping paper for every occasion.

Europeans, would take to the idea of inexpensive "everyday" greeting cards they could send to friends and family not just on holidays, but throughout the entire year. His vision of colorfully illustrated cards expressing sentiments, friendship and even sympathy would create an entirely new market for greeting cards in America.

Convinced that the sending of casual "me to you" messages would eventually catch on as a social custom, Hall introduced his first everyday card in 1919. It featured a line from American poet Edgar Guest: "I'd like to be the kind of friend you've been to me." This simple yet heartfelt verse captured a feeling that many people wanted to share, and it became an immediate bestseller.

Encouraged by the success of this initial venture, the Hall brothers expanded their card themes to include birthday wishes, anniversary tidings, inspirational greetings and get-well messages. World War I added to the brothers' success, as folks back home rushed to send "missing you" cards to loved ones stationed overseas.

By the early 1920s, the all-occasion cards were being sold in stores throughout the East and Midwest, and the Halls moved to a new Kansas City location that employed 120 workers. By now, sending "me to you" cards had indeed become a social custom, something which did not go unnoticed by the Halls' main competitor, American Greetings, which had also begun selling all-occasion cards. In response to the increased competition and to further expand and gain national recognition, Hall re-christened the company Hallmark—a name that suggested the highest quality.

In the decades that followed, Hall continued to strive to make the Hallmark name synonymous with excellence. In 1944, Hallmark executive C.E. Goodman coined the now legendary Hallmark advertising slogan, "When you care enough to send the very best." To ensure his cards lived up to this promise, Hall called upon the talents of popular artists and writers of the day, such as Norman Rockwell, Grandma Moses, Ogden Nash and Pearl Buck. He even sold cards designed by Winston Churchill and Jacqueline Kennedy Onassis.

Always looking for new ways to sell his cards, Hall began studying American shopping habits and discovered a large potential market selling cards through chain drug, food and discount retailers. In 1959, he introduced Ambassador Cards, a special line created to be sold solely through these rapidly growing retail channels.

A die-hard autocrat and staunch perfectionist, Hall insisted on giving his stamp of approval to every single greeting card design and verse before it was added to the product line. Even after his retirement in 1966, when his son, Donald, took over the helm, Hall continued to put in full days at the office when he wasn't vacationing. At the time of Hall's death in 1982, the company he founded more than 70 years earlier was turning out 8 million greeting cards each day, including the card that started it all—the Edgar Guest friendship verse, which remains one of Hallmark's strongest sellers to this day.

Ruth Handler

Co-owner of
Mattel Inc.
Founded: 1945

"When I conceived Barbie, I believed it was important to a little girl's self-esteem to play with a doll that has breasts."

—Ruth Handler

Barbie's Mom

When Mattel co-founder Ruth Handler first proposed that the company make a grown-up doll, the marketing staff at Mattel balked at the idea. Little girls like playing with baby dolls, they proclaimed. And they were certain that adult women wouldn't want their children to have a doll with breasts. But the budding business dynamo wasn't one to give up easily. It took her nearly three years, but Handler finally convinced the company to make the doll. It was probably the best decision they ever made. Barbie, as Ruth would name the 11½-inch doll, was an instant hit, not only making Mattel an undisputed leader in toy manufacturing, but also creating a $1.9 billion per year industry.

The company that would eventually become one of the world's leading toy manufacturers began rather inauspiciously in a garage in El Segundo, California. The original founders, Harold Matson and Elliot Handler (pictured), dubbed the venture "Mattel," creating the name by combining letters of their first and last names. Mattel's first product was picture frames, but Elliot developed a side business making dollhouse furniture from picture frame scraps.

Believing the company was doomed to fail, Matson sold out to his partner, and Handler's wife, Ruth, joined him as co-owner. Encouraged by the success of their doll furniture, the Handlers switched the company's emphasis to toys and began making a line of musical products, including a child-sized ukulele and a patented hand-crank music box, which generated much of the company's revenue in the '50s and '60s.

The company did reasonably well but was far from an industry powerhouse. It was in 1956 that Ruth Handler hit upon the ingenious idea that would rocket Mattel to the forefront of the toy industry and fascinate four generations of young girls.

Handler got the inspiration for the Barbie doll while watching her young daughter, Barbara, and her friends playing with paper dolls. The girls liked to play adult or teenage make-believe with the dolls, imagining them as college students, cheerleaders and adults with careers. It dawned on Handler that make-believe and pretending about the future are important parts of growing up. In researching the market, she discovered a void and became determined to fill the niche with a 3-D doll.

Mattel designers had their doubts, going so far as to say that making such a doll was impossible. While vacationing in Europe, Handler discovered a German doll named Lilli—a quasi-pornographic novelty gift for men. She brought three dolls and sent Mattel designers to Japan telling them to "find us a manufacturer."

Everything You Ever Wanted To Know About Barbie But Were Afraid To Ask

- Barbie's full name is Barbara Millicent Roberts, and her hometown is Willows, Wisconsin.
- Barbie's first career was as a teen fashion model. Since then, she's had more than 75 different jobs, including astronaut.
- The bestselling Barbie doll ever was Totally Hair Barbie, with hair from the top of her head to her toes.
- Close to 1 billion fashions have been produced for Barbie and her friends since 1959. Currently, about 120 new ensembles are designed for Barbie each year.
- More than 40 leading fashion designers, including Bob Mackie, Bill Blass, Gianni Versace and Missoni, have created Barbie costumes.
- The military series of Barbies—Army, Navy, Air Force and Marine Corps—underwent revision by the Pentagon to ensure the most realistic costumes.
- Barbie accessories include a plane, a yacht and 46 houses.
- Barbie has had 17 dogs, 12 horses, five cats and three ponies.
- More than 1 billion Barbies have been sold since 1959. Placed head to toe, they would circle the Earth more than seven times.

Ruth Handler

Handler's vision for the doll, which she called Barbie (her daughter's nickname), was that she be the "ideal" woman. According to legend, Barbie's face and figure were created from a combination of the best features of the day's most popular stars, including Audrey Hepburn's famous eyebrows.

By 1959, Barbie was a reality and ready to hit the stores. But there were a few snags. In early market research, it was revealed that mothers hated the doll, one reportedly saying, "Wow! That's really a daddy's doll, isn't it?" Toy retailers were also less than impressed with Barbie. When the doll was introduced at the 1959 Toy Fair in New York City, retailers had never before seen a doll so completely unlike the baby and toddler dolls that were popular at the time, and many refused to carry it.

Undaunted, Handler went directly to young girls with television ads that presented Barbie as a real person. Thanks to this innovative marketing approach, within three months of her debut, Barbie dolls were selling at a rate of 20,000 per week. Demand for the doll was so great that it took several years for the supply to keep up with the demand. Barbie was so successful that she enabled Mattel to go public in 1960, and within five years, Mattel would join the ranks of the Fortune 500.

Over the next few years, an entire industry sprang up around Barbie. Designers continually worked to create new clothes for Barbie that reflected the changing fashions of the day. But they didn't stop at merely clothes. Barbie soon had her own dream house, a car, a plane, a yacht and dozens of other accessories, not to mention a host of "friends," including dolls named Midge, Skipper and Christie. Barbie even got her own boyfriend, Ken, named after Handler's son. Ironically, ranging from $5 and up, most of Barbie's clothes and accessories cost more than the doll itself (Barbie cost $3). In fact, today Barbie accessories generate nearly 40 percent of Mattel's revenue.

Since her "birth," approximately 1 billion Barbies have been sold in four decades, making Handler's "child" the bestselling fashion doll in every major global market, with worldwide annual sales topping $1.9 billion.

In 1999, at a gala event celebrating Barbie's 40th birthday, Handler was asked if she was surprised by Barbie's tremendous success. "I always thought Barbie was very, very basic," she replied. "She was as basic a toy for play as was possible to have, and I had faith that she would be a great toy. But I never thought that any toy could ever last this long or grow this big."

After a personal victory over breast cancer in the mid-1970s, Ruth Handler retired from Mattel. She went on to use her experience and expertise to start Ruthton Corp., which is dedicated to the development and manufacturing of breast prostheses called "Nearly Me." By meeting with department store buyers, promoting the products herself across the country, and talking candidly with other breast cancer survivors, Handler built her second company into a success. In 1991, she sold Ruthton Corp. to a division of health and beauty aids giant Kimberly-Clark.

William Harley, Arthur Davidson, Walter Davidson & William Davidson

Co-founders of
The Harley-Davidson
Motor Company
Founded: 1901

"*In 1901, these two boyhood friends embarked on a quest to 'take the work out of bicycling.'*"

Riding High On The Hog

The Harley-Davidson motorcycle has become an American icon. Recognized around the world, it is a symbol of America's inventiveness, rugged individualism and pioneering spirit. Ironically, what would become one of the world's largest and most widely recognized motorcycle manufacturers was born out of pure and simple laziness.

Around the turn of the century, a new invention was sweeping across America—the bicycle. This two-wheeled wonder enabled individuals to travel farther and faster than ever before possible, and millions took off to explore the country with pedal-power.

But this wasn't enough for 21-year-old draftsman William Harley (pictured, standing) and 20-year-old pattern-maker Arthur Davidson (pictured, middle). In 1901, these two boyhood friends embarked on a quest to "take the work out of bicycling." Their dream was to build a motorized bicycle that would enable people to travel reliably and as fast as the technology of the time would allow.

Realizing that to fulfill their dream they would need a skilled mechanic, the duo enlisted the help of Arthur's brother, Walter Davidson (pictured, right), a railroad machinist whom they lured from his job in Kansas by promising him a ride on their motorcycle. After arriving in Milwaukee, Walter discovered that he would have to help William and Arthur build their motorcycle before he could ride it. But he decided to stay on anyway. The eldest Davidson brother, William, then a tool-room foreman at a Milwaukee railroad shop, also offered to pitch in.

Working out of their first factory, a 10-foot by 15-foot wooden shed in the backyard of the Davidson family home with "The Harley-Davidson Motor Company" painted on the door (William

Harley was given top billing because it was his idea to build a motorcycle in the first place), the four men produced their first three motorcycles in 1903. Like all their early motorbikes, the

Marching Orders

In 1916, General "Black Jack" Pershing was sent to Mexico to capture Francisco "Pancho" Villa. The Mexican revolutionary had been raiding towns on both sides of the U.S.-Mexican border, and Pershing's orders were to stop Villa any way he could. Pershing's men had difficulty chasing Villa's bandits on horseback through the rugged Mexican terrain, so they asked The Harley-Davidson Motor Company for help. The company loaded 12 motorcycles onto a railroad car and shipped them to Pershing. These specially designed motorcycles were equipped with a sidecar gun carriage that served as a machine gun platform.

Although Pershing never caught Villa, the motorcycle proved its worth in combat, and when America entered World War I, Harley-Davidson was drafted. In 1917, Harley was supplying about half of its motorcycles to the military. But by the end of the war, all of Harley-Davidson's production was going to the military—more than 20,000 motorcycles in all.

Harley-Davidson motorcycles would once again be pressed into service of the country in World War II. Almost immediately after the Japanese attacked Pearl Harbor, Harley-Davidson converted its factories to support America's fighting forces. During the war, more than 90,000 Harleys, the company's entire production output, were shipped overseas for Allied troops.

Because they could go virtually anywhere, U.S. armored divisions used Harley-Davidsons for reconnaissance, to probe for enemy mines, scout for ambushes, secure bridges and establish forward positions. In a tank attack, motorcycles either led or followed the tanks, riding a full throttle with their machine guns blazing.

The wartime exploits of the dashing motorcycle riders gave the bikes an air of glamour and adventure back home, creating a growing mystique around the motorcycles that would greatly boost sales after World War II.

1903 Harley-Davidson had a bicycle crank, a single-cylinder engine, pedals and a leather drive belt. To start one, riders simply pedaled the bike until enough engine compression had built up, then soared away with power.

Harley-Davidson's next few years can be summed up in two words: growth and development. The partners produced three motorcycles in 1904 and seven more in the following year. The company was growing so fast that the Davidson backyard could no longer contain it. In 1906, Harley and the Davidson brothers built a new factory on Juneau Avenue in Milwaukee and produced a record 50 machines. The company formally incorporated in 1907 and, by 1909, they had doubled the size of their factory, hired 35 employees and increased production to around 1,000 motorcycles per year.

Obsessed with improving his invention, Harley began working on a design for a two-cylinder engine. After a false start in 1907, he perfected the model in 1909. The new engine, called a V-Twin, could propel a motorcycle at a lightning speed of 60 mph. Thanks to the success of the V-Twin, the company quickly developed a reputation for building reliable, unusually fast motorcycles; and by 1910, annual production rose to 3,200 machines.

To build excitement and promote sales, Harley-Davidson sponsored a racing team dubbed "The Wrecking Crew," who became known for their seat-of-their-pants racing style. While the fame generated by The Wrecking Crew kept the company in the news and stimulated sales, to stay ahead of the competition the company began reinvesting much of its profits into engineering and product enhancements.

Harley-Davidson's next big breakthrough came in 1912, when Harley perfected a chain drive to replace the outdated leather drive belt. A few years later, in 1916, Harley came up with the step-starter, which eliminated the need for pedals and finally broke the motorcycle from the parentage of the bicycle.

But many people, including the U.S. government, still relied on bicycles for an inexpensive means of transportation. Always looking for other ways to market his company's product, Arthur became determined to convince government officials that motorcycles could replace bicycles at the U.S. Postal Service and many other government agencies. Arthur's strategy worked, and by

1914, the USPS had more than 4,800 Harleys delivering mail. The military was also attracted to the rugged, fast bikes, and Harley sales soared.

By 1920, production reached 28,189 bikes annually, and Harley-Davidson became the world's largest motorcycle manufacturer, with dealerships in 67 foreign countries. Harley was riding high, but problems lay ahead. The country experienced a mild depression in the early 1920s, which caused sales to slip. In addition, the motorcycle faced competition from Henry Ford's cheaper, imminently more practical Model T.

As part of their survival plan, Harley-Davidson convinced America's police departments that the fast, nimble motorcycle was an ideal vehicle for law enforcement. By the middle of the decade, more than 2,900 sheriffs and state patrols were using Harley-Davidsons. Boots, breeches and saddlebags gave motorcycle cops a "Wild West" image that thrilled young boys and captivated the public's interest. Walter recognized the allure of this "motorcycle look," and launched a campaign to sell Harley-Davidson accessories and clothing. The ingenious marketing move

The Wrecking Crew

Today, the idea of a motorcycle manufacturer sponsoring a racing team seems like a common-sense marketing strategy. But back in the 1900s, when The Harley-Davidson Motor Company sponsored a racing team dubbed "The Wrecking Crew," the idea was revolutionary. Known for their death-defying "board track" racing, these fearless daredevils competed on wooden tracks that featured banked turns of up to 60 degrees.

Making the transition from straightaways to banked curves at speeds of up to 80 mph was difficult and often deadly. Accidents were frequent and usually fatal for both riders and spectators, so The Wrecking Crew abandoned board tracks in favor of dirt tracks, which proved to be just as popular though less dangerous. The Wrecking Crew was just as successful on dirt tracks as they'd been on board tracks, and from 1915 on, they were the team to beat.

Harley & Davidson

helped the company survive the down days of the 1920s and created a booming market for Harley-Davidson accessories that remains a major part of the company's success to this day.

Through smart marketing and further improvements, including a larger engine and front brakes, Harley-Davidson sales began to slowly increase, and by 1928, more than 22,000 motorcycles were being produced per year. Optimism had returned. But this attitude proved premature.

The stock market crash of 1929 sent motorcycle sales into a tailspin. Production plummeted to just under 4,000 bikes by 1933. To reverse the slide, Harley gave the bikes a facelift, replacing the standard block-letter Harley-Davidson logo with a new art-deco tank design featuring a graceful stylized eagle. The company also began offering bikes in an array of different color schemes.

Development continued, and in 1936, Harley unleashed its EL model. Boasting an engine that could deliver twice as much power, a new frame, a new suspension and a new tank design, the EL was a major breakthrough for the company. These new bikes hit the road and started to rev up sales. Production climbed back to almost 10,000 units per year, where they would remain until the end of the decade.

The coming of World War II would further increase Harley production and sales. Harley built and shipped more than 90,000 of its military-version motorcycles overseas for use by the Allies.

Following World War II, Americans eagerly returned to motorcycle riding. To meet the exploding demand for its motorcycles, the company purchased additional manufacturing facilities in the Milwaukee suburb of Wauwatosa in 1947. By the time Arthur Davidson, the last of the original founders, died in 1950, Harley-Davidson had become the undisputed king of the road.

Over the next four and a half decades, as a second generation of management rose through the corporate ranks to replace the company's founding fathers, Harley-Davidson would experience a series of ups and downs, resulting from image and mechanical problems as well as competition from the Japanese. But by being faithful to the tradition of quality and development established by its founding fathers, Harley-Davidson stands as the sole survivor of what was once a group of 300 U.S. motorcycle manufacturers.

Hugh Hefner

Founder of Playboy
Enterprises Inc.
Founded: 1953

*"**I**f you have to sum up the idea of Playboy, it is antipuritanism. Not just in regard to sex, but the whole range of play and pleasure."*

—Hugh Hefner

THE ULTIMATE PLAYBOY

ailed as a groundbreaking crusader by his supporters and derided as an irresponsible hedonist by his critics, Hugh
M. Hefner was one of the harbingers of the sexual revolution that
swept through the United States in the 1960s. He was also an
extraordinarily astute entrepreneur who, in addition to publishing
one of the world's most successful magazines, built a tremendously profitable business empire—a conglomeration of clubs, casinos
and resorts known as Playboy Enterprises Inc. In the nearly half-
century since the Midwestern son of a puritanical mother and
workaholic father began espousing the playboy lifestyle, Hefner
would watch as the tremendously successful business he master-
minded nearly crumbled in the 1980s, only to be revived in the
late 1990s.

From the very beginning, Hef, as he likes to be called, knew he
wanted to be involved in publishing. His first experience came in
high school, when he wrote and drew cartoons for his high school
newspaper. He even started his own magazine. But at graduation
time in 1944, instead of pursuing his dream of a job in publishing,
Hef enlisted in the U.S. Army, where he spent the next two years
working stateside as a clerk.

Upon his return to civilian life, Hefner was unable to find
employment as a journalist, nor could he sell his idea for a comic
strip about a college student named "Fred Frat." Instead, he was
forced to take a number of more mundane jobs, including one as
the personnel director for a Chicago cardboard-carton manufacturer and one as an advertising copywriter for a Chicago department store. But just when he was ready to give up his dream, he
received a job offer from *Esquire* magazine that he hoped would

turn his life around. During his tenure at *Esquire*, Hefner learned how to publish and distribute a magazine. *Esquire*, however, would prove to be another dead end. In 1952, the magazine moved its offices to New York City, leaving the would-be publisher behind in Chicago.

Even though his departure from *Esquire* was a disappointment, Hefner left armed with the conviction that the time was ripe for a new men's magazine that catered to urbane tastes like *Esquire* did but was more daring, especially in the area of sex. He began this new project with the kind of zeal he hadn't experienced since his days writing for his high school newspaper. "For the first time in my life, I felt free," Hefner reveals in a *Saturday Evening Post* interview. "It was like a mission—to publish a magazine that would thumb its nose at all the restrictions that had bound me."

Unlike *Esquire*, Hefner's magazine would feature photographs of nude women. And despite a plan to publish the first pictorial in 3-D, the focal point of the premiere issue was an infamous nude calendar photo of Marilyn Monroe. The blond bombshell had posed for the picture prior to becoming a star, and while just about everyone in America knew of the photo's existence, no magazine dared to publish it. The risk of being prosecuted for distributing obscene material through the U.S. mail was too great. But it was a risk Hefner was willing to take.

With a personal investment of only $600 and enough charm to convince his printer to give him credit,

Hef's First (Magazine, That Is)

Like many entrepreneurs, Hugh M. Hefner began pursuing his dream at an early age. As a child, he wrote mystery stories and drew cartoons. His favorite topics, mystery and horror, formed the basis of his first publishing effort. While in high school, he started a magazine called Shudder, which featured short stories, comic strips, book and movie reviews, a "monster of the month," and, in a preview of things to come, offered readers a chance to join a members-only club with annual dues of 5 cents.

the 27-year-old Hefner published the first issue of *Playboy* in December 1953. It was an instant success, selling out its entire press run of 53,991 at 50 cents a copy.

The success of the first issue proved that *Playboy* did have a future, and Hefner began refining his creation. Wanting *Playboy* to be known for more than just its photos, Hefner turned his attention to improving the literary content of the magazine. Soon *Playboy* was publishing fiction and nonfiction articles from such acclaimed writers as Ray Bradbury, Vladimir Nabokov, Carl Sandburg, Tennessee Williams, P.G. Wodehouse, John Kenneth Galbraith and Ken W. Purdy.

The combination of nude photos of "the girl next door," high-caliber writing, and columns geared toward helping young urban men enjoy a sophisticated lifestyle proved to be a popular mix. By 1960, *Playboy's* circulation exceeded 1 million and was growing rapidly.

Inspired by his success, Hefner ventured into other fields. Two other magazines, *Show Business Illustrated* and *Trump*, failed as did a TV show, "Playboy's Penthouse." But several other ventures succeeded, most notably, Playboy Clubs International, a chain of members-only nightclubs whose main attraction was "Bunnies"—gorgeous hostesses and waitresses dressed in satin corsets with "bunny ears" and cotton "tails." Hefner also opened several casinos in London, which became major moneymakers for the Playboy empire.

Throughout the 1970s, *Playboy's* success spawned a host of imitators, including Bob Guccione's *Penthouse* and Larry Flynt's *Hustler*, which began eating away at *Playboy's* circulation base. Hefner's response was to search for a way to separate *Playboy* from what he considered to be "lowbrow" competitors. He found it in 1976, when *Playboy* published an article in which presidential candidate Jimmy Carter admitted to having "lusted in his heart." The interview stirred one of the biggest controversies of the campaign, reinforced *Playboy's* reputation as a publication of substance, and clearly separated it from its imitators. With his empire once again secure, Hefner spent the rest of the disco era living the "California dream" in his West Coast mansion.

But as the '70s rolled into the '80s, Hefner's dream rapidly became a nightmare. With the election of Ronald Reagan, a new wave of conservatism swept the nation, and circulation figures dropped. In addition, Playboy Enterprises was dealt a crushing blow when complaints from competitors forced the closing of its lucrative London casinos. To make matters worse, in 1982, the New Jersey Gaming Commission denied Hefner a license to operate his recently constructed $150 million hotel-casino in Atlantic City. The overwhelming success of the casinos had been masking the losses Playboy had incurred in other business areas, including its resorts, clubs, and record and movie ventures. The final blow came in 1985 when Hefner suffered a stroke.

Hef recovered, but Playboy was in crisis. It needed new leadership. A new direction. So in 1988, Hefner turned over the business operations of Playboy Enterprises to his daughter, Christie. Under Christie's direction, *Playboy* magazine broadened its editorial focus by featuring special sections on fashion and entertainment. She also started the premium cable channel Playboy TV. The success of these ventures was furthered in 1994 when Playboy launched its own pay Web site. While the company may never again reach its former grandeur, Playboy Enterprises is still a major player in the adult entertainment world. As for Hefner himself, even though he has officially stepped down as chairman of Playboy Enterprises

The Naked Truth

Hugh M. Hefner certainly wasn't the first to publish a magazine that featured photos of nude women. But what set Playboy apart was the philosophy behind it. From the very beginning, Hefner intended the magazine to be a handbook for single urban men. His goal was to emphasize the fact that you could live life with a little style, to show that sex was not a major hang-up, and to make sex be considered a natural part of life. The result was a magazine that projected the model of a sophisticated man of the world, for whom sexuality was just one of many pleasures to be enjoyed...pleasures which also included expensive stereo equipment, good food and fine wine. As sociologist Camille Paglia points out, "The apparent hedonism of the Playboy ethic was a real turn for the first time against America's Puritan heritage."

after nearly 50 years of fostering unprecedented social change, he continues to play an important role in the empire he created and plans to do so well into the 21st century.

Jim Henson

*"**N**obody creates a fad. It just happens. People love going along with the idea of a beautiful pig. It's like a conspiracy."*

—Jim Henson

Founder of Henson Associates
Founded: 1958

The Muppet Master

Jim Henson can be credited with many accomplishments. A brilliant innovator, he stretched the capabilities of advancing technology to adapt the ancient art of puppetry to the modern medium of television, transforming both in the process. As a pre-eminent popular artist, he contributed a lovable collection of endearing and enchanting characters to the diverse visual vocabulary of the 20th century. But perhaps his greatest accomplishment was the delight and wonder he brought to children and adults alike, championing the qualities of fancifulness, warmth and consideration in an often coarse and cynical age.

Henson began his television career in 1954 while still a high school student. Hearing that "The Morning Show," a local Washington, DC, program, was looking for a puppeteer, he fashioned a crude puppet out his mother's old green coat and a couple of pingpong balls and landed the job.

The following year, as a freshman at the University of Maryland, he was given his own twice-daily, five-minute TV show called "Sam and His Friends." Realizing that traditional solid-head puppets wouldn't translate well to television, Henson, with the help of fellow classmate Jane Nebel (whom Henson would later marry), invented a new type of puppet that could be more expressive.

Dubbed Muppets (which, according to one story, came from combining the words puppet and marionette), Henson's puppets featured extremely wide, over-biting mouths and flexible arms that could be moved by rods. Made of foam rubber and covered with fleece, wool, flannel or other soft material, the Muppets were pliable, so their faces could be manipulated to imitate human facial expressions. In addition to the Muppets, the show also introduced many of what would become Henson trademarks—

music, off-the-wall humor and technical tricks. At the time, Henson doubted that anyone really watched his show. But he couldn't have been more wrong. In 1958, he won an Emmy for "Best Local Entertainment Show." The success of "Sam and His Friends" led to guest appearances on such national network programs as "The Steve Allen Show," "The Jack Paar Show" and the "Ed Sullivan Show." Henson also began making commercials for sponsors throughout the country. To help out, Jim and Jane brought on puppeteer and writer Jerry Juhl in 1961.

By 1963, increasing demand for national television appearances and an ever-growing list of commercial clients prompted Henson to seek out the talents of master puppet builder Don Sahlin and a young puppeteer named Frank Oz. The trio worked to develop the first nationally known Muppet character, Rowlf the Dog, who appeared regularly on "The Jimmy Dean Show" from 1963 to 1966.

Impressed by Henson's ability to create short, funny puppet skits, in 1969 public television show producer Joan Ganz Cooney

All Together Now

Shortly before his death, Jim Henson had agreed to sell the rights to all but his "Sesame Street" characters to Walt Disney Co. for an estimated $200 million. The money certainly would have made Henson the richest puppeteer in history, but that wasn't his reason for making the deal. He hoped that in the hands of Disney, his endearing creatures would have, in his own words, "greater longevity."

But after Henson's death, Disney pulled the plug on the deal, contending that Jim Henson was his company. Enraged at what he considered to be an insult to his father's memory and wanting his father's dream for the Muppets' longevity to become reality, Henson's son, Brian, sued Disney, leading the organization in a spirited continuation of his father's iconoclasm. Disney eventually conceded, agreeing to an out-of-court settlement. Henson's creations are now part of the pantheon of children's favorites that also includes Mickey Mouse, Donald Duck and Goofy.

asked him to create a family of characters to populate her new children's show, "Sesame Street." Henson hesitated to accept Cooney's offer because he didn't want to be pigeonholed as a children's entertainer, but he eventually agreed.

While Henson was always careful never to take credit for the achievements of "Sesame Street"—the show itself was the creation of the Children's Television Workshop (CTW)—few would dispute that it was primarily Kermit the Frog, Bert and Ernie, Big Bird, Grover and the other Muppets who made "Sesame Street" so captivating. Even Cooney herself once remarked that while CTW had a collective genius, Henson was the only individual genius. "He was our era's Charlie Chaplin, Mae West, W.C. Fields and Marx Brothers," she says. "And indeed, he drew from all of them to create a new art form that influenced popular culture around the world."

During its 30 years on the air, "Sesame Street" has been shown in countless countries, and Henson's Muppets have entranced hundreds of millions of children. In fact, given the number of his fans and the intensity of their devotion, Kermit the Frog may possibly be the most popular children's character of the century, eclipsing even Walt Disney's Mickey Mouse.

Based on the popularity of "Sesame Street," Henson began developing his own program, "The Muppet Show." But despite the Muppets' success on "Sesame Street" and their proven appeal to both adults and children, Henson was unable to convince any major U.S. network to carry it. Even with its more sophisticated satire and wit, network executives still felt "The Muppet Show" was too child-oriented. Finally, in 1975, British impresario Sir Lew Grade offered Henson the chance to bypass the networks and join forces with his internationally syndicated ACC group. Grade even promised Henson complete artistic control over 24 shows per year. It was an offer Henson couldn't pass up. As part of ACC, Henson would get the financial backing he needed to produce the show, yet still have the freedom to offer it to network affiliates as a syndicated program.

Starring such unforgettable characters as Miss Piggy, Fozzie Bear, Gonzo the Great, Rizzo the Rat, Statler and Waldorf and, of course, Kermit the Frog, "The Muppet Show" was an instant hit. At its peak, it drew a weekly audience of more than 235 million viewers from around the world, and some of the biggest names in show business vied for guest appearances. The show's list of guest stars read like a Who's Who of Hollywood, boasting celebrities such as Bob Hope, Orson Welles, Telly Savalas, Dean Martin, Diana Shore, Raquel Welch, Brooke Shields, Steve Martin, John Denver and Rudolf Nureyev (who danced "Swine Lake" with Miss Piggy).

One of the reasons for Henson's sustained appeal was his refusal to stick with the status quo. Once something showed the slightest trace of stagnation, he immediately dropped or revamped it. True to form, when he felt "The Muppet Show" itself growing stale, he promptly ended it in 1981, after a five-year run.

With "The Muppet Show" behind him, Henson took his creations to the big screen, producing five Muppet feature films—"The Muppet Movie," "The Great Muppet Caper," "The Muppets Take Manhattan," "The Muppet Christmas Carol" and "Muppet Treasure Island"—as well as two fantasy films, "The Dark Crystal" and "Labyrinth," which were inspired by the illustrations of Brian Froud.

Throughout the 1980s, Henson continued to create memorable television specials and series, including "Fraggle Rock," the multi-award-winning animated cartoon "Muppet Babies," "Jim Henson's Greek Myths," and "Jim Henson's The Storyteller"—which featured stories based on authentic folk tales, several of which were written by Academy Award-winning writer/director Anthony Minghella.

Tragically, Henson's 34-year conquest of children's imaginations ended on May 16, 1990, when he died of complications brought on by an extremely aggressive

Mad About Muppets

During his 34-year career as a puppeteer, Jim Henson created more than 400 different Muppets and provided the voices for Kermit the Frog, Ernie (of Bert and Ernie fame), TV host Guy Smiley, Rowlf the Dog, the Swedish Chef and the lovable curmudgeon, Waldorf.

form of pneumonia. Today, Jim Henson's legacy lives on through the activities of The Jim Henson Company. Led by the Henson family, The Jim Henson Company has dedicated itself to continuing the work Jim had so successfully accomplished over the years.

Milton Hershey

"*Give them quality. That's the best kind of advertising in the world.*"

—Milton Hershey

Founder of The Hershey Foods Corp.
Founded: 1894

THE CANDY MAN

During the late 19th and early 20th centuries, a time when ruthless businesspeople created empires of steel, oil and railroads on the backs of a hapless rural population forced into grim factory towns, Milton S. Hershey followed a different path to success. Unlike Carnegie, Rockefeller, Vanderbilt and the other cold-blooded "robber-barons" who offered their workers callous treatment and back-breaking labor for menial wages, Hershey offered his employees dignity and prosperity, inspiring bounteous love and loyalty in his workers and making himself wildly rich in the process.

Even so, Hershey's path to sweet success was fraught with obstacles and setbacks that would have crushed lesser men. But through perseverance, ingenuity and his amazing ability to bounce back from failure, he built one of the great American fortunes from the ground up and brought joy to millions with a beneficent wonder that would immortalize his name—Hershey's chocolate.

Hershey began his candy-making career at age 15 when he was apprenticed to Lancaster, Pennsylvania, confectioner Joseph H. Royer. Hershey blossomed under Royer's tutelage, acquiring many of the skills and tools he would later use to build his own empire.

In 1876, with $100 he'd borrowed from his aunt, Hershey opened his first candy shop in Philadelphia. For six years he worked day and night to keep the business alive. Working 15 to 16 hours a day, Hershey would make caramels and taffies at night, then sell them from a pushcart to crowds at the Great Centennial Exposition, which was being held to celebrate the 100th anniversary of the Declaration of Independence. But in February 1882, after a winter dogged by illness and mounting debt, Hershey sold the business and headed to Denver to join his father in the great Colorado silver rush.

Surprisingly, the riches Hershey found in Colorado came not from the ground but from a cow. While working for a confectioner in Denver, Hershey learned that adding fresh milk to caramel greatly improved its quality and extended the candy's shelf life—a discovery that would be crucial in later years.

Hershey left Denver for Chicago, where he started another candy shop. But failure continued to haunt him, and the venture quickly fell through. After a similar experience in New Orleans, Hershey headed to New York City and opened yet another store. Despite his best efforts, the company continually lost money. When a group of kids stampeded his delivery wagon and made off with his entire stock, Hershey was bankrupt.

Hershey returned to Lancaster to find that his relatives had given up on him, refusing even to take him in, let alone lend him money to start another business. But Hershey would soon find salvation in the form of an old friend and employee.

Henry Lebkicher, who had briefly worked for Hershey in his Philadelphia store, not only offered Hershey a place to live but also lent him the money he needed

Let Them Eat Chocolate

It may seem surprising today, when the cost of the average chocolate bar is about 50 cents, but at one time, chocolate was considered a luxury. Before the early 1900s, all chocolate was handmade through a time-consuming and costly process that made chocolate a very expensive treat, affordable only to the rich. But Milton S. Hershey was determined to change that. Like Henry Ford, whose assembly line process modernized the automobile industry, Hershey modernized the chocolate industry. By developing and using innovative machinery that eliminated the need to make and wrap chocolate by hand, Hershey introduced the first method for mass-producing chocolate at affordable prices, allowing everyone to experience the joys of his magical creation, the Hershey Bar.

Share The Wealth

Milton S. Hershey firmly believed that an individual is morally obligated to share the fruits of success with others. As a result, he made many philanthropic contributions to society, the most prominent of which is the Hershey Industrial School. Saddened because they had no children of their own, Hershey and his wife, Catherine, established the school in 1909 so poor, orphaned boys could have a good home and a better chance at life. To ensure its future, Hershey donated an estimated $60 million to the school in trust, as well as 40 percent of his company's common stock. The school's charter mission was to train young men in useful trades and occupations, but over time its vocational emphasis shifted to college preparation and business curricula, and several of its graduates went on to become executives and officers of the Hershey Foods Corp. Known today as the Milton Hershey School, the 10,000-acre institution provides housing and education for nearly 1,000 boys and girls whose family life has been disrupted.

to bring his candy-making equipment from New York. The pair then scraped together enough capital to start the business that would firmly establish Milton Hershey as a candy-maker—the Lancaster Caramel Co.

Drawing from his experiences in Denver, Hershey began experimenting with using fresh milk in the candy-making process and created a unique confection he called "Hershey's Crystal A" caramels. Impressed with the quality and shipping stability of Hershey's new, chewy, milk-based caramels, an English importer placed a large candy order, enabling Hershey to secure a $250,000 loan with which he quickly began expanding his business.

By 1893, in addition to the original Lancaster factory, the now incorporated Lancaster Caramel Co. had plants in Mountjoy, Pennsylvania; Chicago; and Geneva, Illinois, which together employed more than 1,300 workers. Hershey's persistence had finally paid off. And this would prove to be just the beginning.

During a visit to the 1893 World's Columbian Exposition in Chicago, Hershey witnessed a demonstration of chocolate-rolling machinery from Germany that sparked a new determination in him. Hershey turned to a friend and said, "Caramels are a fad, but chocolate is permanent. I'm going to make chocolate."

The next year, using the very same machinery he'd seen at the exposition, Milton started the Hershey Chocolate Co. and began producing more than 114 different types of chocolate candies, including the product that would make his name famous the world over—the milk chocolate Hershey Bar. Previously manufactured only in Switzerland and Germany, milk chocolate was new to the United States, and the Hershey Bar became an instant phenomenon. It was so successful that Hershey sold Lancaster Caramel Co. for $1 million and turned his attention solely to chocolate.

For several years, Hershey had been perfecting a plan for mass-producing milk chocolate. Now with the wealth generated from the sale of the caramel company, he could put that plan into action. Inspired by the utopian "city of the future" created for the Columbian Exposition, Hershey set out to build not just a chocolate factory, but the ideal town where the work force could live, play, work and prosper. Because of its rich supply of clean water, proximity to some of the finest dairy farms in the country, and plenty of land for expansion, Hershey chose his birthplace, Dairy Church, Pennsylvania, as the site for his dream city.

In 1903, Hershey broke ground for his new factory and set into motion the events that would turn his dream into a reality. The factory was modern in every way, with high-tech machinery that eliminated the cost and tedium of making and wrapping chocolate by hand and made possible the mass production of high-quality milk chocolate at affordable prices.

The community Hershey built for his employees (officially renamed Hershey, Pennsylvania, in 1905) was just as impressive and modern. It featured affordable housing with sewage and electricity, paved streets (with names like Chocolate Avenue and Cocoa Avenue), schools, department stores, a trolley system, churches, a library, a hospital, a zoo, an open-air theater and even an amusement park. Both the community and the company prospered, and by 1915, the chocolate plant alone covered 35 acres; company sales rocketed from $600,000 in 1901 to $20 million by 1921.

When the stock market crashed in 1929, Hershey refused to

let the dark shadow of the Depression fall over his idyllic community. While other companies fired employees and cut back their operations, Hershey embarked on an ambitious building plan devised solely to keep his workers employed. They constructed a new high school, a sports arena, a community building and a lavish 170-room hotel. Legend has it that during construction of the hotel, Hershey was watching a steam shovel in operation when a foreman proudly commented that it could do the job of 40 workers. Hershey told the foreman to get rid of the shovel and hire 40 workers.

Both the company and the town survived the Depression and continued to flourish, thanks to Hershey's singular vision and amazing inventiveness. Hershey would put that inventiveness to use for his country during Word War II, when he oversaw the development of the high-energy Field Ration D bars carried by GIs serving in the war zones. The 4-ounce nonmelting chocolate bars packed 600 calories and could support soldiers if no other food was available. Hershey would later say that the four Army/Navy "E for Excellence" awards bestowed on the Field Ration D bars were among the proudest achievements of his life.

Hershey remained at the helm of his chocolate empire until 1944, when he finally retired as chairman of the board at the age of 87. He spent the 88th and final year of his life still experimenting with new confections, including celery, carrot and potato ice creams and a surprisingly successful beet sorbet.

Shortly after Hershey's death in 1945, the chairman of the board of the National City Bank of New York would proclaim, "Milton Hershey was a man who measured success not in dollars, but in terms of a good product to pass on to the public, and still more in the usefulness of those dollars for the benefit of his fellow man."

William Hewlett & David Packard

*Co-founders of
Hewlett-Packard Co.
Founded: 1939*

*"What I'm most proud of is the fact that
we really create a way to work with
employees, let them share in the profits, and
still keep control of it."*

—William Hewlett

MAVERICK MANAGERS

Over the years, the name Hewlett-Packard (HP) has become synonymous with high-tech innovation. From its early days in 1939 right up to the present, HP's growth has been fueled by one technological breakthrough after another. But what really sets HP apart isn't technology but the visionary management style created by HP founders William Hewlett and David Packard (pictured, left). Their policy of showing sensitivity to their employees' needs and giving their workers the chance to be creative in solving technical and business problems has made HP one of the most successful and admired companies in the history of American industry.

Bill and Dave, as HP employees affectionately refer to them, first met in the early 1930s while studying radio engineering at Stanford University in Palo Alto, California. Both avid outdoorsmen with a rabid fascination for electronics, the two became fast friends, spending many weekends camping and fishing in the wilds of the Colorado mountains.

After getting their degrees, Hewlett went on to graduate study at both Stanford and MIT, while Packard took a job in vacuum-tube engineering at General Electric. In 1939, Hewlett returned to Palo Alto, and he and Packard quickly renewed their friendship. Encouraged by Stanford professor and mentor Fred Terman to start a business of their own, the two young engineers raised $538 in start-up capital, set up shop in the one-car garage behind Packard's Palo Alto house, and flipped a coin to decide the company's name. Hewlett won the toss, and Hewlett-Packard was born.

The duo's first venture was an automatic foul-line indicator for bowling alleys. Although it was ingenious, the product really had no market. Undaunted by this initial failure, the two began working on a design Hewlett had outlined in his master's thesis—they created an audio oscillator, which they dubbed the HP200A. (Packard would later reveal that the name was selected to give customers the impression that they weren't dealing with an upstart company offering its first product.) The HP200A was designed to test sound equipment—and also tuned harmonicas. The second feature didn't do much for sales, but Walt Disney, at work on "Fantasia," bought eight of the devices.

Inspired by the sale to Disney, Hewlett and Packard decided to try selling their new product via mail order, so they sent out letters, mostly to university laboratories.

Packard The Patriot

For David Packard, the pursuit of excellence has always been more important than the pursuit of wealth. Hewlett-Packard's (HP) employee-centric management philosophy is one example of this. Another is the invaluable service Packard provided to his country during the Vietnam War. When President Richard Nixon was elected, he needed a skilled administrator to serve as deputy secretary of defense—one who could refine and reform the Pentagon's costly and bureaucratic procurement and management practices, as well as help implement Nixon's strategy for turning over responsibility for conduct of the war in Vietnam to Vietnamese forces.

Packard eagerly accepted the position, voluntarily decreasing his salary from nearly a million dollars a year to about $30,000. Even with the sacrifice, congressional critics cried foul, pointing out that HP did $100 million in defense-related business each year and that Packard owned nearly one-third of the stock in the company. To avoid a conflict of interest, Packard agreed that on the day he quit the Pentagon his Hewlett-Packard stock would not be worth one cent more than it was the day he walked in. As a result, during the three years Packard spent in Washington, he gave up nearly $22 million worth of stock-related profits.

When Packard resigned from his Pentagon post to return to HP in 1971, Defense Secretary Melvin Laird called him "the best thing that has happened to the Department of Defense since it was established."

William Hewlett & David Packard

A few orders trickled in, so they sent out more letters. At the same time, they began work on a new product. "We figured that if people needed the HP200A as a source of sound, they would also need something to measure it," Hewlett explains in an interview in *Electronic News*. "So we brought out a voltmeter to measure what happened."

During World War II (in which Hewlett served as a chief signal officer), Hewlett-Packard expanded rapidly to meet the needs of various defense projects. What began as a trickle of orders turned into a stream, and then a flood, which boosted company sales to $1 million by 1943. During that time, the company began developing what would become known throughout Silicon Valley as "The HP Way." This paternalistic set of practices and policies offered HP workers generous benefits, including medical insurance to cover catastrophic health problems, something that was virtually unheard of in business at the time.

After World War II, orders dipped, but the emerging technology of electronics quickly filled the void. Inundated with orders, HP was propelled into going public in 1957. As HP's product line expanded, so did its number of employees. More responsibility had to be delegated. The partners further refined "The HP Way" by establishing a novel management philosophy in which managers at all levels were given a wide berth to develop plans, make decisions and follow them up.

As Hewlett explains in *Electronic News*, "Dave and I set up this philosophy of management by objective. We felt that fundamentally, people wanted to do a good job, but they needed guidelines. So we set up corporate objectives."

In addition to increased autonomy for managers, the partners also increased the number of benefits they offered their employees. HP became the first U.S. company to offer workers flexible hours. It also introduced profit-sharing and established such management innovations as open offices and employee "coffee talks." This maverick management philosophy broke down the barriers between management and employees, encouraged creativity and innovation, and fostered the respect and trust of the workers.

As the number of HP's employees grew from the hundreds into the thousands, to maintain a small-business atmosphere, Hewlett and Packard divided the company according to product types, with each division having its own marketing, production and research groups. Support functions such as sales and advertising were handled by outside contractors. As a result, HP continued on the fast track throughout the 1960s, with the company growing from a single entity in Palo Alto to more than a dozen manufacturing divisions organized into four product groups.

The objectives Hewlett and Packard established in 1957 remained relatively unchanged until the company entered the computer market. As long as the company was in the instrument business, what one division did really didn't affect another. But the move into computers required a more integrated plan. "If you're going to have a new processor, you've got to have terminals and disks that operate with it," Hewlett explains in *Industry Week*. "So you can't have the same degree of autonomy that the old instrument-based division did." Despite this, realizing that autonomy was one of the main reasons for the company's success, Hewlett and Packard struggled to give their workers as much autonomy as possible. For example, instead of telling the disk division exactly what type of disks to create, Hewlett and Packard would simply give the division a general description of what was needed and let them optimize the design.

While HP continued to grow and prosper throughout the 1970s, Hewlett and Packard, both now approaching their 60s, began a careful withdrawal from active management. In 1977, Packard stepped down as chairman of the board. The following year, Hewlett handed over the title of president and CEO to HP executive John Young but stayed with the company as chairman of HP's executive committee.

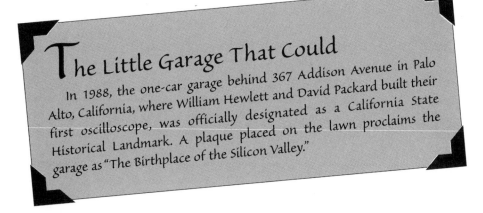

The Little Garage That Could

In 1988, the one-car garage behind 367 Addison Avenue in Palo Alto, California, where William Hewlett and David Packard built their first oscilloscope, was officially designated as a California State Historical Landmark. A plaque placed on the lawn proclaims the garage as "The Birthplace of the Silicon Valley."

William Hewlett & David Packard

He then became vice chairman of the board in 1983, where he remained until his retirement in 1987.

In 1990, Hewlett and Packard briefly returned to active management duties to spearhead an overhaul that is widely credited with revitalizing the company and preventing the losses and lay-offs that plagued IBM and Digital. Hewlett left shortly after he helped right the listing company. Packard remained on as chairman until three years before his death in 1996.

Today, William Hewlett and David Packard are hailed as two of the nation's most respected businessmen and philanthropists. From a tiny mail order business started in a Palo Alto garage, they built a company whose technical excellence, innovative management practices and consistent commercial success will remain an inspiration and model for generations of high-tech entrepreneurs to come.

Howard
Hughes

*"**B**efore being devoured by his eccentricities, Hughes was a true entrepreneurial genius."*

Founder of Hughes Aircraft Co.
Founded: 1932

TROUBLED TYCOON

Quite possibly the most mysterious, elusive and down-right bizarre billionaire the world has ever known, Howard Hughes is generally remembered as an eccentric recluse who was terrified of germs and spent the last years of his life shrouded in secrecy and rumor. Yet before being devoured by his eccentricities, Hughes was a true entrepreneurial genius who achieved remarkable accomplishments as a movie producer, an aviator and an industrialist. He inherited a fortune, and over several decades, transformed it into one of the most diverse empires in the annals of American business.

Hughes was born into wealth on December 24, 1905. His father, an ex-outlaw oil wildcatter, developed a revolutionary drill bit for the oil industry and used the resulting fortune to found Hughes Tool Co. Tragically, Hughes was orphaned at a young age. His mother died when he was 16, and his father followed her to the grave two years later, leaving Hughes an estate worth close to $1 million. Hughes disliked the administrative side of business and hired a young accountant named Noah Dietrich to run Hughes Tool Co. in 1925. Over the next five years, Dietrich turned Hughes' $1 million inheritance into a $75 million empire.

With Dietrich in charge of his company, Hughes was free to indulge in other pursuits. At the age of 21, he became a film producer. His first film, "Swell Hogan," was so bad it was never released, but he did better with his next two films, "Everybody's Acting" and "Two Arabian Knights," which won an Academy Award. He would go on to make such notable minor classics as the World War I aviation epic "Hells Angels," "The Front Page" and "Scarface."

Hughes temporarily abandoned the movie industry in 1932 to indulge in another of his passions—aviation. Hughes dreamed of breaking the world airspeed record, and he founded Hughes

Aircraft Co. to design and build a plane specifically for that purpose. The result was the revolutionary Hughes H-1 racer, a breakthrough in aerodynamics that did indeed set a new world airspeed record of a then-astonishing 352 mph in 1935. Sixteen months later, Hughes set another record when he flew the H-1 nonstop from Burbank, California, to Newark, New Jersey, in just seven hours and 28 minutes.

Hughes next set his sights on conquering the globe. In 1938, he and a four-member crew piloted a Lockheed Model 14 around the world in three days, 19 hours and 8 minutes. The flight not only set a new record but also helped pave the way for the fledgling commercial airline industry. After his around-the-world flight, Hughes began to worry that other aircraft companies were outpacing Hughes Aircraft. To remedy this, he purchased a controlling interest in TWA and began designing experimental aircraft for the military.

He also returned to moviemaking with the controversial film "The Outlaw." Starring a scantily clad 19-year-old, busty newcomer Jane Russell, censors initially banned the picture. When Hughes finally received permission to show it, he shrewdly opted to wait two years, allowing public curiosity to build. Rightly condemned as a ludicrously bad film, "The Outlaw" nevertheless made millions.

During World War II, Hughes teamed up with Henry Kaiser and won a government contract to build three huge "flying ships," which were supposed to serve as troop carriers. Only one was ever completed, the famous Spruce Goose. The government canceled the contract for the flying boats when it became obvious that they could not be completed in time for use in the war.

Bonfire Of The Biographies

After his record-breaking around-the-world flight, a national magazine wrote an in-depth biography of the daredevil tycoon. Determined to keep his private life private, Howard Hughes bought all 175,000 copies of the magazine and burned them in an airplane hangar.

In 1946, Hughes' life took a terrible and irreversible turn. While testing a new aircraft in the skies over Los Angeles, his plane lost power and crashed into a Beverly Hills home. Hughes was dragged from the burning wreckage by a passing Marine, and it was later determined that he had broken nearly every bone in his body. Hughes eventually recovered physically, but his spirit would never be the same. During his recovery, he needed so much codeine to tolerate the pain that he became addicted to the painkiller and would remain so for the rest of his life.

After the accident, Hughes' behavior became more and more strange. So much so that when the Spruce Goose finally rolled off the assembly line in 1947, the military refused to believe that the behemoth could fly, and the U.S. Senate accused Hughes of perpetrating a hoax for his own amusement. To prove the Spruce Goose was no hoax, Hughes himself took the massive plane for a test flight on November 2, 1947. It would be his last major public appearance and his swan song as an aviator. Five years later, Hughes spun off his aircraft division from Hughes Tools and used the money to found the Howard Hughes Medical Institute in Florida.

Always a loner, Hughes became ever more reclusive. By 1963, he was so unwilling to show himself in public that when his 78 percent stake in TWA sparked an antitrust suit, Hughes refused to appear in court or even give a deposition. His failure to appear led to a default ruling against him, and he was forced to sell his TWA stock for $546 million.

To avoid paying taxes in California, Hughes moved to Las

Vegas and used the money from the sale of his TWA stock to buy the Desert Inn and Casino, which became his home and headquarters. Over the next four years, he purchased several other hotels and casinos, a local television station, Alamo Airlines and nearly 25,000 acres of property surrounding Las Vegas. These new properties, combined with Hughes Tool and other real estate holdings in Arizona and California, gave Hughes an estimated net worth of $1 billion.

In November 1970, Hughes moved to the Bahamas, again to avoid taxes. He never returned to the United States. Drug addiction and deteriorating mental and physical health forced him further into seclusion. During the last years of his life, the wealthy hermit scuttled between secret retreats in Nicaragua, Canada and England before finally settling in Acapulco, Mexico. Years of drug use and a poor diet finally took their toll in 1976, when Hughes, an emaciated 94-pound wreck, died of kidney failure while in flight from Acapulco to Houston, where he was being taken for medical treatment.

Hughes remained controversial even in death. His failure to leave a valid will spurred a slew of forgeries and a free-for-all among potential heirs. In the end, the big winner was the IRS, which gobbled up 60 percent of Hughes' estimated $2 billion empire for estate taxes.

Howard Hughes should have lived the all-American dream. He was a true American hero and innovator. Yet he is remembered not for tremendous achievements, but for the tragedy his life became. It seems Hughes was living proof of the old adage, "Money can't buy happiness."

H. Wayne Huizenga

*"**I** enjoy building something good and having a successful product and making money."*
—H. Wayne Huizenga

Chairman of AutoNation Inc.
Founded: 1995

THE BILLIONAIRE GARBAGEMAN

H. Wayne Huizenga is considered by many to be one of the greatest idea men in the history of American business. With his uncanny ability to pick a fragmented industry ripe for consolidation and create a company that dominates that industry so quickly that his competitors are left out in the cold, Huizenga has made himself a billionaire. Voted by *Forbes* magazine as one of "Corporate America's Most Powerful People," he presides over a multibillion-dollar business empire that includes everything from professional sports teams to the nation's largest car retailer. And it all started with a single garbage truck.

The fact that Huizenga would become one of the world's most successful entrepreneurs is no surprise. In fact, entrepreneurship runs in his family. His Dutch immigrant grandfather started a garbage business in Chicago, and his father was head of his own construction company. When he was a boy, Huizenga's father told him, "You can't make money working for someone else."

Young Wayne took his father's advice to heart and set out to make his mark on the business world. In 1962, at the age of 25, Huizenga started the Southern Sanitation Service by borrowing $5,000 from his father and coaxing a local trash hauler in Fort Lauderdale, Florida, to sell him a used truck and a few accounts. Each day, Huizenga would set out on his route at 2 a.m., picking up garbage and toting it to the dump until early afternoon. Then he'd shower, put on his best suit, and spend the rest of the day calling on homeowners, supermarkets and retail stores to solicit business for his company. "I didn't know anything about the business," he admits in an interview in *The New York Times Magazine*. "I just worked hard and gave good service."

The approach worked, and by 1968 Huizenga owned 20 trucks and was servicing customers as far south as Key West. It was around that time that a relative, Dean Buntrock, who was running the disposal firm originally founded by Huizenga's grandfather, suggested merging his company with Southern Sanitation. Huizenga agreed, and Waste Management was formed.

Buntrock's vision was to create a nationwide sanitation company. To accomplish this goal, he and Huizenga embarked on a buyout spree, acquiring 90 trash haulers in a nine-month period. It was during this time that Huizenga developed the key strategies and skills he would later use to run his other companies. The buyouts were made mainly with Waste Management stock.

The Midas Touch

Like the legendary King Midas, nearly everything H. Wayne Huizenga touches seems to turn to gold. With the exception of the Florida Marlins, few of his ventures have ever lost money. Huizenga is quick to share the credit with his managers and partners. But it seems to be Huizenga himself who is solely responsible for his success. The fact that many of the businesses he started have floundered since Huizenga left supports this contention.

Consider the case of Waste Management. When Huizenga departed the company in 1984, it boasted revenue of more than $1 billion. Shortly after his departure, earnings began to drop rapidly, and the company would have gone out of business had it not been bought out by USA Waste Services. A similar result happened with Blockbuster. After Huizenga sold the company to Viacom in 1994, the embattled video giant experienced a troubled five-year run that led to Viacom selling 20 percent of Blockbuster to the public in 1999, with plans to sell all of Blockbuster by the end of the year. Discovery Zone and Boston Market, both at one time connected to Huizenga, have also had their problems.

This has prompted some critics to claim that Huizenga builds companies that have little lasting value. Huizenga instead points the finger at his successors. "I left these companies in great shape," he told U.S. News & World Report, "and to be blamed for their problems years after I left is ridiculous.

Huizenga and Buntrock felt that diluting their ownership stakes was better than taking on oppressive interest payments that could bury the company in a downturn. They also generally kept the former owners on as managers, believing that if their companies were good enough to acquire, so was their expertise. Thanks to this strategy, Waste Management eventually became the largest garbage removal company in the country, making Huizenga and Buntrock millionaires.

By 1984, Waste Management revenue was topping $1 billion. But Huizenga had grown tired of the garbage business, and he retired at age 46. His retirement wouldn't last long, however. Restless and worth at least $21 million thanks to his share in Waste Management, Huizenga began buying small local businesses. During a three-year period, he acquired more than 100 businesses ranging from bottled water and lawn-care services to hotels and office buildings. As one writer remarks, "[Huizenga] so dominated Fort Lauderdale that a typical resident could pass an entire day using nothing but his services." By 1986, Huizenga's collection of businesses had

In Good Company

One of the secrets of H. Wayne Huizenga's success is his ability to delegate responsibilities to others who have greater expertise than he does in certain areas. When he bought into Blockbuster, he saw it as a sort of video McDonald's—a one-product venture that could easily be duplicated and franchised. However, Huizenga had little knowledge of the retail business, so he sought help from the ranks of fast-food giants, where he found and recruited former McDonald's and KFC real estate manager Luigi Salvaneschi.

Salvaneschi's major contribution to Blockbuster's success was the site-selection mind-set he had pioneered at McDonald's: blitz major markets, add stores quickly, and never say "market saturation." In an interview for The New York Times Magazine, Salvaneschi told Richard Sandomir that Huizenga's special skills are in financing and accounting, but beyond that, "he knows what makes things go, hires good people and stands back to let them work."

annual revenue of $100 million. But he had yet to strike the deal that would make him a household name and a business legend.

In 1987, John Melk, a former employee, and Don Flynn, a Waste Management senior vice president, convinced Huizenga to look into a small chain of video stores called Blockbuster. Originally, Huizenga balked. He'd always associated video stores with dingy, pornographic ventures. But when he saw that Blockbuster stores were clean, well-lit and staffed with clean-cut employees, one word popped into his head: "McDonald's." Like the famous hamburger chain, Blockbuster, Huizenga realized, was an easy, one-product concept that could be marketed aggressively—and profitably—nationwide. Within one week, Huizenga, Melk and Flynn owned a controlling interest in Blockbuster.

Now in charge, Huizenga embarked on what had become his standard strategy: acquisition on a grand scale. When he bought into Blockbuster in 1987, it owned eight stores and franchised 11. Just one year later, Blockbuster was the largest video-rental chain in the world. By the second quarter of 1991, the store count had reached 1,654, plus 27 stores in the United Kingdom and 51 in Canada.

Huizenga was making money so quickly that he couldn't spend it all on the company, so he went on another buying spree, this time purchasing all or part ownership of the Miami Dolphins, Joe Robbie Stadium, the Florida Marlins, the Florida Panthers, the Super Club Retail Entertainment record chain, Republic Pictures, Sound Warehouse and Music Plus. Huizenga had become one of the wealthiest men in America, worth almost $700 million. But once again, Huizenga felt the urge to move on. So in 1994, he sold Blockbuster to Viacom for $8.4 billion and began seeking out a new industry to conquer.

He found it in 1995, but it wasn't exactly a new industry. In fact, it was one that Huizenga was very familiar with. Investing $64 million of his own money and raising an additional $168 million, he bought the Atlanta-based sanitation company Republic Waste Industries. The move confused many Wall Street pundits. They simply couldn't understand why Huizenga would return to the trash business. In truth, he wasn't. "I was just looking for a shell [company], and this happened to come up," he explains in a Forbes interview. "It could have been anything."

At the time, the venture, which Huizenga promptly renamed Republic Industries, was a small company struggling in the trash-hauling and electronic-security businesses. True to form, Huizenga greatly expanded both aspects of the business, making them lucrative cash cows. Flush with cash, Huizenga trained his sites on his next target, the retail automotive industry, and began building a nationwide network of new- and used-car outlets. Over a period of six months, he bought 65 auto dealerships with 109 outlets selling 31 brands, opened 11 used-car superstores called AutoNation USA, and purchased three rental-car agencies, including Alamo and National.

But unlike his storied successes in trash-hauling and video rental, Huizenga has found the auto business a bumpy ride. By 1999, Republic, now renamed AutoNation Inc., owned 412 new-car dealerships and 29 used-car stores, and was operating nearly 4,000 rental car locations worldwide, making it the world's number-one auto retailer and the United States' second-largest provider of vehicle-rental services.

Yet the company's earnings were disappointing. After peaking at 45 in 1997, AutoNation's stock dropped to around 15, where it remained for nearly two years. In an attempt to jolt the company out of its rut, Huizenga sold off most of his auto-rental businesses in August 1999 and announced plans to refocus AutoNation on new-car sales. With sales still slumping, Huizenga's next step was to spin off his remaining rental businesses into a separate company, close 23 used-car operations and combine the rest with new-car dealerships. Despite this "restructuring" AutoNation posted a 1999 fourth-quarter loss of $279.6 million. But Huizenga isn't discouraged. He's convinced that with the right plan, he can turn AutoNation into another legendary success story. "We haven't been able to get all cylinders running at one time," he told *Business Week*. "But now, we think we have the business model."

If anything, Huizenga seems to take the loss in stride. That's his style. Even though he is one of the world's richest men, money isn't the driving force behind his entrepreneurial ventures. What drives him is the thrill he gets from one-on-one competition between himself and a rival. That's why at a time when most people his age are considering retirement, Huizenga presses on and promises to remain one of the business world's most influential and successful entrepreneurs well into the next century.

Steve Jobs

Co-founder of
Apple Computer Inc.
Founded: 1976

"We started out to get a computer in the hands of everyday people, and we succeeded beyond our wildest dreams."

—Steve Jobs

THE COMEBACK KID

Steve Jobs' vision of a "computer for the rest of us" sparked the PC revolution and made Apple an icon of American business. But somewhere along the way, Jobs' vision got clouded (some say by his ego), and he was ousted from the company he helped found. Few will disagree that Jobs did indeed impede Apple's growth, yet without him, the company lost its sense of direction and pioneering spirit. After nearly 10 years of plummeting sales, Apple turned to its visionary founder for help, and a little older, little wiser Jobs engineered one of the most amazing turnarounds of the 20th century.

The adopted son of a Mountain View, California, machinist, Steve Jobs showed an early interest in electronics and gadgetry. While in high school, he boldly called Hewlett-Packard cofounder and president William Hewlett to ask for parts for a school project. Impressed by Jobs, Hewlett not only gave him the parts, but also offered him a summer internship at Hewlett-Packard. It was there that Jobs met and befriended Steve Wozniak, a young engineer five years his senior with a penchant for tinkering.

After graduating from high school, Jobs enrolled in Reed College but dropped out after one semester. He had become fascinated by Eastern spiritualism, and he took a part-time job designing video games for Atari in order to finance a trip to India to study Eastern culture and religion.

When Jobs returned to the United States, he renewed his friendship with Wozniak, who had been hard at work trying to build a small computer. To Wozniak, it was just a hobby, but the visionary Jobs immediately grasped the marketing potential of such a device and convinced Wozniak to go into business with him. In 1975, Wozniak and the 20-year-old Jobs set up shop in Jobs' parents' garage, dubbed the venture Apple, and began working on the prototype of the Apple I.

Although the Apple I sold mainly to hobbyists, it generated enough cash to enable Jobs and Wozniak to improve and refine their design. In 1977, they introduced the Apple II—the first personal computer with color graphics and a keyboard. Designed for beginners, the user-friendly Apple II was a tremendous success, ushering in the era of the personal computer. First-year sales topped $3 million. Two years later, sales ballooned to $200 million.

But by 1980, Apple's shine was starting to wear off. Increased competition combined with less than stellar sales of the Apple III and its follow-up, the LISA, caused the company to lose nearly half its market to IBM. Faced with declining sales, Jobs introduced the Apple Macintosh in 1984. The first personal computer to feature a graphical-user interface controlled by a mouse, the Macintosh was a true breakthrough in terms of ease-of-use. But the marketing behind it was seriously flawed. Jobs had envisioned the Mac as a home computer, but at $2,495 it was too expensive for the consumer market. When consumer sales failed to reach projections, Jobs tried pitching the Mac as a business computer. But with little memory, no hard drive and no networking capabilities, the Mac had almost none of the features corporate America wanted.

For Jobs, this turn of events spelled serious trouble. He had clashed with Apple's board of directors, and in 1983, he was ousted from the board by CEO John Sculley, whom Jobs had hand-picked to help him run Apple.

Bad Call

Apple may have never existed if Hewlett-Packard had been on the ball. After developing the circuit board that would become the heart of the Apple I, Steve Wozniak offered it to Hewlett-Packard, who turned it down saying that it wasn't "a salable product."

Steve Jobs

Garage Sale

To generate the $1,350 in capital they used to start Apple, Steve Jobs sold his Volkswagen microbus, and Steve Wozniak sold his Hewlett-Packard calculator.

Stripped of all power and control, Jobs eventually sold his shares of Apple stock and resigned in 1985.

Later that year, using a portion of the money from the stock sale, Jobs launched NeXT Computer Co., with the goal of building a breakthrough computer that would revolutionize research and higher education. Introduced in 1988, the NeXT computer boasted a host of innovations, including extremely fast processing speeds, superb graphics and an optical disk drive. But priced at $9,950, the NeXT was too expensive to attract enough sales to keep the company afloat. Undeterred, Jobs switched the company's focus from hardware to software. He also began paying more attention to his other business, Pixar Animation Studios, which he had purchased from George Lucas in 1986.

After cutting a three-picture deal with Disney, Jobs set out to create the first computer-animated feature film. Four years in the making, "Toy Story" was a certified smash hit when it was released in November 1995. Fueled by this success, Jobs took Pixar public in 1996, and by the end of the first day of trading, his 80 percent share of the company was worth $1 billion. After nearly 10 years of struggling, Jobs had finally hit it big. But the best was yet to come.

Within days of Pixar's arrival on the stock market, Apple bought NeXT for $400 million and reappointed Jobs to Apple's board of directors as an advisor to Apple chairman and CEO Gilbert F. Amelio. It was an act of desperation on Apple's part. Because they had failed to develop a next-generation Macintosh operating system, the firm's share of the PC market had dropped to just 5.3 percent, and they hoped that Jobs could help turn the company around. At the end of March 1997, Apple announced a quarterly loss of $708 million. Three months later, Amelio resigned, and Jobs took over as interim CEO. Once again in charge of Apple, Jobs struck a deal with Microsoft to help ensure Apple's survival. Under the arrangement, Microsoft invested $150 million for a nonvoting minority stake in Apple, and the companies agreed to "cooperate on several sales and technology fronts." Next, Jobs installed the G3 PowerPC microprocessor in all Apple computers, making them faster than competing Pentium PCs. He also spearheaded the development of the iMac, a new line of affordable home desktops, which debuted in August 1998 to rave reviews. Under Jobs' guidance, Apple quickly returned to profitability, and by the end of 1998, boasted sales of $5.9 billion.

Against all odds, Steve Jobs pulled the company he founded and loved back from the brink. Apple is once again healthy and churning out the kind of breakthrough products that made the Apple name synonymous with innovation. Jobs once described himself as a "hopeless romantic" who just wanted to make a difference. Quite appropriately like the archetypal romantic hero who reaches for greatness but fails, only to find wisdom and maturity in exile, an older, wiser Steve Jobs returned triumphant to save his kingdom.

John
Johnson

John
John
John
John
Johnson
Johnson
Johnson
Johnson
John
John
John
John
John
Johnson
Johnson
Johnson
Johnson

"When I see a barrier, I cry and I curse, and then I get a ladder and climb over it."

—John Johnson

Founder of Johnson Publishing Co. Inc.
Founded: 1942

THE VOICE OF BLACK AMERICA

John Johnson rose from poverty to become one of the world's most influential media pioneers by creating the largest black-owned publishing company in the United States. But more important, through the landmark magazines he founded, *Ebony* and *Jet*, Johnson gave African-Americans a voice and a face, and, in his words, "a new sense of somebody-ness," of who they were and what they could do at a time when blacks were virtually invisible in mainstream American culture.

Johnson credits much of his success to his mother. Born in Arkansas City, Arkansas, Johnson's father died when he was only 6, forcing everyone in his family to work to survive. "I was a working child," he explains to Jim Hoskins, author of *Black Stars: African-American Entrepreneurs*. "I learned how to work before I learned how to play."

Nevertheless, Johnson's mother realized the importance of education and insisted that he attend school, which he did through the eighth grade. But there was no high school for blacks in Arkansas City. To ensure her son would receive a good education, Johnson's mother toiled as a cook for levee workers until she'd saved enough money so she and John could move to Chicago, which had become a mecca for blacks seeking to escape the poverty and prejudice of the South.

Johnson and his mother arrived in Chicago in 1933. It was the middle of the Great Depression, and due to lack of work, they were forced to rely on welfare for two years. That experience shamed Johnson and sparked in him a burning desire to succeed. "Both my mother and I were determined that we weren't going to stay on welfare," Johnson explains. "We always worked toward doing better, toward having a better life. We never had any doubts that we would."

Johnson displayed his determination to succeed as a student at Chicago's DuSable High School, graduating with honors in 1936. At a National Urban League dinner to honor Johnson and other students who had distinguished themselves, Johnson met Harry H. Pace, president of Supreme Life Insurance Co. of America, which was then the largest black-owned business in the North. Impressed by the young man, Pace asked Johnson about his plans for the future. Johnson explained that he wanted to go to college but could not afford the tuition. Pace offered Johnson a part-time job at Supreme to help him pay for tuition. This would prove to be a major turning point in Johnson's life.

The following September, Johnson enrolled at the University of Chicago and began working at Supreme. He started as an assistant on the *Supreme Liberty Guardian*, the company's in-house newsletter, and was eventually promoted

Branching Out

Like many entrepreneurs, John Johnson built a multimillion-dollar empire by recognizing a demand and filling it. It was a strategy that would lead him to success not only in publishing but also in the cosmetics industry. In 1958, Johnson began sponsoring the Ebony Fashion Fair, the world's largest touring fashion show, which has donated more than $46 million to black charities. Early on, he had trouble finding cosmetics shades dark enough for his models.

After unsuccessful attempts to convince Estee Lauder and Revlon to produce cosmetics specifically for black women (both companies now do), Johnson started his own cosmetics company, Fashion Fair, and promoted it through direct mailings to Ebony and Jet subscribers. Today, Fashion Fair is the world leader in the field of cosmetics for women of color. Johnson considers it one of his greatest triumphs. "I not only proved that there was a market when they said there wasn't one," he says in a Forbes interview, "but so far the giants have not been able to shake my position."

to editor of the *Guardian*. One of Johnson's tasks was to comb black newspapers and magazines from around the country and brief Pace on what he learned. But Johnson soon found that his wealth of knowledge put him in the spotlight on the social circuit—African-Americans were hungry for news of the black world beyond any connection with crime, which was what the white media usually focused on.

This discovery gave Johnson the idea of publishing a magazine for general black audiences. In 1942, he founded Johnson Publishing Co. and set out to publish his first magazine, *Negro Digest*. But when the 24-year-old tried to find a bank that would lend him money, he was waved away by bankers who contemptuously called him "boy."

Undaunted, Johnson decided to go directly to the public for start-up money. Putting up his mother's furniture as collateral, Johnson borrowed $500, which he used to mail out offers to Supreme Life's 20,000 policyholders for discount charter subscriptions. Three thousand people sent in the $2 annual subscription, giving Johnson $6,000 to pursue his dream.

To convince a distributor to take on the magazine, Johnson got 30 fellow employees and friends to ask for *Negro Digest* at newsstands along Chicago's South Side. He also reimbursed friends who bought up most of the copies, convincing dealers the magazine was in demand. He then took those copies and resold them. This ploy was repeated in Detroit, New York City and Philadelphia. Circulation grew slowly at first. Then Johnson began publishing a series of articles titled "If I Were A Negro," in which prominent whites imagined being black. First Lady Eleanor Roosevelt was among those who contributed to the series, which caused a dramatic jump in circulation. Within a year, *Negro Digest* was selling 50,000 copies per month.

Inspired by his success, Johnson started his second magazine, *Ebony*, in 1945. *Ebony* and Johnson showed that blacks led successful middle-class lives, which played a major role in convincing white corporations to advertise in the black media, as well as persuading advertisers to use black models. Using meticulous market research, Johnson and his staff showed white advertisers that it was in their best interest to reach out to black consumers, and they proved that ads featuring black models had a greater response rate than ads featuring white models. "These things are accepted today, but they were new in the '40s," Johnson explains in a 1985 *Ebony* interview. "There were no major black models before *Ebony*, and there were few black salespeople for major companies before *Ebony*. I don't think we're completely responsible, but I don't know anyone who is more responsible."

Johnson discontinued *Negro Digest* in 1950 (he would revive it 10 years later as *Black World*) and started an advice magazine called *Tan*. By 1971, Johnson had changed the title of *Tan* to *Black Stars* and expanded its editorial content to include features on black entertainers. The following year, he began publishing it as a pocket-sized weekly under the name *Jet*.

Inside Scoop

Few will argue that John Johnson played a major role in the civil rights movement during the 1960s. In fact, the first issue of Negro Digest featured contributions by Langston Hughes and early civil rights leader Walter White. And many agree that the civil rights movement itself would not have been as broadly understood by the masses in this country if it weren't for Ebony and Jet. Writers for the magazines attended civil rights movement meetings in churches across the South and gave readers an insider's view of the struggle. As former Johnson Publishing advertising executive Ronald Sampson explained in an interview in Chicago magazine, "The general news media was covering it as a confrontation. Ebony and Jet were inside the churches and were able to tell what went on in the meetings."

Nevertheless, the focus of Ebony has shifted over the years, prompting some critics in the black community to argue that Johnson devotes too much space to good news. "I know what some people are trying to say—that I don't put out an 'opinion' magazine. But you can't think about race 24 hours a day. You've got to take a rest," Johnson told Nancy Millman of Chicago. "Ebony started out as a magazine about achievement and success. We wanted black people to feel good about themselves. And in that sense I think we have succeeded—and continue to succeed."

After *Jet*, Johnson branched out into other projects, including a book division, a book club and a high-end cosmetics line for blacks. He also purchased two radio stations, making him the first African-American in Chicago to own a broadcasting outlet. In addition to his own ventures, Johnson is also a major shareholder in *Essence*, a magazine for black women.

Thanks to Johnson's determination and unique vision, he has become one of the most successful and wealthy black men in America today. Led by its flagship publication, *Ebony* (with a circulation of 2.1 million), the family-owned Johnson Publishing Co. is one of the largest minority-owned businesses and the largest black-owned publishing firm in the world. Looking back on his accomplishments, Johnson says, "There is no secret to success. You have to have a bit of luck, and you have to be at the right place at the right time. I was fortunate enough to have a mother who taught me very fundamental things about success. She taught me that you have to earn success, which means you have to prepare yourself, you have to work hard, you have to have commitment, and you have to have faith. You have to believe that things are possible. If there is a secret, the secret is in all those things."

Will Keith Kellogg

*"**B**ehind the name lies a fascinating story of two very different brothers whose sibling rivalry ranks up there with that of Cain and Abel."*

Founder of Kellogg Co.
Founded: 1906

THE CORNFLAKE KING

When Will Keith and John Harvey Kellogg invented the first flaked cereal in 1894, they turned the American diet on its ear. Before long, the Kellogg name was gracing breakfast tables across the country. But behind the name lies a fascinating story of two very different brothers—one an eccentric doctor, the other a sober businessman—whose sibling rivalry ranks up there with that of Cain and Abel.

Will Keith Kellogg was born in Battle Creek, Michigan, in April 1860. His father, John Kellogg, a successful broom maker and staunch Seventh Day Adventist, believed Christ's Second Coming was imminent and therefore placed little emphasis on education. So as soon as young Will Keith was old enough, he was put to work in his father's factory. Will Keith discovered that he had a natural knack for business, and by age 14, he was the company's youngest traveling salesman. Five years later, he was managing a broom factory in Dallas.

John Harvey Kellogg took a very different path. A flamboyant physician, author and inventor, Dr. Kellogg had gained world renown as head of the Battle Creek Sanitarium. Offering radical treatments that promised to revitalize the body, mind and spirit, the San (short for Sanitarium) had become a mecca for those looking to improve their health. As patronage at the San increased, the good doctor decided he needed someone to keep the books and help him run the place. For this he turned to his younger brother, Will Keith, who had returned to Michigan in 1880. In addition to his business knowledge, there was another reason John chose Will Keith—he knew that the shy young man posed no threat to his control of the San.

At the core of Dr. Kellogg's "biologic living" program was a firm belief in vegetarianism. But he had difficulty convincing his patients to give up meat. So John established an experimental kitchen and put Will Keith to work inventing a palatable substitute for meat made from wheat. For years, John had been trying to duplicate a cereal product made in Denver called Shredded Wheat. Unfortunately, Shredded Wheat didn't go over very well with the San's visitors. Most claimed it tasted like "baled hay."

Will Keith searched for a way to turn wheat into something more tasty, and he hit upon the idea of creating a wheat flake. However, the mushy wheat batter simply refused to cooperate. After several unsuccessful attempts, Will Keith went home to ponder the problem. When he returned to the lab several days later, he found that the batter had molded. In disgust, he gave the crank of the "flaking machine" a turn—and to his surprise, out came perfect flakes. Apparently the mold had given the batter the "rise" it needed to flake.

Will Keith quickly discovered that the process worked just as well with oats, rice and corn. But although it was Will Keith who had stumbled upon the answer, it was John who took all the credit, claiming the idea had come to him in a dream. To Will Keith's frustration, John insisted that the new cereal be sold only to the San's patients. Where Will Keith saw dollar signs, John only saw good health. The two brothers hadn't been very close to begin with, and now their differences began to open a chasm between them.

In 1891, a would-be entrepreneur named Charles W. Post arrived at the San for treatment

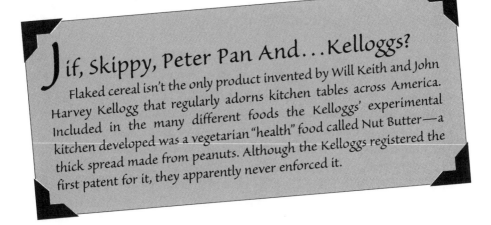

Jif, skippy, Peter Pan And…Kelloggs?

Flaked cereal isn't the only product invented by Will Keith and John Harvey Kellogg that regularly adorns kitchen tables across America. Included in the many different foods the Kelloggs' experimental kitchen developed was a vegetarian "health" food called Nut Butter—a thick spread made from peanuts. Although the Kelloggs registered the first patent for it, they apparently never enforced it.

The Bashful Benefactor

Although he was never known as the warmest of men, over the years Will Keith Kellogg quietly established a reputation as a giver to local charities, and he would often look for ways to help people in need. During the Depression, he ran his factory on four six-hour work shifts to create more jobs.

Will Keith also showed a great concern for children, especially rural children. In 1930, he set up the Child Welfare Foundation (CWF) to help the vast number of children living in poverty. Dedicated to improving the health and education of children across the country, the CWF was eventually renamed the W.K. Kellogg Foundation. Upon his death, Will Keith willed most of his 60 percent interest in Kellogg Co. to the foundation to ensure that it would continue. Today, the W.K. Kellogg Foundation is one of the world's largest private charities, thanks to its 34 percent ownership of Kellogg Co.

of a severe case of dyspepsia (a digestive system disorder). Post saw a potential gold mine in the products being created in the San's experimental kitchens and became particularly fascinated with the Kelloggs' attempts to create a coffee substitute made from cereal. When alerted to Post's curiosity, John replied, "Let him see everything we're doing. I shall be delighted if he makes a cereal coffee."

Post did just that, and in 1895, he began marketing Postum, a cereal coffee made from grain and molasses—like Kellogg's. Postum was a great success, especially in the winter. But Post needed a product to sell in the summer, so he began marketing a cereal called Grape Nuts. By 1901, Post had made his first million.

Post's success rankled Will Keith, who hated the idea of the upstart Texan getting rich on the San's creation. After several unsuccessful attempts to get his brother to sell the San's cornflakes commercially, Will Keith decided to strike out on his own. Looking for a way to make the cornflakes taste better, he added malt flavoring to the recipe. When Dr. Kellogg—who promoted a sugar-free diet—found out, he was furious. But Will Keith didn't care. He was sure he'd found the formula for his success, and in 1906, he separated from his brother and formed The Battle Creek Toasted Corn Flake Co. The business acumen Will Keith had displayed in his youth re-emerged, and by 1910 his was a million-dollar business.

Will Keith's success infuriated John, who resented the commercialization of "his" creation and name. In retaliation, Dr. Kellogg changed the name of his company to Kellogg Food Co. In turn, Will Keith changed his company to Kellogg Toasted Corn Flake Co., and to differentiate his flakes from those of his brother and other competitors, he added his signature to every box along with the slogan, "Beware of imitations. None genuine without this signature." It marked the beginning of what would become a decade-long court battle over who owned the Kellogg name.

In 1910, Will Keith sued John. Then in 1916, John sued Will Keith. Finally, the "battle of bran," as it was known, reached the Michigan Supreme Court, which granted the younger brother the right to sell cereal under the Kellogg name. Defeated, John moved to Florida and rapidly faded into obscurity.

Finally emerging from his brother's shadow, Will Keith quickly became a dominant figure in American business. A true marketing genius, he began giving away free samples of his cereal, which caused sales to explode. By the 1920s, Kellogg Co. led the pack in what had become a multimillion-dollar industry.

Throughout the years of Will Keith's growing success, he had not seen or spoken to his older brother. But when he heard reports of John's increasingly eccentric behavior, he traveled to Florida to check on his brother's condition. Will Keith was appalled to find that his brother was quickly losing touch with reality. John Harvey Kellogg died a year later, in 1943, at the age of 91. Before his death, he sent Will Keith a letter of reconciliation in which he apologized for his behavior. But Will Keith never saw it. He had become almost completely blind, and his protective staff never informed him of the letter. On his own deathbed in 1951, Will Keith was finally told of the letter. Struck that he had never known about his brother's change of heart, he sat up in bed and cried, "My goodness, why didn't someone tell me before this?"

The Kellogg brothers' inability to collaborate drove them apart, but ironically, that's what allowed each to do what he did best. Today, the company that Will Keith Kellogg started nearly a century ago reigns as the No. 1 maker of ready-to-eat cereals.

Calvin Klein

"*Anything I wanted to do, I did. If there's something I want to do, nothing stops me.*"
—Calvin Klein

Founder of Calvin Klein Ltd.
Founded: 1968

A STYLISH OBSESSION

His casual chic style brought American fashion into its own and onto a par with Paris. He single-handedly created the designer jeans craze of the 1970s, and then revolutionized fashion advertising in the 1980s. Today his name adorns everything from underwear to perfume. And his stylish designs and business acumen have built a fashion empire. But unlike his clothes, Calvin Klein's rise to the top of the fashion world has been anything but uncomplicated.

Born on November 19, 1942, Klein was largely influenced by his mother who instilled in him a love of art and fashion. While other kids played stickball, Klein preferred to tag along with his mom while she shopped at discount clothing stores in New York City. A loner who taught himself how to sketch and sew, Klein claims he always knew he wanted to be a fashion designer.

After graduating from New York City's Fashion Institute of Technology in 1962, Klein married Jayne Centre and went to work in the garment district as a $75-per-week apprentice sketching designs from the European runways for coat mogul Dan Millstein. The tactic of copying was typical for fashion at that time, because no original ideas were coming out of America. But Klein wanted to change that. He dreamed of starting his own fashion company, and nothing was going to stop him—not even the fact that he was nearly broke and still working at his father's grocery store to make some extra cash.

In 1968, at the age of 26, with $2,000 of his own money and a $10,000 loan from his boyhood friend Barry Schwartz, Klein founded his own company, Calvin Klein Ltd., with Schwartz as his partner. Their first order came literally by accident, when a coat-buyer from department store titan Bonwit Teller got off on the wrong floor and wandered into Klein's workroom. Impressed by his line of trench coats, the buyer placed a $50,000 order, telling the young designer, "Tomorrow you will have been discovered." And indeed, it was that order from Bonwit, along with a glowing editorial he received in *Vogue*, that put the Calvin Klein name on the map.

In 1973, Klein leapt from making only coats to designing a line of sportswear, creating what would become known as "The Calvin Klein Look" and giving birth to American leisurewear. With youthful silhouettes, a pristine use of color and fine fabrics, his relatively affordable sportswear first caught the attention of American women who were fed up with outrageous and impractical Parisian couture. Shortly after, men became attracted to the relaxed, masculine look of Klein's designs, which were in tune with the health and bodybuilding craze that was sweeping America at the time.

Klein had finally hit the big time. The money poured in as his clean, muted, simple designs became hits with both the buying public and the fashion press, who gave him the prestigious Coty Award in 1973, 1974 and 1975. But success did not come without a price. In 1974, it cost him his marriage.

After his divorce, Klein embarked on a self-described "wild period," spending his nights partying at disco club Studio 54, where cocaine and casual sex were part of the scene. As his power and notoriety grew, Klein maintained a high public profile, worrying little about the liabilities of fame—until 1978, when his 11-year-old daughter, Marci, was kidnapped. Although she was released unharmed, both Klein and

Good Press, Bad Press

At the same time his advertisements for jeans and fragrances were being criticized, Calvin Klein's clothing was receiving critical acclaim for its clean, modern lines. Time magazine called him the "Frank Lloyd Wright of fashion," and named him one of the 25 most influential Americans in 1996.

his daughter were left indelibly scarred. The once-publicity-hungry Klein gave up partying and became a virtual recluse.

The year 1980 marked a turning point for Klein's empire. A series of commercials by photographers Doon Arbus and Richard Avedon that featured 15-year-old model Brooke Shields cooing, "Nothing comes between me and my Calvins," made Klein's new line of tight jeans a nationwide phenomenon, selling 200,000 pairs the first week alone.

The provocative commercials marked a revolution in clothing advertising. It was a more sensual approach to marketing that would later be emulated by Klein's competitors. The commercials also prompted criticism from feminist leaders such as Gloria Steinem, who proclaimed they were pornographic and inspired violence against women. The negative publicity only served to fuel sales.

Klein would once again court controversy in 1982, when he put his name on the waistband of a line of men's underwear and started a campaign featuring near-naked men dressed only in his designer skivvies. Many publishers rejected the sexy ads. But once again, the controversy spilled over into Klein's favor, and stores simply couldn't keep the underwear in stock.

In 1983, Klein and his partner bought Puritan Jeans, their jeans licensee, for $65.8 million. It was Klein's first and nearly fatal misstep. Lifestyles were changing as the reality of AIDS emerged and halted the casual sexuality of the 1970s. As a by-product of this, the demand for tight-fitting designer jeans waned. By 1984, the designer jeans business had dried up, leaving Klein deep in debt. He refinanced the debt with $80 million in junk bonds, leaving his empire in serious danger of crumbling. To make matters worse, rumors were spreading that Klein was dying of AIDS.

The rumors ceased when Klein married his second wife, model Kelly Rector, in 1986. But Klein was experiencing a dark period in his personal life. He had become addicted to vodka and Valium. When Klein's office announced that he had gone to the Caribbean on an extended vacation, the rumors about AIDS resurfaced, so the truth was revealed—Klein had been admitted to the Hazelden Clinic in Minnesota for alcohol and drug abuse.

Klein came out of rehab facing bankruptcy but was saved by a pal from his Studio 54 days—multibillionaire David Geffen. Given a new start, Klein spawned numerous product lines, including a more affordable clothing line called CK, and licensed his name on sunglasses, watches, handbags and more. All the new products did well, but Klein's ads continued to spark controversy.

In 1995, he launched a series of jeans ads featuring real teens, some as young as 15, in sexually provocative poses. Dubbed "kiddie porn" by the press, several television stations pulled the ads, and the FBI and Justice Department began investigating the company for possible violations of child pornography laws. The ads were universally denounced, but in the end, the Justice Department ruled they were not pornography.

Klein pulled the ads, and in spite of the negative press, came out smelling like a rose—his cK one perfume and CK jeans selling well, his brand-new headquarters store opening in New York City, and his company with the healthiest financial picture in many years. Indeed, the man who popularized name-brand jeans, clean American lines, and men's underwear for women is unquestionably a stylish survivor as he enters the 21st century as one of the world's top fashion designers.

Philip Knight

*"Play by the rules.
But be ferocious."*
—Philip Knight

*Co-founder of Nike Inc.
Founded: 1972*

HE JUST DID IT

In 1993, the man whom *The Sporting News* voted "the most powerful person in sports" wasn't an athlete, a manager or a team owner. He was Philip Knight, the dynamic iconoclast who for nearly 30 years has shod the feet of sports legends and "weekend warriors" alike. In less than a decade, his marketing savvy and uncompromising competitiveness had transformed the athletic-shoe industry and made Nike one of the most successful and widely recognized brand names in the world.

Knight first came up with the blueprint for what would become the world's No. 1 athletic-shoe company while working on his master's degree at Stanford University. Assigned to write a term paper on starting a small business in an area he knew well, the former University of Oregon track star naturally chose running. He outlined a plan for breaking the stranglehold Adidas had on the running-shoe market by using cheap Japanese labor to manufacture a cheaper, better-quality running shoe.

Shortly after graduating in 1962, Knight decided to put his plan into action. He flew to Japan to visit Onitsuka Tiger Co., manufacturer of an Adidas knockoff sold in Japan. Introducing himself as the head of Blue Ribbon Sports, a company that existed only in his mind, Knight told Tiger executives that his firm was the ideal choice to import their shoes into the United States. He convinced Tiger to send him some samples, promising to place an order after his "partners" examined them.

Back in the United States, Knight borrowed money from his father to pay for the samples, and he sent a few pairs to his former University of Oregon coach, Bill Bowerman, who quickly became his partner. Putting up $500 each, Bowerman and Knight officially formed Blue Ribbon Sports and purchased 200 pairs of Tigers, which Knight began selling from his car at high school track meets throughout the Pacific Northwest.

By the early 1970s, sales had reached $3 million, and Knight decided it was time for Blue Ribbon to break with Tiger and start designing its own shoes. In 1972, Blue Ribbon launched its Nike line, named after the Greek goddess of victory. Emblazoned with a "swoosh" logo Knight paid a Portland State art student $35 to design, the shoes featured a unique "waffle sole"—created by Bowerman—that offered better traction with less weight.

Knight's marketing strategy was simple. Rather than rely on advertising (which he admittedly loathed), he would get top athletes to endorse his shoes, and then let his sales force sell the product. His strategy and the timing of the launch couldn't have been better. That summer, the Olympic track and field trials were held in Eugene, Oregon, with none other than Bill Bowerman as coach of the American Olympic team. Knight took full advantage of the opportunity, putting Nikes on the feet of several top finishers. When they made national television, so did the shoes they were wearing. One of the most visible runners wearing Nikes was American record-holder Steve Prefontaine. A cocky, anti-establishment type, Prefontaine became

Sole Man

Although Philip Knight was certainly the marketing genius behind Nike Inc.'s success, he wouldn't have had much to market without Bill Bowerman. It was Bowerman's design innovations that kept Nike on the leading edge of athletic-shoe technology. Bowerman constantly fiddled with running shoes, searching for ways to improve them. He would slice them up, take a toe from one, stitch it to the heel of another and then attach both to an upper with duct tape and rubber cement. His methods were admittedly unorthodox. And so was the way he came up with Nike's heralded "waffle sole." As Bowerman often tells the story, "I was looking at my wife's waffle iron, and I thought it looked like a pretty good traction device." So he grabbed a bottle of liquid urethane, poured it on the iron, and the waffle sole was born.

The Knight Stuff

The culture Philip Knight fostered at Nike Inc. during its early days was anything but corporate. Executive conferences were referred to as "buttface meetings," because direct confrontations and yelling were encouraged. Tequila fountains irrigated sales conferences. During a company golf tournament, a sales rep distributed marijuana paraphernalia from his golf cart. And when tattoos became the rage, scores of Nike workers had themselves branded with the famous Nike "swoosh."

Some viewed Knight's encouragement of such antics as mere childishness. But it would prove to be a stroke of motivational genius. As one veteran Nike employee put it, "It was a holy mission, you know, to "swoosh" the world. We were Knight's crusaders. We would have died on the cross."

the first of a team of edgy athletes that Knight recruited to endorse his shoes.

As Knight had planned, athlete endorsements played a major role in boosting Nike sales throughout the 1970s. For instance, after tennis "bad boy" John McEnroe hurt his ankle and began wearing Nike three-quarter-top shoes, sales of that style leapt from 10,000 pairs to more than 1 million. And the sudden popularity of jogging combined with Nike's canny marketing created a demand where none existed before. No longer would any old pair of shoes do for that jog around the block; people wanted to wear what the best in the world were wearing...and that was Nike (as Blue Ribbon was rechristened in 1978).

Nike experienced continued success throughout the early 1980s, thanks mostly to the tremendous sales of its Air Jordan line. Commercials glorifying Michael Jordan's high-flying, slam-dunking antics made the gaudy black and red sneakers a hot item, selling more than $100 million worth in the first year alone. By 1986, total sales hit $1 billion, and Nike surpassed Adidas to become the No. 1 shoe manufacturer worldwide.

Amazingly, Knight stumbled only once in his stellar career. In the late 1980s, Nike's strategy of focusing on hard-edged, hard-core athletes ignored the growing market for aerobics shoes. When British shoe manufacturer Reebok pitched their leather shoes as a fashion item for the trendy aerobic workout crowd, they quickly overtook Nike in the top spot.

Between 1986 and 1987, Nike sales dropped 18 percent. Knight was forced to face the fact that while Nike technology appealed to sports professionals, other consumers might rank appearance over function. In response, Nike came up with Nike Air—a multipurpose shoe with an air cushion in the sole. The commercial produced to unveil the new line featured the Beatles' song "Revolution." (The rights to that song cost Nike $250,000.) Nike Air may or may not have been a revolution in footwear, but it certainly revived sales. Nike regained the lead from Reebok in 1990 and has remained there ever since.

But as Nike has grown into a huge multinational enterprise, it has become a magnet for controversy. In 1990, it came under fire from Jesse Jackson, who maintained that while African-Americans accounted for a large percentage of Nike's customers, Nike had no black vice presidents or board members. Jackson launched a boycott that led to the appointment of Nike's first black board member. That same year, stories of teenagers being killed for their Air Jordans sparked outrage at what was perceived as Nike's overzealous promotion of its shoes. More recently, Knight has been accused of exploiting factory workers in Asia, some of whom are paid less than $2 per day by the subcontractors who manufacture Nikes. But despite this negative publicity, Nike sales have remained strong.

Philip Knight, now in his late 50s, has come to be viewed as one of the master marketers of the age. When asked by a reporter how he achieved such fame, in a veiled reference to the Reebok torpedo that forced him to rethink his marketing strategy, Knight replied, "How did John Kennedy become a war hero? They sunk his boat."

Ray Kroc

"The definition of salesmanship is the gentle art of letting the customer have it your way."

—Ray Kroc

Founder of McDonald's Corp.
Founded: 1955

Photo Courtesy: McDonald's Corp.

Burger Baron

When Ray Kroc was a child, his father took him to a phrenologist—a practitioner who claimed he could predict the future by reading the bumps on a person's head. Kroc's chart revealed that his future would be in the food-service industry. Whether through psychic power or sheer luck, the phrenologist proved to be correct. Uniquely adroit at identifying popular trends, Kroc would go on to lay the foundation for the modern fast-food industry and champion the world's No. 1 fast-food chain.

Like many entrepreneurs, Kroc began working early in life. While still in grammar school, the would-be fast-food king started a lemonade stand in front of his home in the Chicago suburb of Oak Park. He also worked in a grocery store, and he spent a summer behind the soda fountain in his uncle's grocery store. Through these early experiences, Kroc began to view the world as one big place to sell to.

By the time he was a teenager, Kroc had no patience for school, so he quit to take a job as a salesperson for Lily-Tulip Cup Co. He was a natural. Young, ambitious and willing to work hard for long hours, Kroc quickly became the company's top salesperson. In the course of selling cups, Kroc met Earl Prince, a client who had invented a five-spindle milk-shake-mixing machine called a Multimixer.

Fascinated by the speed and efficiency of the machine, and recognizing a cash cow when he saw one, Kroc, then 37, left Lily and obtained exclusive marketing rights to the machine. He spent the next decade and a half crisscrossing the country peddling the Multimixer to drugstore soda fountain and restaurant owners.

As Kroc approached his 50th birthday, however, sales began to drop. During the early 1950s people were leaving the cities for the suburbs, forcing many neighborhood soda fountains to close. Ray was losing customers by the dozens. But one small restaurant in

San Bernardino, California, ordered eight machines. Intrigued by the order, Kroc left for California to see for himself what kind of restaurant needed to churn out 40 milk shakes at a time. There he found a small hamburger stand run by two brothers, Dick and Mac McDonald.

The McDonald brothers' restaurant was unlike any Ray had ever seen. In contrast to the popular drive-in restaurants of the time, it was self-service, had no indoor seating, and the menu was limited to cheeseburgers, hamburgers, fries, drinks and milk shakes, all of which were produced in an assembly-line fashion that enabled customers to place their orders and receive their meals in less than a minute.

Kroc quickly calculated the financial rewards possible with hundreds of these restaurants across the country. But when he approached the McDonalds with the idea, they told him they weren't interested in doing it themselves. So Kroc offered to do it for them. The brothers agreed and gave Kroc the exclusive rights to sell the McDonald's method.

Ray opened his first McDonald's in April 1955 in the Chicago suburb of Des Plaines. He used the meticulously

Hamburger U

Ray Kroc believed that the success of his company lay in his franchisees following "the McDonald's Method" to the letter. To ensure this, he developed a 75-page manual that outlined every aspect of running a McDonald's operation. Nothing was left to interpretation. Burgers had to be exactly 1.6 ounces, served with a quarter ounce of onion, a teaspoon of mustard and a tablespoon of ketchup. Fries had to be cut at nine-thirty-seconds of an inch thick. The manual even specified how often the restaurant needed to be cleaned.

In 1961, Kroc came up with a way to gain even greater control over his franchisees. In the basement of a McDonald's in Elk Grove, Illinois, he opened a training center that would eventually become Hamburger University, where students earned their degrees in "Hamburgerology" with a minor in french fries.

clean and efficient restaurant as a showcase for selling McDonald's franchises to the rest of the country. For each franchise he sold, Ray would collect 1.9 percent of the gross sales. From that he would give the McDonalds one-half percent. Kroc sold 18 franchises his first year in business but was shocked to discover he was barely making enough money to cover his expenses. In his haste to acquire the rights to the McDonalds' methods, he had made them a deal they couldn't refuse. Unfortunately, it was a deal on which he couldn't make any money.

Then Kroc met Harry Sonnenborne, a financial genius who showed Kroc how to make money—not by selling hamburgers, but by selling real estate. Under Sonnenborne's plan, Kroc set up a company that would purchase or lease the land on which all McDonald's restaurants would be located. Franchisees then paid Kroc a set monthly rental for the land or a percentage of their sales, whichever was greater. By owning the land the franchises were built on rather than just the franchises themselves, Kroc was guaranteed a profit. With his real-estate formula in place, Kroc set out to fulfill his goal—opening 1,000 McDonald's from coast to coast.

But there were problems. Kroc continually clashed with the McDonald brothers over changes he wanted to make in their original formula. Kroc became increasingly frustrated and decided he wanted control of McDonald's all to himself. So in 1961, he bought out the McDonalds for $2.7 million—cash. Kroc thought the deal included the original McDonald's restaurant in San Bernardino, but the brothers said it did not. Infuriated, Kroc confided to a long-time employee, "I'm not normally a vindictive man, but this time I'm going to get those sons-of-bitches." And he knew just how to do it. Without the rights to their own name, the McDonalds were forced to rename their restaurant The Big M. So Kroc opened a brand-new McDonald's one block away and put The Big M out of business.

With the McDonald brothers out of his way, Kroc was free to run the company as he saw fit. By 1965, he had opened more than 700 restaurants in 44 states. In April of that year, McDonald's became the first fast-food company to go public. Stock was issued at $22 per share. Within weeks it climbed to $49 a share, making Kroc an instant multimillionaire. By the end of the decade, Kroc had met and surpassed his goal, with nearly 1,500 McDonald's operating worldwide.

By the 1970s, McDonald's was the largest food supplier in the country and would remain so through the next two decades. At the time of his death on January 14, 1984, a new McDonald's was opening on average every 17 hours. Ten months later, McDonald's sold its 50-billionth burger.

Like many of the 20th century's most influential entrepreneurs, Ray Kroc was not a creator. When Kroc came onto the scene, convenience food already existed in many forms, from local diners to hot dog stands. But it was Kroc who had the cunning ability to grasp all the complexities of the fast-food concept and deliver it in the best possible way.

Sandra Kurtzig

Founder of
ASK Computer
Systems Inc.
Founded: 1974

*"I think luck is seizing opportunities.
There are opportunities all around.
There are millions of good ideas, but it's
those people who seize the ideas and seize
the opportunities that appear lucky."*

—Sandra Kurtzig

THE FIRST LADY OF COMPUTERS

In today's male-dominated software industry, women founders and CEOs are practically nonexistent. But while software titans like Microsoft's Bill Gates, Netscape's Marc Andreessen and Oracle's Larry Ellison have become the poster boys for Silicon Valley success, the first multimillion-dollar software entrepreneur was a woman. Starting with just $2,000, Sandra Kurtzig built a software empire that at its peak boasted $450 million in annual sales. And it all started as a part-time job.

Like many Silicon Valley companies, ASK Computer Systems Inc.'s beginnings were humble. In 1972, Sandra Kurtzig quit her job selling computer timeshares for General Electric so she could devote more time to starting a family. An admitted workaholic, Kurtzig knew she couldn't give up working altogether, so in hopes of making a little extra money and "to keep her mind occupied," she launched what she thought would be a small, part-time contract software-programming business in her snug second bedroom. "I never intended it to be outside the bedroom, let alone the world," she admits in an *Industry Week* article.

Her first client asked her to create a program that could track inventory and provide manufacturing information in a timely way. Realizing that other manufacturers might find such a program useful, she recruited several bright computer and engineering graduates and directed them to write standardized applications aimed at solving the problems of local manufacturers. "I knew what manufacturers wanted because of my technical background," Kurtzig told *Forbes* magazine, "and I could translate those needs into easy-to-use software."

Initially, Kurtzig was unable to convince Silicon Valley venture capitalists to invest in her start-up, so she was forced to launch ASK on retained earnings alone. To gain access to the minicomputers her company needed, she convinced executives at a nearby Hewlett-Packard plant to let her and her programmers use one of the company's series 3,000 minicomputers at night. "They let us in at 6 p.m., and we came with sleeping bags and stayed until 6 a.m." It wasn't long before Kurtzig's part-time job was taking up 20 hours a day. By 1978, ASK had its first salable products—a package of programs called Manman (short for manufacturing management), which improved inventory control and production management.

Kurtzig then struck a deal with Hewlett-Packard to sell its minicomputers pre-loaded with

Dear Sandra

In her autobiography, CEO Building a $400 Million Company From the Ground Up, Sandra Kurtzig offers the following advice to would-be entrepreneurs:

- **Believe in yourself.** If you don't believe in yourself, no one else is going to believe in you. You're not going to be able to communicate well if you don't believe in your idea.
- **Surround yourself with good people.** Have a good team and don't be afraid to share the glory and the responsibility and the authority. It takes a lot of hard work, and as the company gets bigger, it doesn't take any less. The work is just different.
- **Be willing to make mistakes.** You just have to make fewer mistakes than your competition.
- **Don't get wrapped up in your success.** When we went public, all of a sudden we were the fair-haired children of the peninsula and we were the overnight success. But it took six or seven years of hard work and 20-hour days to become the overnight success.
- **You're still the same person you were when you started.** You still stand in line at the post office, you still put your pants on one leg at a time, and just because all of a sudden everybody thinks you're great, don't let it go to your head. If you do, when your business has problems, you won't be able to cope with it.

Sandra Kurtzig

her programs. This breakthrough turnkey system meant ASK could market a complete product to computer-wary managers several years before computers would become common tools of the industry.

Without money for a sales force, marketing, advertisements or brochures, ASK built its customer base by selling systems to big corporate clients like Hewlett-Packard and Hughes Electronics "on our personality, our ideas, our energy, our hard work and our commitment to their success," Kurtzig explains. The strategy worked. Kurtzig's association with HP enhanced ASK's credibility with prospective customers and afforded the company access to promising industrial markets. The system was an instant hit, and ASK sales soared from $2.8 million in 1979 to $39 million in 1983, making it the 11th-fastest-growing company in the country between 1978 and 1982.

Meanwhile, Kurtzig took the company public in 1981. Between 1981 and 1983, following a small equity offering and a 2-for-1 split, earnings per share doubled, which meant a windfall for Kurtzig that made her worth $65 million.

But even with her tremendous success, Kurtzig was growing tired of the fast-track life. "When you are the CEO, you live it seven days a week, 24 hours a day," she explains. "And you can't ever go on vacation and not think about the meetings you're missing—or should be attending—or without feeling guilty about what you're not doing." Wanting to devote more time to her children and realizing that she couldn't do that and keep up her whirlwind pace at ASK, Kurtzig resigned from most of her duties in 1985, keeping only her title of chairman.

Feeling that other parts of her life "needed fulfilling," Kurtzig spent the next four years dabbling in other pursuits, including a brief association with ABC's "Good Morning America," building a home in Hawaii, writing her autobiography, and, of course, spending time with her sons.

For a while, ASK continued to prosper despite the departure of its founder. Over the next four years, profits grew by $1.5 million, hitting $13.5 million by the end of fiscal year 1989. But there were storm clouds forming on the horizon. Sales seemed to be flattening out after reaching $79 million. More ominous, ASK's product line was flat. The company was still living off a software package whose last overhaul coincided with Kurtzig's decision to relinquish day-to-day control. In the fall of 1989, when it became clear ASK was facing the first of what would likely be several quarters of flat sales, ASK's board of directors persuaded Kurtzig to rejoin as CEO in hopes that she could turn the company around. It was an offer she couldn't refuse. "When push comes to shove," she says of her return, "well…ASK is my baby, and ASK is what I know."

Kurtzig's first step after returning to ASK was to bring entre-preneurial-minded people onto the board. To increase employee participation, she asked research and development employees to rate the performance of the division's managers. The top-rated managers were rewarded with greater responsibility. Those who received low ratings were given their pink slips. She also put an end to the practice of senior managers giving themselves hefty raises and bonuses.

Womanagement

One of the reasons for Sandra Kurtzig's tremendous success was her refusal to accept the status quo. When she first started ASK, it was a generally held belief that in order to compete in a male-dominated industry, a woman had to think like a man. But Kurtzig felt different-ly. Rather than following the classic rigid, hierarchical "male" approach to management, she adopted a policy of being honest with her employees, sharing information rather than withholding it, and keep-ing her office door open.

"I have a style of walking around and stroking people," Kurtzig explains in a 1990 Time magazine article. "Whenever possible, I try to compliment them in front of their peers and go up and hug them. A woman can show the warmth that a man often can't." Thanks to Kurtzig and other female managers, a woman's emotional range and empathy, which were once looked upon as distinct disadvantages, are now viewed by many as potential resources. "The best way to negoti-ate," Kurtzig insists, "is to understand what the other side wants. With men, it's often all or nothing. They can end up where it's the last time either side will do business with the other."

Sandra Kurtzig

Most important, she repositioned the firm as a database provider and re-engineered the company's software to run on a variety of different computers. By 1992, ASK was back on top, boasting sales of $450 million, making it the largest public company ever founded and run by a woman.

Comfortable that her company was back on track, Kurtzig once again retired, letting professional management take over the company she'd nurtured back to health. Two years later, ASK was purchased by Charles Wang's firm, Computer Associates.

Today, Sandra Kurtzig is chairman of the board of E-Benefits, an insurance and human resources service provider she founded with her son's Andrew and Ken (pictured, left to right) in 1996. Though no longer considered a "major player" herself, Kurtzig was instrumental in laying the groundwork of the modern business-to-business software industry. Her innovative approach of creating easy-to-use software for complex manufacturing tasks has been a model for virtually every successful software company in the industry today.

Estee Lauder

Estee Lauder Estee Lauder Lauder Estee Lauder Estee Lauder Lauder Estee Lauder Estee Lauder Estee Lauder Lauder Estee Lauder Lauder Estee Lauder Estee Laude Estee

"I didn't get here by dreaming or thinking about it. I got here by doing it."

—Estee Lauder

Founder of Estee Lauder Inc.
Founded: 1946

The Sweet Smell Of Success

Estee Lauder built a cosmetics empire on the motto, "There are no homely women, only careless women." By convincing those "careless women" they could become beautiful—with a little help from her products—she took on the giants of the cosmetics world and won. Starting with little more than a dream, through extraordinary ambition, impeccable taste, perseverance, innovative marketing and hard work, this creative visionary became the wealthiest self-made woman in America and created a family dynasty that continues today.

Thanks to the romantic, mythical background she created for herself, little was known of Lauder's childhood life until 1985. For years, she gleefully misled the media with stories claiming she was a countess of genteel European background. Only when an unauthorized biography threatened to expose the truth did Lauder "come clean," rushing into print an autobiography titled *Estee: A Success Story*.

Born Josephine Esther Mentzer in 1908, the would-be Grand Dame of Beauty grew up in the Corona section of Queens, New York. Her background was indeed European—her parents, Max Mentzer and Rose (Schotz) Mentzer, were Jewish immigrants from Hungary and Czechoslovakia, but they were far from high society. Her father owned a hardware store, above which the family lived.

In her autobiography, Lauder admits that as a child she was ashamed of her parents' "old-country ways" and heavily accented English. "Both were European in every straight-laced way," she writes, "and I desperately wanted to be 100 percent American." Working in her father's store instilled in Lauder an understanding of retailing and entrepreneurship at a young age. But what she really dreamed of was "being an actress—name in lights, flowers, handsome men," she explains.

Shortly after World War I erupted, Lauder's uncle, John Schotz, came to live with the family. A chemist who specialized in making his own "secret" skin-care products, Schotz set up a make-shift laboratory in the tiny stable behind the Mentzer's house and began concocting his creams with young Estee at his side. "I recognized in my Uncle John my true path...I watched and learned."

Determined to become a scientist, Lauder hawked her uncle's wares to her classmates at Newton High School, going so far as to give them complete makeovers to prove the

Beauty Secrets

Estee Lauder has become famous for such "Lauderisms" as "Create your own style" and "Don't be afraid of the trial-and-error approach," which she claims were part of the ticket to her success. In her 1985 autobiography, Lauder offered the following 15 rules as advice to aspiring entrepreneurs.

1. Find the proper location.
2. When you're angry, never put it in writing.
3. You get more bees with honey.
4. Keep your own image straight in your mind.
5. Keep an eye on the competition.
6. Divide and rule.
7. Learn to say no.
8. Trust your instincts.
9. Act tough.
10. Acknowledge your mistakes.
11. Write things down.
12. Hire the best people.
13. Break down barriers.
14. Give credit where credit is due.
15. Train the best sales force.

Guerrilla Sales

Those who know her have described Estee Lauder as a woman you simply can't say no to. Quite often, this is attributed to her irresistible charm. But the real reason Lauder has succeeded where others have failed is that she simply refuses to give up. When she wants something, she's been known to resort to some highly creative tactics to get it. She used one such tactic to break the prestigious Galleries Lafayette account in Paris. When the manager refused to stock her products, Lauder "accidentally" spilled her Youth Dew on the floor during a demonstration in the middle of a crowd. As the appealing scent wafted through the air, it quickly aroused the interest of customers, who began asking where they could purchase the product. Seeing this, the manager capitulated and gave Lauder her initial order.

quality of her uncle's products. She learned marketing and merchandising at an early age, saying, "To sell a cream, you sold a dream in the early days."

But before she could realize her dream of becoming a glamorous skin-care specialist, Estee met and married Joseph Lauter, a moderately successful textile salesman, and moved with him to Manhattan. Shortly thereafter, the couple adopted the original Austrian spelling of their surname, Lauder, which would later add credence to Estee's false claim that she was born in Vienna.

Throughout the early years of her marriage and even after the birth of her first child, Leonard, in 1933, Lauder continued to refine and improve her uncle's creams, cooking up concoctions on her kitchen stove. To create a market for her product, she gave free demonstrations and makeovers at salons, hotels, the subway and even in the street. She also began visiting the homes of her clients, where she would make up their friends and sell more cream. It wasn't long before Lauder was a fixture on the guest lists of New York City's most influential hostesses.

Realizing that social contacts were vital in the beauty business, Lauder decided to make her childhood dreams come true by becoming an elegant lady of refinement and distinction. Through fabrications and embellishments of the truth and by dressing like her customers and imitating their behavior, Lauder made herself into a sophisticated and debonair lady of beauty—a role that quickly became indistinguishable from reality. But in her single-minded quest for sales, her marriage suffered, eventually ending in divorce in 1939.

After her divorce, Lauder moved to Miami Beach, Florida, where she continued to sell her skin products to affluent vacationers. She also had several affairs with wealthy men she hoped could help with her business. But it was not to be. After three years of searching for a rich prince to make her dreams come true, she grew tired of the chase and realized that she dearly missed her ex-husband. Ironically, it was sickness that brought the couple together again. When Leonard came down with the mumps, Joseph and Estee reunited as loving mother and father. A new spark ignited, and they remarried in 1942, agreeing to make a go of the cosmetics business together—with Estee in charge of marketing and product development and Joe overseeing finances, manufacturing and administration.

The couple opened their first store in New York City in 1944. After a brief time off in December of that year to give birth to their second son, Ronald, Estee returned to work almost immediately, officially forming Estee Lauder Inc. in 1946. In need of manufacturing and storage facilities, the Lauders converted a Manhattan restaurant into a factory. Estee sold during the day and cooked up the creams and oils for her products on the restaurant's stoves at night.

In what would prove to be an ingenious marketing move, Estee decided to sell her products only through upscale department stores. Her first target was Saks Fifth Avenue. She convinced Saks to place a large order for her skin creams, which the store sold out of within two days. Her success with Saks convinced Estee that she could compete with such cosmetics giants as Revlon, Helena Rubinestein and Elizbeth Arden. She became a persuasive traveling salesperson dedicated to penetrating every fine department store in the United States.

Her ambition and dedication began to pay off in the early 1950s as the Estee Lauder line became a regular feature at such prestigious stores as I. Magnin, Marshall Field's, Nieman-Marcus and Bonwit Teller. But the company was still small compared to the titans. Determined to change this, Lauder embarked on an innovative promotion strategy. Turned down by one ad agency after another because of the small size of their account, the Lauders invested their entire $50,000 advertising budget in samples to be offered through direct mail, charity giveaways and as gifts with purchases. (Lauder's "free gift with purchase" technique would become a company trademark and later, a standard industry practice.) The result was thousands of new customers.

But the real turning point came in 1953, when Lauder introduced her first fragrance—Youth Dew, a bath oil that doubled as a perfume. Priced at just $8.50, Youth Dew was an affordable luxury for most women, and sales zoomed from a few hundred dollars a week to several thousand. By the mid-1950s, Youth Dew accounted for 80 percent of Estee Lauder's sales and had transformed the fledgling company into a multimillion-dollar business.

Throughout the 1960s, Lauder continued to broaden her product line, introducing (among other things) male toiletries under the Aramis brand name and the first line of fashion-oriented, allergy-tested cosmetics, Clinique. In addition, Lauder set out to conquer the rest of the world, convincing Harrod's of London and Paris' Galleries Lafayette to carry her products. By the mid-1970s, Lauder's products were on the market in more than 70 countries worldwide. The company continued to prosper throughout the 1980s and '90s, becoming the third-largest cosmetics company in America—with 10,000 employees and sales in excess of $2 billion. By 1999, Estee Lauder products accounted for nearly 50 percent of all retail beauty aids sold in America.

The once struggling skin-cream huckster is now retired, with an estimated net worth from her innovation—beauty in a jar—of $5 billion, according to *Fortune* magazine. Although her son Leonard and her grandchildren now occupy the executive suites, Estee Lauder remains the firm's creative genius and driving spirit. A classic entrepreneur and innovator who refused to listen to experts, Lauder's risk-taking mentality and refusal to settle for anything less than the very best changed the world of cosmetics distribution. But Lauder herself explains the secret of her success more simply: "I was a woman with a mission and single-minded in the pursuit of my dream."

Charles Lazarus

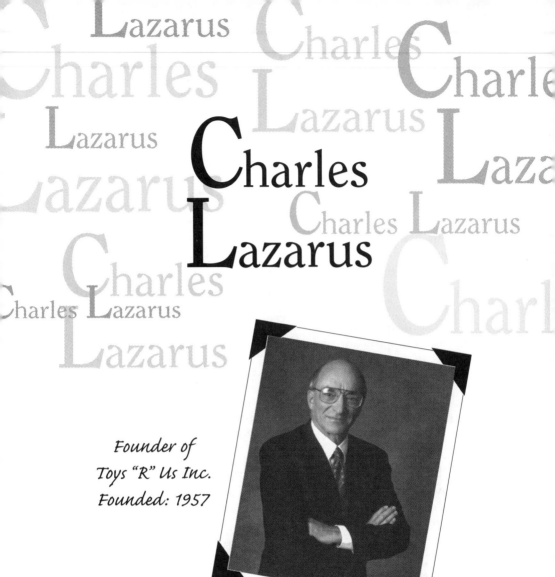

Founder of
Toys "R" Us Inc.
Founded: 1957

"Listening to the customer is probably the best thing in the world. Almost all that we have here and now, and how we expanded the business came from the customer saying 'I need...' or 'I want...'"

—Charles Lazarus

TOY TITAN

Mention the name Toys "R" Us, and children's faces immediately light up. And that's just the way Charles Lazarus likes it. The first retailer to mass-merchandise toys at across-the-board discount prices, Toys "R" Us Inc. has been called one of the biggest success stories in retailing in the past 20 years. And its founder, Charles Lazarus, has been called one of the few geniuses in the business. Ironically, what led Lazarus to pioneer the first one-stop-shopping supermarket for toys was a disgruntled mother and a broken doll.

After returning from World War II, Lazarus decided to go into business for himself, so he rented his father's former bicycle-repair shop on the ground floor of the house where he had been born and grown up. "I came out of the service after the war, and everyone I talked to said they were going to go home, get married, have children and live the American dream," Lazarus explains. "I had saved a few dollars in the service, so I decided that I would open a store in my father's bicycle-repair shop. But instead of selling bikes, I would sell cribs, carriages, strollers, high chairs…everything for the baby. My instincts told me the timing was right." His instincts proved to be correct, and thanks to the postwar baby boom, Lazarus experienced several very good years.

As he learned the ins and outs of running his first store, Lazarus began to realize that the key to his success lay in listening to his customers' needs and fulfilling them. Early on, a woman asked him for some toys to go along with a crib she was buying. Having none, he quickly added a few basic playthings to his stock. It wasn't long before a customer came in to replace a doll her baby had smashed. Lazarus quickly realized that people who bought toys returned for more. Those who bought cribs or high chairs generally didn't return. Lazarus got the message and switched to selling mostly toys, an industry where there was little organized competition.

Sales rapidly increased, and Lazarus began searching for new and better ways to take advantage of the now booming toy market. That's when he hit upon the idea of selling toys in a bigger environment. Expanding his shop into an empty supermarket next door, he lined the shelves with box after box of toys, which he offered at discount prices. The combination of selection and pricing was an immediate success.

"It was amazing," he remembers. "We were probably the first ones selling toys and juvenile products at a discount. Here we were, located in the middle of Washington, DC—and customers had to go find parking, which was really hard to do. But one customer told another, and all the word-of-mouth really worked for us."

It worked so well that by the early 1950s, Charles had made enough money to open a second store. Shoppers flocked to his "cash-and-carry" stores, knowing that they would find a vast array of toys and almost every style of stroller or crib in stock and at reasonable prices. But toys were still his bestsellers.

So in 1957, Lazarus opened a second "toy supermarket," which he named Toys "R" Us, with the "R" backwards. The second store was certainly a risk. Although his first "cash and carry" toy store had been a success, specialty retailing and off-price positioning were revolutionary concepts in those pre-mall, pre-discount days. Plus, toy retailing was seasonal. Department stores, which dominated the toy business at the time, made 70 percent of their sales during the six weeks before Christmas. In order to survive, Toys "R" Us would have to be able to successfully sell toys year-round, something that was unheard of in the industry

Against The Grain

From the very start, Charles Lazarus approached retailing differently than most of his competitors did—especially when buying and pricing merchandise. For example, many retailers set their selling price based on what they paid wholesale. But not Lazarus. He would decide at what price he thought he could sell great volumes of the product, and then he would determine what price he would pay the wholesaler.

Charles Lazarus

Thinking Outside The Jack-In-The-Box

Charles Lazarus realized early in his career that the way customers perceive you is one of the most important factors in success. And Lazarus was a master at projecting the image he wanted for Toys "R" Us Inc. By creating stores with row after row of shelves stacked to the rafters with toys, he gave his customers the impression that his store had a virtually limitless selection, and no matter what toy they were looking for, Toys "R" Us would have it.

Along with selection, Lazarus also wanted his customers to feel they would always get the best price at Toys "R" Us. He often sold hot products for little or no profit to maintain this low-cost image. For instance, in 1977, an electronic game called "Simon" was one of the most popular toys on the market. It was also in short supply. While some stores took advantage of the demand and charged more than $30 for the game, Lazarus charged less than $20. Why? Because he figured that shoppers would believe everything else in his stores must also be bargain-priced.

at the time. But once again, Lazarus' timing couldn't have been better. The growing popularity of television, and thus television advertising, gave rise to the phenomenon of "hot toys"—toys that every kid wanted and "just had to have," regardless of what time of year it was. So Lazarus made sure parents knew exactly where to find them, and at discount prices: Toys "R" Us.

In 1966, Lazarus had four stores that together sold about $12 million worth of toys each year. To finance further expansion, he sold the whole operation to Interstate Sales for $7.5 million in cash. As part of the deal, Lazarus stayed on as head of the toy division. Toys "R" Us continued to flourish under Lazarus' direction, but the same was not true of Interstate. A victim of ill-managed growth, the company was forced to file for bankruptcy in 1974.

Lazarus convinced the bankruptcy court to let him oversee Interstate during this crucial period. Through a combination of persistence, careful business decisions and heavy investments in talent and technology, Lazarus began the task of restructuring. He sold off or liquidated the unprofitable operations, retaining his toy stores, and in just four years Interstate emerged from bankruptcy and was renamed Toys "R" Us.

Fueled by the energy and enthusiasm of the remarkable comeback, in 1983, Toys "R" Us opened even more stores in the United States, started a chain of children boutiques called Kids "R" Us and began expanding internationally, opening stores in Singapore and Canada. In 1993, the company continued its international expansion by opening stores in Australia, Belgium, the Netherlands, Portugal and Switzerland.

Lazarus remained at the helm of Toys "R" Us until 1994, when he relinquished his CEO title to Michael Goldstein. He remains with the company as chairman emeritus, devoting his time to the international focus of the business, serving as a sort of Toys "R" Us ambassador to foreign countries where the company hopes to open new stores.

But as it enters the 21st century, Toys "R" Us faces growing competition from deep discounters such as Wal-Mart and warehouse clubs like Price/Costco. Ironically enough, these companies have grown to prominence using the same one-stop-shopping strategy pioneered by Lazarus more than 37 years ago.

William Levitt

*"**A**ny damn fool can build homes. What counts is how many you can sell for how little."*
—William Levitt

Co-founder of Levitt & Sons
Founded: 1929

THE SULTAN
OF SUBURBIA

Like many brilliant entrepreneurs, William Levitt didn't come up with the idea that made him rich. He stole it. Although it is true that Levitt perfected the assembly-line approach that enabled his workers to churn out houses at an incredible rate, long-forgotten developers in California had been doing something similar for years. Levitt's true genius was that he foresaw the unprecedented demand for middle-class housing that followed World War II and, by applying a panoply of assembly-line techniques to housing construction, positioned himself to make the most of the situation. His unique vision of a planned community with well-built but affordable houses jump-started the suburbanization of America and dramatically changed the way homebuilders built and homebuyers bought.

Ironically, the man who would become known as the "Pioneer of Suburbs" never intended to be a builder. His dream was to be a commercial aviator. But he drifted into the housing business after his father, Abraham, and brother, Alfred, designed and built a house on a lot William owned but had been unable to sell. With a house on the lot, William quickly made the sale. Realizing a good thing when he saw it, he immediately joined forces with his father and brother to form Levitt & Sons in 1929.

With Abraham handling the landscaping and community planning, Alfred designing the homes and William dealing with management, financial matters and sales, the company experienced moderate success throughout the 1930s. By the end of the decade, Levitt & Sons had built 2,500 homes ranging in price from $9,100 to $18,500.

When World War II erupted, William put his business career on hold to serve in the Pacific with one of the Navy's Seabee combat construction units, where he earned a reputation for bending rules and even disobeying orders if it would help him accomplish his objectives.

Shortly after William returned to the family business in 1945, the company entered its greatest era of success. Millions of newly liberated GIs, many with wives and children, were eager to buy homes. Unfortunately, wartime shortages had crippled the housing industry, and there simply weren't enough homes to meet the demand. Sensing a tremendous opportunity, the Levitts purchased 1,000 acres of land on Long Island, 25 miles east of Manhattan, and embarked on a bold venture to build 17,000 homes. It was quite an optimistic goal at a time when most developers averaged four to five houses a year. But the Levitts had a plan.

They broke down the construction process into 27 separate tasks and assigned each task to a group of workers who would go from house to house repeating their specific task at each site. Trucks would deliver parts and materials to homesites placed at 60-foot intervals. Then the carpenters, tilers, painters and roofers arrived each in turn. There was even one employee who did nothing but bolt washing machines to the floors. When the process was in high gear, houses were completed at the rate of 36 per day. (Even at that pace, Levitt was hard-pressed to keep up with demand. During the first weekend, Levitt sold more than 300 houses.)

Affordable But Not Equal

William Levitt's dream of affordable, well-built housing was not for everyone...at least not initially. As late as the 1950s, he refused to sell homes to African-Americans. He once offered to build a separate development for blacks, but he would not integrate white developments, believing that integration would cause him to lose 90 to 95 percent of his white customers. Levitt defended his policy by saying, "We can solve a housing problem or we can try to solve a racial problem. But we can't do both." Levitt would eventually relent, of course, but decades later, many of the communities he created remain predominantly white.

A Family Affair

Although it is William Levitt who is generally credited with the success of Levittown and the innovations that made it possible, he could not have accomplished either without his brother and father. In fact, Alfred and Abraham Levitt first experimented with many of the standardization and cost-reduction techniques that were later used at Levittown while building 1,600 homes for military and civilian personnel stationed at the Norfolk Naval Base in Virginia in 1942.

To keep down lumber costs, the Levitts bought their own forests and built a sawmill in Oregon. They purchased appliances directly from the manufacturer, cutting out the distributor's markup. They even made their own nails. The Levitts' methods kept costs so low that in the first few years, their cookie-cutter two-bedroom houses—which featured fireplaces, radiant-heated floors, up-to-date kitchen equipment, laundry rooms and televisions—could be sold for just $7,900...a price that still allowed the Levitts a profit of about $1,000.

In its first year, William's dream community, which he rather arrogantly dubbed "Levittown," made the company a profit of approximately $5 million. In 1949 alone, the Levitts built 4,600 houses and sold them for a total of more than $42 million. Clearly their mass-production technique was the key to the company's future. It also dramatically changed the housing industry. After seeing the Levitts' success, builders across the country began turning cornfields into bedroom communities, mimicking the Levitts' cost- and time-cutting methods. The suburbanization of American was on.

From the late 1940s to the late 1960s, the Levitts experienced phenomenal success, building additional Levittowns in Pennsylvania, New Jersey, New York and Florida. William assumed more control when Alfred left the company in the mid-1950s, and then complete control when Abraham died in 1962. By the late 1960s, William had become one of the richest men in

America, with a fortune estimated in excess of $100 million. He lived in a lavish 30-room mansion on his "La Coline" estate in Mill Neck, New York, and spent much of his time on his 237-foot yacht, La Belle Simone, named after his third wife. But after nearly four decades of unprecedented success, Levitt's luck was about to change.

In 1968, after his company had built more than 140,000 homes around the world, Levitt sold Levitt & Sons to International Telephone and Telegraph (ITT) for $92 million in stock, most of which went directly into his pocket. The deal barred him from the domestic construction business for 10 years, so using his ITT stock as collateral, Levitt embarked on a series of building projects in Iran, Venezuela, France and Nigeria. But the success he'd achieved in the United States eluded him. Even worse, in just four years, the value of his ITT stock dropped 90 percent, leaving him millions of dollars in debt.

In the late 1970s, Levitt made several abortive attempts at a comeback, including two developments in Florida, both of which failed, forcing him to refund thousands of prospective homebuyers' deposits because the homes were never built. The final blow came in 1981, when New York State Attorney General Robert Abrams charged that Levitt had illegally siphoned money from the Levitt Foundation, a charitable organization started by his family years earlier. Levitt was eventually forced to repay $5 million to the foundation.

By 1982, with much of his fortune gone, Levitt had settled into a restless retirement. He died at the North Shore University Hospital in Manhasset, New York, January 8, 1994. Despite his financial problems in his later years, William Levitt, along with his father and brother, revolutionized the housing industry. The mass-market construction methods they helped to make industry standards enabled millions of middle- and working-class Americans to own their own homes and reshaped the face of the nation.

George Lucas

"Everybody has talent. It's just a matter of moving around until you've discovered what it is."

—George Lucas

Founder of Lucasfilm Ltd.
Founded: 1971

STAR WARRIOR

No other 20th-century filmmaker has had a greater impact on the film industry than George Lucas. His zeal for innovation forged a new relationship between entertainment and technology that revolutionized the art of motion pictures. His uncanny business acumen turned film licensing and merchandising into a multibillion-dollar industry. And his "Star Wars" trilogy ushered in the era of the Hollywood mega-blockbuster.

Lucas was born in Modesto, California, on May 14, 1944. As an adolescent who, as he says, "barely squeaked through high school," Lucas aspired to be an auto racer. He changed his mind about a racing career, however, when a near-fatal accident crushed his lungs and sent him to the hospital for three months just days before his high school graduation. The experience changed Lucas. "I realized that I'd been living my life so close to the edge for so long," he says. "That's when I decided to go straight, to become a better student, to try to do something with myself."

Lucas enrolled at Modesto Junior College, where he developed a fascination with cinematography. Deciding on a career in film, he applied to the prestigious University of Southern California (USC) film school. USC was a milestone for Lucas. "Suddenly my life was film—every waking hour," he says in a 1997 *Playboy* interview. He concentrated on making abstract science fiction films and mock documentaries, which caught the attention of director Francis Ford Coppola, who invited Lucas to sit in on the shooting of "Finian's Rainbow." Coppola also persuaded Warner Bros. to make a film of one of Lucas' student movies. The full-length feature, "THX-1138," a bleak Orwellian tale, was released in 1971 to modest reviews and a lukewarm reception at the box office. But studio executives were impressed with Lucas' obvious talent.

"THX-1138" had earned Lucas a reputation as a skilled but mechanical filmmaker devoid of humor and feeling. His second film, "American Graffiti," which was based on his own coming of age in Modesto, would change that. Filmed on a shoestring budget of just $780,000, the film became a smash hit soon after its release in June 1973 and eventually grossed $120 million.

The film got rave reviews and made Lucas a Hollywood sensation. It also proved to be a defining moment for Lucas, as both a filmmaker and a businessman. Studio honchos pulled rank and made changes to Lucas' final version. The changes were minor, but the scars were lasting. "I'm very aware as a creative person that those who control the means of production control the creative vision," he says. "It's not a matter of saying 'You're going to let me have the final cut,' because no matter what you do in a contract, they will go around it. Whereas if you own the cameras and you own the film, there's nothing they can do to stop you." And that's exactly what Lucas set out to do.

When negotiating with 20th Century Fox in 1975 for his next movie, "Star Wars," Lucas cut his directing fee by $500,000 in exchange for things Fox regarded as nearly worthless: ownership of the film's merchandising and all sequel rights. It turned out to be a brilliant move, one that assured Lucas the real independence and creative control he'd been seeking. "Star Wars" shattered all box office records, earning Lucas about $40 million in its initial release—merchandising would later bring him tens of millions more. Most important, Lucas owned the sequels, and thus a franchise. To maximize its value, he financed his first sequel, "The Empire Strikes Back," himself, borrowing heavily to cover the $30 million production costs. Given the success of "Star Wars," it was a good bet, but a huge risk—if the film bombed, Lucas would be bankrupt. "Empire" did exceptionally

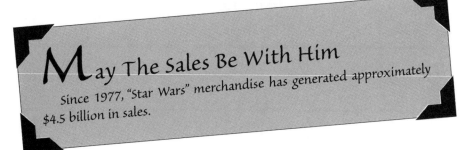

May The Sales Be With Him

Since 1977, "Star Wars" merchandise has generated approximately $4.5 billion in sales.

well, however, as did the third film in the trilogy, "Return of the Jedi," which Lucas also financed.

Lucas further increased his fortune in the 1980s by producing the three Indiana Jones movies, for which he earned well over $100 million. Then, at the very top of his game, he largely abandoned moviemaking and poured his fortune into digital experiments that, he sensed correctly, would transform the movie business.

His main focus was Industrial Light & Magic (ILM), which he created in 1975 when he couldn't find an outside company to do special effects for "Star Wars." ILM's first breakthrough was a motion-control camera, which could revolve repeatedly around stationary objects while remaining in constant focus, thus simulating flight. To generate cash, Lucas turned ILM into a service company. Having created a market for special-effects-laden films, he began taking on work from other filmmakers. This way he could keep developing techniques while other people funded his research.

Charging up to $25 million per movie, ILM was almost immediately profitable, supplying the special effects for such blockbusters as "Jurassic Park" and "Twister." Lucas funneled ILM profits into related businesses that sprang from his research. Skywalker Sound emerged as the industry's top audio post-production company, which then branched out to providing a digital sound system for movie theaters and homes under the name THX (in honor of his first film). And with the founding of LucasArts Entertainment, Lucas then moved into video games, producing such top-sellers as the "Star Wars"-inspired Rebel Assault, X-Wing and Dark Forces.

A Touch Of Magic

Just how much impact has George Lucas had on the movie industry? He directed or produced four of the top 10 grossing films of the 20th century. His Industrial Light & Magic has played a key role in 11 of the top 20 box office hits of all time, including "Titanic," "E.T.," "Jurassic Park" and "Forrest Gump."

By the mid-1990s, Lucas decided to return to filmmaking and began work on the script for the "Star Wars" prequel, "Star Wars: Episode I, The Phantom Menace." To create a buzz for the new movie, he embarked on a carefully planned marketing strategy. In 1997, he re-released the "Star Wars" trilogy as a special edition, which scored $475 million at the box office. The huge popularity of the films built a new audience for "The Phantom Menace." Just as important, it provided Lucas with the $115 million he needed to finance production, guaranteeing him both complete creative control and greater profits. Again, it was a gamble. But again, it paid off.

Released on May 19, 1999, the film broke all box office records, taking in an estimated $42 million on its opening day. By September, it had become the top-grossing movie of the summer, raking in $419.4 million, more than twice as much as its closest competitor.

The success of "The Phantom Menace" firmly established Lucas as one of the most powerful—and profitable—people in Hollywood. But the admitted workaholic isn't about to rest on his laurels. Plans for "Star Wars" Episodes II and III are already on the table, as well as plans for a fourth Indiana Jones movie.

During his nearly 30 years as a filmmaker, George Lucas has advanced the art of motion pictures by taking risks and continually pushing the envelope. He has changed the way Hollywood makes films by setting the standard for what a modern commercial movie can be. And it's not over yet, young Jedi.

Henry Luce

"*The human adventure does, as I believe, have meaning and purpose.*"
—Henry Luce

Founder of Time Inc.
Founded: 1923

EDITORIAL EXPLORER

Henry Luce was undoubtedly the most influential journalistic innovator of the first half of the 20th century. As editor in chief of *Time*, he helped create a new form of journalism, inventing the newsweekly and laying the groundwork for the modern mass print media. By the time he was 40, Luce had carved out an empire that included three wildly popular magazines, national radio programming, and newsreels that appeared every day in 8,000 movie theaters across America. At the height of his power, his words could sway government policy and mold public opinion.

Luce was born in 1898 in Tengchow (now P'eng-lai), China, where his father—a Presbyterian minister and missionary—headed a small college for Chinese converts to Christianity. Luce spent his entire childhood in China, and as a result, grew up with an idealized image of America as "an unfinished masterpiece of democratic liberalism and capitalism." It was an image he would never fully abandon.

Luce emerged from his youth with a deep sense of moral certainty, an unquenchable ambition and limitless curiosity. He read voraciously and developed an almost obsessive attraction to travel. It was his thirst for knowledge and experience that helped determine the direction of his career in life.

After graduating from Yale in 1920, Luce spent a year in England studying at Oxford before returning to the United States, where he took a job as a reporter alongside fellow Yale alum Britton Hadden. While working together, the two drew plans for an idea they had first discussed at Yale—a new type of weekly magazine that wouldn't simply report the news but would also interpret it for those who did not have the time, the energy or the knowledge to interpret it for themselves. Sensing what would become the country's scarcest commodity, Luce named the magazine *Time*, and designed it to be read in less than an hour.

"It'll never work," acclaimed journalist, editor and author H.L. Mencken told Luce before *Time's* launch. But the ambitious young man remained undaunted. He and Hadden amassed $86,000, and with a staff consisting only of themselves and three other full-time writers, they published the first issue of *Time* on March 3, 1923.

Time quickly attracted a growing readership, doubling its circulation within a year. A major reason for the magazine's success was its uniqueness. Unlike other national periodicals such as *Collier's* and *Scribner's*, which tended to be more literary, *Time* was an urgent, news-driven appraisal of the week's events written in a distinctive style (originated by Hadden) that featured brevity, brashness and shock, and captured the imagination of the growing college-educated public.

By 1928, Luce and Hadden were looking for new worlds to conquer and began working on a concept for a business magazine to be called *Fortune*, which, Luce declared, would provide entrepreneurs with a literature of their own. He insisted that his new publication be superbly researched and richly produced. To give *Fortune* more clout, he priced it a $1 per issue—a lavish sum for a magazine at that time.

But before the first issue could be published, Hadden died unexpectedly of blood poisoning in 1929. Luce was stunned, but he quickly pulled himself together and resumed work on *Fortune*, which first hit newsstands in February 1930, shortly after thousands of fortunes had instantly disappeared in the worst stock market crash in American history. Despite its unfortunate timing, *Fortune* was a success and made

Lasting Impressions

Henry Luce is credited with innovating many of the techniques that have become standard journalistic practices. He was the first publisher to emphasize personalities in the news. In Time, he started the concept of group journalism by introducing the reporter-researcher-writer team. And in Life, he created the photographer-writer team.

Stick To Your Guns

Henry Luce believed so strongly in his editorial vision that he often took enormous risks to grow his titles. In 1936, when Life debuted and became an instant blockbuster, the cost of printing 1 million copies per week surpassed revenue, and Time Inc. started losing millions. For fear of alienating his subscribers, Luce refused to scale back production or alter the quality of the magazine. Instead, he encouraged his printer and paper suppliers to find more efficient publishing methods by guaranteeing them a fair margin of profit despite Time's losses. The strategy worked. By 1939, Life had not only become profitable, but it was the most widely circulated magazine in the world and would remain so until the 1960s.

Luce an important figure on Wall Street. Luce continued to expand his empire by acquiring *Architectural Forum*, and he began producing "The March of Time," a series of newsreels that were heralded as the most imaginative of the era.

With *Time* established as the leader in the field of weekly journalism and *Fortune* boasting a readership that included some of the country's top businesspeople, Luce turned his attention to photojournalism and introduced *Life* in 1936. With marvelous photographs, snappy captions, and stories ranging from the maudlin to the spectacular, *Life* became an instant phenomenon. Although its original print run of 466,000 copies was the largest first-issue printing in magazine publishing history, demand for the magazine quickly exceeded the supply, and copies sold at a premium. Within a year, *Life's* circulation exceeded 1 million readers per week.

At the end of the 1930s, Time Inc. boasted three of the top-selling magazines in the country. But Luce had more than business on his mind. He could see the gathering storm in Europe and, through his magazines, began to prepare an isolationist America for a world war he felt was inevitable. In the winter of 1941, he published his famous essay "The American Century," in which he argued that the United States could determine the outcome of the war, then build a free and orderly world after an Allied victory. The editorial, which ultimately reached tens of millions of Americans, sparked a fierce debate between internationalists and isolationists. But that debate became moot when the Japanese attacked Pearl Harbor and catapulted America into World War II.

Time flourished during wartime, and at the end, it emerged as one of the largest and wealthiest publishing enterprises in the world. In 1954, hoping to profit from the population's search for leisure and pleasure, Luce launched the hugely successful *Sports Illustrated*. By the end of 1955, *Time* was earning revenues of more than $200 million a year and would continue to grow until Luce's retirement in 1964. At the time of Luce's death in 1967, *Life's* circulation was 750 million and *Time* had a circulation of 350 million.

Today, *Time* and the competitors it spawned bear faint resemblance to the original. But they still owe a great debt to the founder of newsmagazine journalism. Henry Luce's vision of a magazine that would explain and interpret complex events for a broad audience led to news analysis as opposed to straight reporting, and changed journalism forever.

J. Willard Marriott

J. Willard Marriott

Marriott

*Founder of
Marriott
International Inc.
Founded: 1927*

*"Success seems to be connected to action.
Successful people keep moving. They
make mistakes, but they never quit."*

—J. Willard Marriott

FROM ROOT BEER TO RICHES

With a philosophy of hard work, clean living, and a sometimes obsessive commitment to perfection, J. Willard Marriott turned a nine-stool root beer stand into one of the fastest-growing, most diversified and most profitable companies in the highly competitive American food and lodging business.

Like many of the 20th-century's early entrepreneurs, Marriott was born into poverty and went to work early in life. The son of a poor Mormon sheepherder, he began tending his father's flocks at the age of 8. By 14, he was taking sheep to market by rail from Ogden, Utah, to cities as far away as San Francisco and Omaha. Marriott may have remained on the ranch if not for the Mormon Church's requirement that all members perform missionary service.

At the age of 19, Marriott traveled east to preach the Gospel. For two years he wandered New England, finally ending up in Washington, DC. After experiencing the hot, humid Washington summer, he thought to himself that if he could find a nice cold drink to sell there, he could make a lot of money. But the idea would have to wait. When Marriott returned to Utah, he discovered that his father, along with most sheepherders, had gone bankrupt because of an economic downturn that had caused the price of sheep to plummet.

Having witnessed enough poverty and wanting to build a better future, Marriott, who never graduated high school, decided to complete his education. He talked his way into Weber State College, a community college that had recently been established in Ogden. Marriott cut a deal with the school's president (who just happened to be Marriott's former seventh-grade teacher), under which he would pay for his tuition by teaching theology classes. After two years at Weber, Marriott felt it was time for him to transfer to the University of Utah. To earn money for tuition, he took a job selling woolen underwear to lumberjacks in the Pacific Northwest. During Marriott's senior year at the University of Utah, an A&W root beer stand opened in Salt Lake City. Impressed by its success and remembering his experience as a missionary, Marriott purchased the Washington-area A&W franchise.

With $1,500 of his own money and a $1,500 loan, Marriott opened a nine-stool root beer stand on 14th Street in Washington, DC, on May 20, 1927. With the help of his new bride, Allie, Marriott ran the stand all summer with great success, but as winter approached, sales fell flat. Recognizing the seasonal nature of the soft-drink business, he got permission from A&W to add food service and opened his first Hot Shoppe. That winter, while Marriott waited on customers, his wife cooked chili, tamales and barbecue-beef sandwiches made according to recipes donated by the chef of the nearby Mexican Embassy. Employing shrewd promotional tactics—such as giving out free root beer coupons on street corners—and focusing on offering quality food at low prices, Marriott quickly expanded his operations by adding two more locations.

Always looking for new ways to improve his company, he bought the vacant lot next to one of his Hot Shoppes, removed the curb,

Willard Wisdom

- **On management:** "Take care of your people and they will take care of your customers."
- **On innovation:** "Great companies are built by people who never stop thinking about ways to improve the business."
- **On work:** "No person can get very far in life working 40 hours a week."
- **On success:** "It's the little things that make big things possible. Only close attention to the fine details of any operation makes the operation first class."
- **On entrepreneurship:** "I have always felt that America is the land of unlimited opportunities for those who will 'pay the price.'"

J. Willard Marriott

The Skivvy Challenge

J. Willard Marriott experienced his first business success selling woolen underwear to lumberjacks in the Pacific Northwest. His sales technique was ingenious: He picked out the two biggest, meanest-looking lumberjacks he could find and challenged them to tear a pair of his underwear apart. If they could, he gave them a free pair. If they couldn't, they had to buy a pair. Invariably, the lumberjacks accepted his challenge, and, invariably, they lost.

and began offering the first drive-in service on the East Coast. Waiters, called "curbers," ran food to customers on a tray with a fold-up bracket that clamped to the top of a car door. Customers loved it, and soon all three Hot Shoppes offered drive-in service. The move fueled further expansion, and by 1932, Marriott had seven Hot Shoppes in the Washington area and was close to being a millionaire.

Marriott's next innovation came in 1937. At Hot Shoppe No. 8, which sat near Hoover National Airport (the current site of the Pentagon), Marriott noticed that airline passengers would stop off at the Hot Shoppe to pick up a box lunch to eat aboard the plane. A genius at finding a need and filling it, Marriott decided to pre-box meals and sell them directly to the airlines, giving birth to the in-flight catering industry. Within a year, he was servicing 20 daily flights out of Hoover.

As America readied for war in 1942, Marriott juggled 24 Hot Shoppes in Washington, DC; Philadelphia and Baltimore. While World War II caused Hot Shoppe revenue to drop, it also presented a new opportunity. Marriott began managing cafeterias in government office buildings and war-production factories. When the war ended, prosperity returned, and customers flooded the Hot Shoppes. By 1953, Marriott's nine-stool root beer stand had grown to 56 restaurants, serving a total of 30 million customers per year.

After 30 years in the food business, Marriott took the biggest gamble of his career. He opened his first motor hotel, The Twin

Bridges, near the Washington National Airport, just a stone's throw from Hot Shoppe No. 8, on eight acres of land he had purchased three years earlier. In 1953, travel was on the rise, and airline experts accurately predicted that passenger jets would soon be flying in and out of National Airport. It became obvious to Marriott that the land he had purchased would be an ideal spot for a motor hotel and that such a hotel would represent "the logical extension of Hot Shoppes' traditional concern for the American family on wheels," he later recalled. With a $7 million price tag, the 370-bed Twin Bridges was the largest motel in the world.

By 1963, more than 35 years of virtual nonstop work were beginning to take their toll, and Marriott was ready for a change. He decided the time had come for a handpicked, hand-trained Marriott to run the company, and he tapped his eldest son, Bill Jr., for the job. One year later, the company changed its name to Marriott Hot Shoppes Inc., and Bill Jr. was named president.

In 1967, the company name changed again, to Marriott Corp., and in 1968, it was listed on the New York Stock Exchange. That same year, Marriott acquired the Big Boy Restaurants and, a year later, developed the Roy Rogers chain to compete with McDonald's. The company further diversified with the launch of Sun Line Cruise Ships and Marriott World Travel, then spent $250 million on three Great America theme parks.

Bill Jr. succeeded his father as CEO in 1972. Throughout the 1970s and '80s, Marriott Corp. continued to expand its hotel business, concentrating primarily on business travelers. Marriott remained chairman of the board but left day-to-day operations to his son.

On August 13, 1985, J. Willard Marriott died of heart failure. He left behind a hotel chain, several restaurant chains and flight kitchens serving 150 airlines. His empire was worth more than $3.5 billion. By 1999, Marriott International had become the 13th-largest employer in the United States, the second-largest lodging company in the world, and was operating or franchising more than 1,900 hotels.

Louis B. Mayer

Louis B. Mayer Louis Louis B. Mayer Louis B. Mayer B. M. Louis B. Mayer B. Louis B. Mayer L. B. L. Mayer Louis B. M. Mayer Louis

"**B**e smart, but never show it."
—Louis B. Mayer

Co-founder of Metro-Goldwyn-Mayer
Founded: 1924

THE REAL MGM LION

In Hollywood, there are lots of players. But only a few write a whole new script for the industry. One of these was Louis B. Mayer. By filling his studio with "more stars than there are in heaven," and making what he believed were good, wholesome, family movies, he established Metro-Goldwyn-Mayer as the industry's dominant film factory and ruled Hollywood for nearly a quarter of a century.

A Russian-Jewish immigrant whose family came to the United States in the late 1880s to escape the oppression of czarist Russia, Mayer began his show business career as a theater operator. Although movies were still in their infancy, he foresaw the tremendous financial possibilities in their development. In 1907, he purchased a dilapidated burlesque house just north of Boston in Haverhill, Massachusetts, and transformed it into a 600-seat movie theater.

A keen marketer from the start, Mayer built his patronage by alternating films with stage attractions and within a year he was grossing $25,000. Using his profits, Mayer swiftly took over other theaters in the area, ultimately acquiring control of the largest theater chain in New England. To ensure a steady supply of films for his growing string of theaters, he organized his own distribution company in 1914.

Next Mayer decided to try his luck at production. He moved to Los Angeles in 1918, founded the Louis B. Mayer Pictures Corp., and released a series of tear-jerkers starring the then-popular actress Anita Stewart. Mayer's success in all three aspects of the film industry—exhibition, distribution and production—attracted the attention of Marcus Loew, the owner of Loews'

Theaters, who was negotiating the purchase of the Goldwyn Studio.

Loew needed an experienced executive to oversee the films that would be produced by the newly combined Metro-Goldwyn, and offered Mayer the job of vice president in charge of production. Mayer agreed, but under one condition: that his name be added to the company. And thus, Metro-Goldwyn-Mayer was born.

Mayer, with the help of his dedicated lieutenant and so-called "boy wonder" of the industry, production chief Irving Thalberg, transformed MGM into a film factory, churning out an average of 47 feature films a year. He built up a roster of household names that included Judy Garland, Clark Gable, Joan Crawford, Elizabeth Taylor, Katharine Hepburn, Lana Turner, the Marx Brothers, Ava Gardner and Greta Garbo, and controlled them with a contract system that legally bound the stars to MGM for years.

Mayer worked hard to project himself as a father figure to his extended family of stars, directors and producers, but he was a master manipulator who could be brutally ruthless. When Clark Gable asked Mayer for a raise from $1,000 to $5,000 per week, Mayer blackmailed him, threatening to tell his wife about his affair with Joan Crawford. Gable settled for $2,000.

Yet when it came to defending his "family" against scandal and rumor, Mayer would go to incredible lengths. For instance, when a drunken Gable struck and killed a pedestrian near Hollywood Boulevard, Mayer sent him into hiding, then conspired with the local D.A. to put a minor executive on MGM's payroll for life in exchange for taking the rap.

In The Beginning

One of Louis B. Mayer's early successes came when he offered director D.W. Griffith $50,000 for the exclusive New England rights to "The Birth of a Nation." The deal eventually netted Mayer a record-breaking $500,000.

While Mayer's professional moral code may have been tinged with shades of gray, his movies reflected his penchant for wholesomeness and escapism. Convinced that morality sold, he favored the virtues of patriotism and family over controversial subject matter. With films like the Andy Hardy series (starring Mickey Rooney), Mayer defined American society according to his fantasies. And for quite some time, the strategy worked. Moviegoers flooded MGM's theaters, and critics lauded MGM films.

But as praise and profits soared, storm clouds were gathering on the horizon. Thalberg, who oversaw such MGM blockbusters as "Ben Hur," "Mutiny on the Bounty" and "The Wizard of Oz," was growing tired of playing "second fiddle." Mayer was the highest-paid person in the nation, making more than $1 million a year, and Thalberg felt entitled to an equal share. For his part, Mayer had begun to resent the growing opinion that Thalberg was the true creative genius behind MGM. By the mid-1930s, the rift between the mogul and his protégé grew to the point that they no longer spoke to one another. Thalberg eventually threatened to leave MGM for another studio, but before he could make good on this threat, he died of a heart attack in 1937.

Mayer would continue his arbitrary reign at MGM throughout the late 1930s and early 1940s, producing a host of prizewinning and profitable films. But during the postwar years, Mayer's invincibility began to fade. Audiences were becoming more sophisticated, and Mayer's formula of sappy, sentimental family fare and glossy romantic productions lost its appeal. Even worse, the government forced the industry to divest its lucrative theater chains, and top stars and directors were demanding the profit participation the studios had always denied them.

Star Power

Committed to obtaining the best talent money could buy, Louis B. Mayer scouted pretty girls and dashing men the world over, personally discovering Greta Garbo, Joan Crawford, Rudolph Valentino and Clark Gable.

Looking to boost MGM's profits, Albert Schenck, who had succeeded Marcus Loew, hired Dore Schary from RKO, hoping that he would become a "new Thalberg." But Schary's promotion of realistic dramas with controversial themes clashed with Mayer's sentimental romanticism. When Mayer told Schenck it was either him or Schary, Schenck chose Schary. After nearly 27 years as Hollywood's most powerful producer, Mayer resigned from MGM in 1951.

In the years that followed, Mayer attempted new ventures sporadically but never with much enthusiasm. Still bitter over his ouster from MGM, he tried to take over Loew's company in early 1957 through a complicated stock maneuver, but the effort failed. Mayer died shortly afterward.

Despite his faults, Mayer was a true innovator. Unlike other Hollywood moguls, who were simply trying to make a profit, Mayer was an idealist intent on using the power of movies to exert what he considered the proper moral influence on the American public. As a result, he built MGM into the most prestigious film studio of the 1920s, '30s and '40s, and left behind a legacy of classic films that defined America's aspirations, if not its reality, for many years after his death.

William McGowan

"*The meek shall inherit the earth, but they'll never increase market share.*"
—William McGowan

Founder of MCI Communications Corp.
Founded: 1968

MONOPOLY BUSTER

When William McGowan set out to take on AT&T, people thought he was crazy. Time and again he was told that AT&T was simply too big and too powerful. But through a combination of dogged determination, hard work and a healthy dose of chutzpah, McGowan shattered AT&T's monopoly, kicked open the door to free competition in the long-distance market, and transformed a struggling company into the world's second-largest long-distance carrier.

McGowan was already a multimillionaire when he decided to go head-to-head with AT&T. He'd spent nearly 10 years on Wall Street as an independent financial consultant specializing in the reorganization and turnaround of failing companies. His most notable success was Powertron Co., which he took over for $25,000 in 1959 and sold for $3 million in 1962.

In 1968, a friend introduced him to John D. Goeken, an Illinois entrepreneur who sold mobile radios. Goeken wanted to expand his service by building a microwave system between Chicago and St. Louis. But the Federal Communications Commission (FCC) had held up approval of the project for five years because of strong opposition from AT&T, and Goeken was practically bankrupt.

McGowan realized that if the FCC granted Goeken's application, his firm could eventually compete with AT&T for long-distance telephone service throughout the nation—something no one had ever tried before. As McGowan later told *Money*, "The fact that it had never been done before made the idea all the more irresistible." McGowan bought half interest in Goeken's company, Microwave Communications Inc., for $50,000 and changed the name to MCI Communications Corp.

One year later, the FCC approved MCI's petition to provide

"private line" telephone service along the Chicago-St. Louis route. There was only one problem: To implement its long-distance service, MCI's networks needed to be connected to local telephone networks, which were owned by subsidiaries of AT&T. When AT&T refused to allow any interconnections except at exorbitant prices, MCI filed a lawsuit against the company in 1974, charging that it was violating antitrust laws by restricting access to its local telephone network.

But it would take six years for the suit to come to trial. During that time, McGowan helped develop and get approval by the FCC for a new type of service called MCI Execunet. This ingenious system allowed MCI customers to call up MCI's computers, which would then connect the caller to any other telephone number, completely bypassing AT&T's long-distance facilities. Priced at a fraction of the cost of AT&T's long-distance service, Execunet was a tremendous success. This did not go unnoticed by AT&T.

By approving Excunet, the FCC had unknowingly permitted MCI to implement general long-distance services. AT&T pointed this out to the FCC, which ordered MCI to drop the service. MCI appealed, and a federal court ruled that MCI or any other carrier had the right to offer long-distance service.

When MCI's lawsuit against AT&T finally came to trial in 1980, the court found in MCI's favor, awarding the company $1.8 billion in damages. AT&T appealed, and the damages were reduced to $113 million. However, during the trial, MCI had presented numerous AT&T documents that revealed a long-standing policy to destroy any long-distance competition.

Home Field Advantage

One of the keys to William McGowan's success was that he moved the headquarters of MCI Communications Corp. from Illinois to Washington, DC, knowing that the war with AT&T would be primarily a battle of lobbyists. "I didn't concern myself with technology," he recalls, "just the regulation of the industry".

William McGowan

Junk Bonds Make Good

To finance MCI Communications Corp.'s expansion after the breakup of AT&T, William McGowan convinced junk-bond king Mike Milken and his now defunct firm, Drexel Burnham Lambert Inc., to raise more than $2 billion for MCI in the 1980s. Milken often cited MCI as evidence that the high-risk, high-yield junk bonds they used to raise cash played a major role in enhancing U.S. business, opposing his critics' contention that junk bonds were responsible for scores of corporate bankruptcies.

This prompted the U.S. Department of Justice to file its own lawsuit against AT&T. To avoid a trial, AT&T negotiated a settlement in 1984, agreeing to divest its local "Baby Bell" companies and give up control of the local telephone networks.

After more than 10 years of fighting, McGowan had finally broken AT&T's stranglehold on long-distance service. But it was a Pyrrhic victory. Up to that point, MCI had a basic advantage— it was allowed to transmit its calls across the local operating companies' lines at prices 70 percent lower than what AT&T charged. Under the agreement, all long-distance telephone carriers, including AT&T Long Distance, were granted equal access to the Baby Bell lines. The discounts that had so favored MCI were phased out by the FCC.

For MCI, the change was a disaster. The company had always been a niche-player, billing itself as the low-price provider. It was completely unprepared to compete with AT&T on quality of service. MCI lost millions. The troubles took their toll on McGowan, who suffered a heart attack in December 1986; the following April, he received a heart transplant.

McGowan was sidelined for nine months, but when he got back, he was ready for action. Spurred on by McGowan, MCI management improved quality and service and pushed for more corporate customers. MCI also digitized its phone network, allowing for faster transmission of both voice and data. The company quickly gained a reputation for excellent service and soon boasted the Pentagon, Westinghouse, Chrysler and IBM among its corporate customers. MCI returned to profitability in 1987, and by late 1991 had regained its position as the nation's second-largest long-distance carrier. His dream fulfilled, McGowan stepped down as CEO. He died of a second heart attack a year later.

During his 24-year tenure as head of MCI, William McGowan grew MCI from a nearly defunct mobile radio service to a $9.5 billion telecommunications juggernaut. Today, the company he founded, now called MCI WorldCom, is the largest telecommunications company in the world, with annual earnings of $17.6 billion. But his real legacy is that more than any other individual, McGowan brought about the breakup of AT&T and sparked a telecommunications revolution.

Tom Monaghan

> "*Always keep your eye on the operation.*"
> —Tom Monaghan

Founder of Domino's Pizza Inc.
Founded: 1960

Photo Courtesy: Domino's Pizza Inc.

In 30 Minutes or Less

He is the hero of hungry college students and couch potatoes everywhere—the man who made getting a fresh, hot pizza as easy as picking up the telephone. By pioneering the delivery-only pizza chain, Tom Monaghan turned a single floundering pizza parlor into the nation's second-largest pizza chain. Along the way, he amassed a fortune estimated to top $1 billion. Not bad for a poor kid from Ann Arbor, Michigan, who graduated last in his high school class, was kicked out of seminary school, and enrolled in college six times without getting past the status of freshman.

Tom Monaghan's early life reads something like a Charles Dickens novel. When he was only 4, his father died—on Christmas Eve, no less. His mother felt incapable of caring for her two sons while she attended nursing school, so Monaghan spent most of his youth in orphanages and foster homes. When he was a freshman in high school, he decided he wanted to be a priest. But the seminary's strict discipline proved too much for the rambunctious youth to handle, and he was expelled less than a year later for such heinous transgressions as pillow-fighting and talking in the chapel. Returning to public school, Monaghan graduated 44th in a class of 44. The caption under his photo in the 1955 class yearbook read, "The harder I try to be good, the worse I get; but I may do something sensational yet."

Monaghan dreamed of studying architecture at the University of Michigan, but his poor grades coupled with a lack of money ruled that out. He enlisted in the Marine Corps and by the end of his three-year tour, he had saved $2,000 for tuition. But he naively invested the money in a get-rich-quick scheme with an unscrupulous "oilman." Of course he never saw the money or the oilman again. With only $15 in his pocket, Monaghan hitchhiked from San Diego back to Ann Arbor.

In 1960, Monaghan's luck finally began to change when he and his brother, Jim, borrowed $900 and bought a failing pizza store in Ypsilanti, Michigan. Monaghan threw himself into the business, putting in upwards of 100 hours per week. Eight months into the venture, his brother grew tired of the grind and traded his half of the business for Monaghan's Volkswagen Beetle. "It was a setback, but I took it in stride and was optimistic," Monaghan writes in his autobiography, *Pizza Tiger*. "I made the decision to commit myself heart and soul to being a pizza man. My purpose was clear, and the knowledge that the future success—or failure—of the business rested on my shoulders alone was welcome."

Shortly afterward, Monaghan hit upon the formula that would make his fortune. He simplified the menu, limited the number of sizes and toppings, set strict standards for ingredients, and offered delivery service in 30 minutes or less. "The idea of stressing 30-minute delivery grew out of my insistence on giving customers a quality pizza," Monaghan explains in *Pizza Tiger*. "It didn't make sense to use only the best ingredients if the pizza was cold and tasteless when the customer got it." To motivate his drivers to make their deliveries as fast as possible, Monaghan gave bonuses to those who collected the most cash.

By late 1965, Monaghan was enjoying modest success and bought two more stores. That same

A Very Special Delivery

In the early days of Domino's Pizza Inc., Tom Monaghan not only managed the store—he delivered his product, too. One evening in 1962, he delivered a pizza to a dormitory at Central Michigan University, where switchboard operator Marge Zyback caught his eye. Six months later, Marge took Tom for better, for worse, and for all the pizza she could eat.

Tom Monaghan

The End Of An Era

After a number of fatal accidents, several lawsuits, and numerous complaints from consumer and safety groups that its 30-minutes-or-less policy encouraged reckless driving, Domino's Pizza Inc. discontinued its trademark delivery guarantee in 1993.

year, Monaghan changed the name of all three of his pizzerias to Domino's Pizza.

Domino's Pizza Inc. found a receptive market in college towns and near military bases, and in 1967, Monaghan sold his first franchise, ending the year with a profit of $50,000. Monaghan established an ambitious goal of opening one new store per week—and he nearly met that goal. In the first 10 months of 1969, 32 new Domino's sprang up, mostly in residential areas.

But the rapid expansion proved to be disastrous. Almost all the stores failed, and Monaghan found himself $1.5 million in debt. To avoid bankruptcy, he relinquished control of the company to a local businessperson. He regained control within a year, but the ordeal taught him a valuable lesson. Monaghan vowed that there would be "no more expansion for expansion's sake," reduced his goal to 20 new stores per year, and began selecting his sites more carefully.

The strategy worked, and by the end of the 1980s, Domino's had grown to 290 stores. To celebrate the opening of his 1,000th franchise in 1983, Monaghan realized a lifelong dream by purchasing the Detroit Tigers baseball club for $35 million. The very next year, the Tigers won the World Series.

Domino's remarkable growth continued throughout the second half of the 1980s, and by 1989 the company boasted almost 5,000 stores in the United States and nearly 260 in other countries. That same year, Monaghan shocked the business world by giving up the presidency of Domino's to devote more time to Catholic charities. He remained chairman and CEO until 1998, when he once again surprised the industry by announcing his retirement and selling his 93 percent stake in Domino's to the

Boston-based investment firm Bain Capital for an estimated $1 billion.

Since retiring, Monaghan has become even more active in the Catholic Church, pledging his time and money to charitable endeavors such as building churches and missions in Honduras and Nicaragua, and the founding of a Catholic law school.

As for Domino's, it's doing just fine without its founder. In 1999, it boasted more than 6,200 stores in more than 60 countries, and was the world's No. 1 pizza delivery company and No. 2 pizza chain overall.

Akio Morita

Co-founder of
Sony Corp. of America
Founded: 1960

"Our plan is to lead the public with new products rather than ask them what kind of products they want. The public does not know what is possible, but we do."

—Akio Morita

GADGET GURU

In 1946, in the basement of a former department store, Akio Morita and Masaru Ibuka set out to make Japan's first tape recorders. World War II had just ended, and even basic materials were scarce. For the tape, Morita scrounged some mimeograph paper, which they cut into narrow strips with razor blades. For the magnetic coating, they melted oxalicferrite powder in a skillet to create ferric oxide, then painted it onto the paper strips. The tape sounded terrible, but it worked. And from these humble beginnings, Sony was born.

Over the next 50 years, Sony would go on to become the number one consumer brand name in the world. The man responsible for that amazing feat is Sony co-founder Akio Morita—a brilliant marketer who turned the fledgling company into an international presence.

Morita was born into a wealthy family of sake brewers in 1921. As the oldest of three sons, he was expected to take over the family business. But Morita's interests lay elsewhere. "When I was in high school," Morita would later recall, "my father bought me an electronic phonograph. The sound was fantastic. I was so impressed, I started to wonder how and why such sound came out. That's when my interest in electronics began." Morita studied electronics in his spare time and attempted to build his own radio, phonograph and tape recorder, succeeding in all but the last.

After convincing his father to let his younger brother run the family brewery, Morita enrolled in Osaka Imperial University, where he earned a bachelor's degree in physics. During World War II, he was drafted into the Imperial Japanese Navy, but instead of combat duty, he was assigned to a Naval Research Center at Susaki. It was there that he met the man who would become his business partner, Masaru Ibuka.

After the war, with the equivalent of $500 in capital, Morita and Ibuka formed the Tokyo Telecommunications Co., which was later renamed Sony. The company's early products included vacuum tube voltmeters, amplifiers and a bulky $500 tape recorder that proved to be too expensive for the consumer market. Sony's first real breakthrough came when it produced the first transistor radio in 1955. Bell Laboratories had developed transistors in the United States, but Sony was the first to use them in radios (and later, in other electronic devices as well) for mass production to the public.

From the outset, Morita saw America as the most likely market for Sony's products—business was booming, employment was high and people were eager for new and exciting things. With Sony's first transistor radio in hand, Morita made the rounds to American distributors but found little enthusiasm. Finally, a purchasing agent at the Bulova watch company saw the miniature radios and said he would take 100,000 of them, provided he could market them under the Bulova name.

This was a huge order, worth more than Sony's total capitalization at the time. But Morita was set on building Sony into an international brand. Despite a cablegram from Ibuka and Sony's board instructing him to accept the offer,

Leader Of The Pack

One of the secrets of Sony's success was Akio Morita's dedication to "staying two steps ahead of the competition" in the development of new products. As a result, Sony boasts many industry firsts, including:

- The first AM transistor radio
- The first pocket-sized transistor radio
- The first two-band transistor radio
- The first FM transistor radio
- The first all-transistor television set
- The first home-use VCR
- The first 8-mm video camera

Akio Morita

he turned Bulova down. Later, he would describe this as the best business decision of his career.

Morita eventually found a distributor who agreed to sell the radios under the Sony name, and as he had predicted, Americans loved the newfangled invention. The radio's success led to other firsts in transistorized products, including an 8-inch transistorized television and a videotape recorder. Sony's technological achievements in product design, production and marketing helped transform the "Made in Japan" label from being a synonym for cheap imitations to a symbol of superior quality. In Morita's own words, they made Sony the Cadillac of electronics.

Determined to build a presence in the United States that would dominate the landscape without appearing foreign, Morita moved himself and his family to New York in 1963 to personally oversee the operations of Sony Corp. of America, which had been established three years earlier. Morita reasoned that to sell to Americans effectively, he would have to know more about them and how they lived. He quickly built a solid and valuable network of contacts by socializing and giving parties during the week—a habit he maintained throughout his career.

A master at finding a need and filling it, Morita observed that Americans loved music and would listen to it in their cars and even carry large stereos to the beach and the park. He came up with an idea for a product that offered high-quality sound yet was portable enough to allow the user to listen while doing something else. Thus, one of Sony's most popular and profitable products was born: the Walkman.

The Betamax Blunder

In a 1986 interview, Akio Morita was asked to name his worst business error. After hemming and hawing a bit, he finally replied, "Beta." Sony pioneered the videocassette recorder with the beta format and stubbornly stood by it even when the VHS format began to corner the market. As a result, Sony's highly profitable VCR sales of the 1970s and early 1980s soon dwindled and eventually became a liability.

The Walkman was a big windfall for Sony because its technology proved to be difficult to duplicate. It was more than two years before other companies could introduce competing models. By that time, Sony had sold 20 million units, and the company's reputation and brand recognition soared worldwide.

With Morita as CEO, Sony continued to diversify and became a leader in virtually every aspect of the consumer electronics market, from televisions to CD players. In 1987, the company purchased CBS Records for $2 billion, then before his retirement as CEO in 1989, Morita set into motion the deal that would lead Sony to purchase Columbia Pictures, making Sony a major player in the entertainment industry.

In 1993, Morita suffered a stroke that left him partially paralyzed. He retained his title as chairman until 1995, but continued to wield enormous power over the company he helped found until October 1999, when he died from pneumonia at age 78.

Akio Morita pioneered the marketing concept of brand-name recognition at a time when most companies in Japan were producing products under somebody else's name. With this strategy, as well as his unswerving dedication to provide the best available technology, he helped make the Sony name synonymous with superior-quality consumer electronics.

Jean Nidetch

> "*It's choice, not chance, that determines your destiny.*"
>
> —Jean Nidetch

Founder of Weight Watchers International Inc.
Founded: 1963

THE FIRST WEIGHT WATCHER

Before Richard Simmons dealt meals…before Susan Powter tried to "stop the insanity"…and long before there were "fat blockers," Phen-fen and liposuction, an overweight housewife from Queens, New York, made a life-changing discovery: Staying on a diet was easier when you shared the experience. From this simple but profound revelation, Jean Nidetch launched Weight Watchers and gave birth to the modern diet industry.

Born in 1923, Jean was an overweight child whose overweight mother rewarded her with food. Her entrance into adult life was far from easy. Though she dreamed of being a teacher, her father died shortly after she enrolled in college, and Jean was forced to drop out and work at a number of different jobs to help support the family.

When she was 24, Jean married Marty Nidetch. "I was fat and he was fat," Jean reveals in a 1981 *McCall's* interview. "It was our common bond. I ate all the time to be happy, and yet food only made me sad. I thought God had blessed thin people, and God had cursed me, so my fate was sealed."

Finally, in 1961, desperate to lose weight, the 38-year-old mother of two paid a visit to the New York Department of Health Obesity Clinic, where she was put on a diet of low-fat proteins and plenty of fruits and vegetables. The diet was working, but she found herself continually cheating. To boost her morale, she called up six overweight friends and invited them over to talk. With her friends, she discovered, she could talk freely about her food excesses, and they could do the same.

The six all joined Nidetch's diet and began meeting on a weekly basis. Members of the group started bringing other overweight friends to the weekly get-togethers, and within two months, more than 40 women were meeting at Nidetch's house. Each week they weighed in and talked, and each week the scales recorded a weight loss. Thanks to the help of her friends, by October 1962, Jean had lost more than 70 pounds and reached her goal of 142 pounds.

The experience turned Nidetch into a weight-loss zealot. Having exorcised her own food demons, she replaced her compulsion to eat with a drive to help others achieve what she had. She encouraged her friends to spread the word about their program, and the group continued to grow. When she began receiving phone calls from overweight people, many of them recluses, asking for help, she drove around the New York metropolitan area visiting individuals or groups. Among them were garment executive Albert Lippert and his wife, Felice.

Concerned about their growing girth, the couple had heard about Nidetch's amazing weight-loss program and decided to see for themselves if it really worked. It did. In just one week, Lippert lost 7 pounds, and his wife lost 4. (He would eventually shed 53 pounds while his wife lost 50.) Lippert's marketing instincts were fired by the program's potential, and he became convinced that Nidetch had found the formula for a successful business. "With the [Weight Watchers] plan, I had provided something to myself that I needed and wanted," Lippert recalls. "I knew that there were hundreds of thousands of people out there like myself who could benefit. I was certain it would work."

Though Nidetch admits she would have preached her program "for nothing on a street corner," Lippert persuaded her to enter a partnership with him, and in May 1963, Weight Watchers Inc. opened its first office above a movie theater in Little Neck, New York.

Weighty Numbers

Since its inception in 1963, Weight Watchers International Inc. has taught more than 25 million members how to lose weight. In 1998 alone, approximately 1 million members attended one of 29,000 weekly Weight Watchers meetings in 28 countries worldwide.

Run With It

The success of Weight Watchers International Inc. franchises in the late 1960s and early 1970s inspired Albert Lippert to expand the company into related markets. By 1973, in addition to the franchises themselves, the organization's spin-off enterprises included a monthly Weight Watchers magazine, a daily syndicated TV program called Weight Watchers Forum, a string of summer camps for overweight boys and girls, a line of frozen foods, and a line of diet beverages and desserts.

Within a year, the business had achieved such success locally that there simply wasn't enough room in the small office to hold all the Weight Watchers members. It was at this point that Lippert suggested to Nidetch that they begin selling Weight Watchers franchises.

Using a process that Lippert once likened to giving away razors to sell razor blades, he and Nidetch sold the franchises for a relatively low price but required each franchise owner to pay the company 10 percent of their gross. It wasn't long before franchises they had sold for as little as $2,000 were returning upwards of $100,000 a year. Within five years, the company had 91 franchises in 43 states. In 1968, Nidetch and Lippert decided to go public, and Weight Watchers Inc. became Weight Watchers International Inc.

In 1973, more than 17,000 Weight Watchers members from around the world gathered in New York City's Madison Square Garden to celebrate the 10th anniversary of Weight Watchers. At the gala event, Nidetch announced that she would be resigning as president of the company but would remain on as a consultant.

Over the next few years, Nidetch would continue to preach the Weight Watchers gospel on countless radio and television programs, enthusiastically recounting her success story. By 1977, the company claimed to be recruiting more than 20 million new members a year. This success attracted the attention of H.J. Heinz Co., which purchased Weight Watchers for $72 million in 1978.

As part of the deal, Lippert joined the Heinz board and Nidetch agreed to stay on as a consultant.

By 1999, Weight Watchers had become the world's largest company in the field of personal weight control, and Nidetch had helped change the shape of millions of overweight men and women throughout the world. A testament to her tremendous impact on both the diet industry and the world, *Ladies Home Journal* magazine voted Jean one of the 100 most important women of the 20th century.

David Ogilvy

David David Ogilvy David Ogilvy David David Ogilvy David Ogilvy David Ogilvy David Ogilvy Ogilvy

"**Y**ou cannot bore people into buying your product; you can only interest them in buying it."
—David Ogilvy

Founder of Ogilvy & Mather
Founded: 1948

Master Of The Soft Sell

The eye-patch-wearing "Man in the Hathaway Shirt." Colonel Whitehead and "Schweppervescence." The Pepperidge Farm bakery wagon. All have become advertising icons. And all came from the mind of David Ogilvy. One of the founding fathers of modern advertising, Ogilvy spent his life preaching the benefits of research; long informative copy; and, well, benefits. His firm belief that "the consumer is not a moron" helped start a creative revolution in the 1960s that changed the landscape of American advertising.

Born in West Horsley, England, in June 1911, Ogilvy took a rather circuitous route on the way to becoming an advertising legend. After flunking out of Oxford in 1931, he headed to Paris and took a job as a chef's apprentice at the Hotel Majestic. Monsieur Pitard, the head chef, made an everlasting impression on Ogilvy and helped form his principles on management when he fired a junior chef who could not get his bread to rise properly. "I was shocked by his ruthlessness," Ogilvy recalls in his book, *Confessions of an Advertising Man*, "but it made all the other chefs feel that they were working in the best kitchen in the world."

Returning to England a year later, Ogilvy supported himself by selling cooking stoves door to door. He was so successful that his employer asked him to write an instructional manual for his fellow salesmen. The manual, along with the intercession of his brother, Francis, helped win Ogilvy a copywriting job at the London advertising agency of Mather & Crowley, where Francis was an executive. Advertising became a passion that consumed most of Ogilvy's time. "I loved advertising," he writes. " I devoured it. I studied and read and took it desperately seriously." Ogilvy's dedication soon paid off. Mather & Crowley promoted him to account executive. But Ogilvy had his eye on greener pastures.

Assigned to study American advertising techniques, Ogilvy convinced Mather & Crowley to send him to the United States in 1938. He became fascinated with America and Americans, and at the end of 1939, he resigned from Mather & Crowley to take a position with research guru George Gallup. Ogilvy later called this "the luckiest break of my life," and cited Gallup as one of the major influences on his thinking. Gallup's meticulous research methods and devotion to reality were the foundation of what would become "the Ogilvy approach to advertising."

During World War II, Ogilvy worked for British Intelligence in the United States, collecting economic intelligence on Latin America, and he later served as second secretary at the British Embassy. After mustering out in 1945, Ogilvy and his wife moved to a farm in Amish country in Lancaster County, Pennsylvania. Ogilvy had fallen in love with the area while on a bicycle trip. On a whim, Ogilvy tried his hand at tobacco farming but found it "physically and economically impossible to succeed." So in 1948, with the backing of his former employer, Mather & Crowley, Ogilvy laid the groundwork for the advertising agency that would eventually become known as Ogilvy & Mather.

From the very beginning, Ogilvy eschewed the quick-sale, hard-sell advertising style that was the standard at the time in favor of a more long-term, soft-sell approach. Ogilvy's strategy focused on building brand-name recognition, and featured lengthy, informative, benefit-oriented copy and eye-catching people or symbols. His first major success came

Mr. Manners

Unlike many advertisers, David Ogilvy always used his client's products. "This is not toadyism," he writes in his autobiography, Confessions of an Advertising Man, "but elementary good manners." Ogilvy also resigned accounts when he lost confidence in a product. Rolls-Royce was one of Ogilvy's early clients and a cornerstone of his fledgling agency. But he resigned the account when he felt the quality of the cars, which he loved to drive, was not up to speed.

David Ogilvy

Ogilvy On Advertising

During his career, David Ogilvy was known for his advertising dictums. These terse yet profound sayings, which he called "Obiter Dicta" (Latin for an incidental remark or observation), have become advertising commandments. Some of his more famous "Obiter Dicta" include:

- "The consumer is not a moron. She is your wife. Do not insult her intelligence."
- "Never run an advertisement you would not want your own family to see."
- "Tell the truth, but make it fascinating."
- "Unless your campaign contains a big idea, it will pass like a ship in the night."
- "There's no substitute for homework. The more you know about a product, the more likely you are to come up with a big idea for selling it.

with a campaign he
created for the small Maine clothing company Hathaway.

Ogilvy's copy for the initial ad crackled with a literacy that flattered readers' intelligence. But it was the accompanying photograph that propelled the campaign into advertising history. On a whim, Ogilvy decided to photograph his male model wearing a Hathaway shirt—and an eye patch. When "The Man in the Hathaway Shirt" appeared for the first time in *The New Yorker* magazine in September 1951, it caused an instant sensation. The company could barely keep up with demand for its shirts.

Ogilvy's reputation as a master of image and brand recognition was further enhanced when he took over the account of Schweppes, a British manufacturer of tonic water struggling to gain a foothold in America. He designed a print ad campaign around Colonel Edward Whitehead, the bearded, ever-so-British head of Schweppes' American operations. Within five years, Schweppes was selling more than 30 million bottles a year.

What made the work of Ogilvy & Mather stand out was Ogilvy's insistence that print ads not only put client names, or brand names, in each headline, but "promise a benefit…deliver news…offer a service…quote a satisfied customer…recognize a problem…or tell a significant story." A perfect example of a classic Ogilvy headline is one he wrote in 1958 for Rolls-Royce: "At 60 miles an hour, the loudest noise in this new Rolls-Royce comes from the electric clock." This campaign helped double the company's American sales in a year.

Throughout the 1960s and early 1970s, Ogilvy & Mather achieved tremendous success with a stream of stunning work that not only generated sales for its clients but also excited genuine industry admiration and earned numerous awards. Ogilvy became an icon to agency people, who were newly liberated by the post-war creative revolution he helped spark. By the time Ogilvy stepped down as creative director of Ogilvy & Mather in 1975, it ranked as the world's fifth-largest advertising agency.

Today, David Ogilvy is viewed by many in the industry as the most influential advertiser of the 20th century. His advertising ideas have become icons, his writings and books the bible of what constitutes good and bad advertising. But his greatest legacy, the one that truly shaped the face of modern advertising, was an approach to advertising that regarded the consumer as an intelligent buyer.

Pierre Omidyar

Founder of
eBay Inc.
Founded: 1995

"I never had it in mind that I would start a company one day and it would really be successful. I have just been motivated by working on interesting technology."

—Pierre Omidyar

AN EMPIRE
BUILT ON PEZ

Pierre Omidyar didn't expect to make a dime—let alone become a billionaire—when he set up a small online auction on his private Web site. He just wanted to score some points with his girlfriend. But within five months, what had started out as a hobby had become a $3 billion empire with more than 2 million subscribers, and Omidyar found himself at the head of one of the most popular and profitable Web-based businesses in Internet history. And it all started with Pez dispensers.

Omidyar was born in Paris in 1967 but moved to Baltimore when his father began his medical residence at the Johns Hopkins University Medical Center. A precocious teen, he became interested in computers and would regularly sneak out of physical-education classes to play with his high school's PCs. Rather than punish Omidyar for ditching class, the principal hired him at $6 per hour to write a computer program to print catalog cards for the school library. It wasn't much, but it was a beginning.

His entrepreneurship proved more lucrative a few years later when, while working on a bachelor's degree in computer science at Tufts University, he wrote a program to help Apple Macintosh programmers manage memory. He distributed it online as "shareware," asking users to pay on the honor system, but the few checks that dribbled in barely covered the cost of the post office box he'd rented to collect them.

In 1991, Pierre and three of his friends founded a company to write programs for the pen-computing market. As a lark, he set up an early e-commerce site called eShop on the company's Web site. Pen computing turned out to be one of the more notable technology flops, but the eShop site proved lucrative enough to attract the attention of Microsoft, who later bought the company.

Fed up with start-ups, Omidyar took a job as a developer relations engineer for software-maker General Magic in 1994 and made a little money on the side as a freelance Web page designer. It was about this time that he met his spouse-to-be, Pamela Wesley. An avid collector of Pez dispensers, Wesley complained that she was having difficulty finding like-minded souls on the Internet. Eager to help out, Omidyar included a small online auction service on his personal Web page so Wesley could communicate with, buy from, and sell to other collectors from all over the United States.

Launched on Labor Day 1995, the fledgling auction site that Omidyar dubbed eBay (for "electronic Bay," a reference to the San Francisco Bay area) bore little resemblance to the company that would make Omidyar a fortune. Back then, Omidyar made no guarantees about the goods being offered, took no responsibility and settled no disputes. He simply offered a place where users could go online, interact and bid for items.

Much to Omidyar's surprise, collectors of Barbie dolls, Beanie Babies and household junk of all sorts seized upon eBay almost immediately. By February, the site had become so popular that it outgrew Omidyar's personal Internet account. With the help of his friend and fellow computer programmer Jeff Skoll (who would later become eBay's president). Omidyar moved eBay to a much more expensive business site; to cover his increased costs, he began charging a few cents to list an item and collecting a small commission if it was sold.

Rules Of The Game

A rarity for Internet start-ups, Pierre Omidyar developed a business model that let eBay Inc. become profitable quickly while still delivering what users regarded as good value. Here's how it works. Both buyers and sellers pay to use the service. Each "for sale" listing costs 25 cents to $2. Potential buyers submit bids in an "electronic auction" that runs for multiple days. If the goods are sold, eBay collects a commission of 1.25 percent to 5 percent from the seller.

Traffic on the site continued, and eBay Inc. was immediately profitable. Omidyar began to think he had finally stumbled onto a way to turn his penchant for computer programming into some real cash. "The biggest clue was that so many checks were piling up at my door that I had to hire part-time help to open them all," he told *The New York Times*.

Unknowingly, Omidyar had tapped one of the richest veins in the online world—the desire of people to connect with others who share their interests. And he quickly realized that few interests generate more passion than collecting. "I thought people would simply use the service to buy and sell things," he says. "But what they really enjoyed was meeting people."

Encouraged by this early success, Omidyar quit his day job, and he and Skoll devoted their time to building eBay's community and technology. The duo rationalized that as long as the system worked, the community (and the profits) would continue to grow. And grow they did. By mid-1997, eBay had become one of the most visited sites on the Web, with more than 150,000 users bidding on 794,000 auctions every day. The average eBay shopper was spending nearly 3.5 hours per month on eBay, longer than the average shopper on any other site.

With the company doubling every three months, Omidyar and Skoll decided they needed venture capital backing and a savvy management team. In June 1997, they took the eBay business plan to Benchmark Capital and got a $4.5 million check for a 22 percent share of the company. Benchmark also promised to find a CEO to help run eBay, tapping Margaret Whitham, an executive with the Hasbro toy company, for the top spot.

A Whole Lotta Trading Goin' On

From the company's founding in 1995 until late 1999, $2 billion worth of merchandise was sold through eBay Inc.'s auctions. Some of the stranger (and not necessarily legal) items offered through eBay have included a 1998 Volkswagen Beetle, a Russian space shuttle and a human kidney.

Whitham quickly turned what was a ragtag band of sellers hawking stuff from their basements into a lean, mean corporate machine. She created a new marketing division and placed all firearm and pornography auctions on separate, age-restricted sites. With new marketing energy—and the dirty laundry safely hidden away—she took eBay public on September 24, 1998.

The stock single-handedly revived the market for Internet initial public offerings. On its first day of trading, it rolled out at $18 per share. Four months later, it cracked the $300 mark, thrilling investors and making Omidyar a billionaire.

From its humble beginnings trading Pez dispensers, eBay has become one of the hottest sites on the Internet and has revolutionized e-commerce. Its success has spawned dozens of imitators hoping to cash in on the online auction craze. Yet even with increased competition, eBay's growth has not slowed one iota. By late 1999, eBay boasted nearly 8 million registered users trading an average of 33 million items per year, ranging from Beanie Babies to fine antiques. As for Pierre Omidyar, he's just as amazed by eBay's astounding growth as everyone else. "I didn't set out to create a huge business on eBay. When it happened, I just took advantage of it."

Ross Perot

"*My role in life is that of the grain of sand to the oyster—it irritates the oyster and out comes a pearl.*"

—Ross Perot

Founder of Perot Systems Corp.
Founded: 1962

THE BILLIONAIRE BOY SCOUT

Supersalesman. Enterprising entrepreneur. Patriot. Philanthropist. Presidential candidate. In his long and colorful career, Ross Perot has played all these roles and more. This "can do" bantamweight billionaire from Texas has taken on industry giants such as IBM and General Motors Corp., helped gain better treatment of U.S. prisoners during the Vietnam War, and even spearheaded a commando raid to rescue two of his employees from Iranian terrorists. But perhaps his most important contribution, though not quite as flashy as his other exploits, was his groundbreaking work in the development of the information technology industry.

Born in Texarkana, Texas, in 1930, Perot started working when he was very young. Beginning at age 7 and continuing through high school, he tried his hand at a series of occupations, including bronco busting (he broke his nose…twice), selling Christmas cards, hawking garden seeds, selling magazines and delivering papers on horseback. Somehow he still found the time to become an Eagle Scout, which he would later say was one of the greatest achievements of his life.

Following high school, Perot entered the United States Naval Academy, where he was a battalion commander before serving four years at sea. In 1957, he returned to Texas to join IBM. A natural-born salesman, Perot was soon making higher commissions than any of his colleagues and once met his annual sales quota by January 19th.

Always on the lookout for new avenues of advancement, Perot approached IBM executives and proposed that the company not only sell hardware but also supply customized software and technical support. IBM wasn't impressed. Rankled by the abrupt dismissal of his idea, Perot went to get a haircut. While waiting his turn, he picked up a copy of *Reader's Digest* and came across a quotation from Henry Thoreau's *Walden*: "The mass of men lead lives of quiet desperation." He determined then and there to strike out on his own. On his 32nd birthday—June 27, 1962—with a $1,000 loan from his wife, Margot, Perot founded Electronic Data Systems Corp. (EDS).

EDS did moderately well, counting Frito-Lay among its first clients. But the real breakthrough came in 1965 when the newly formed Medicare and Medicaid programs created a huge market for medical-claims processing. Perot got in on the ground floor as a subcontractor for Blue Cross/Blue Shield. In 1965 alone, EDS won contracts from 11 states to computerize their Medicare and Medicaid billing systems. Finding his niche in the insurance business, Perot sought out new clients in the private sector, and by 1968 EDS was worth $2.4 million. That same year, in what *Fortune* magazine called "the greatest personal coup in the history of American finance," Perot took EDS public and within one week was a billionaire.

Appalled by news footage of American POWs in Vietnam, Perot decided to put his newfound wealth to good use. In December 1969, he chartered two Braniff jets and filled them with 30 tons of food, medicine and gifts for the POWs. Although North Vietnamese officials refused to let the plane land in

Paper Boy Wonder

One of the keys to Ross Perot's success is that, rather than waiting for fate to shine upon him, he makes his own opportunities—a characteristic he developed early in life. At the age of 12, Perot decided he wanted a paper route. Informed that there were no routes available, he offered to create one in one of the most dangerous sections of his hometown of Texarkana, Texas. Convinced that he couldn't succeed, his employer offered him a larger-than-normal commission. But the quick-thinking Perot did succeed. He delivered his papers on horseback, allowing him to easily evade would-be muggers.

Hanoi, the publicity Perot generated resulted in improved treatment for some of the POWs (as they reported years later, after their release).

Throughout the 1970s and '80s, Perot embarked on a number of social ventures, including spearheading Texas' war on drugs, education reform and further efforts to help American soldiers missing in action.

In 1984, on his 54th birthday, Perot sold EDS to General Motors (GM) for $2.5 billion and joined GM's board of directors. GM hoped EDS could consolidate and streamline its computerized information systems, which were scattered throughout more than 100 data centers. But problems quickly arose. GM's tangled bureaucracy made it difficult for Perot to enact what he saw as vital reforms. Frustrated, he began to publicly criticize GM with biting remarks such as, "Revitalizing GM is like teaching an elephant to tap dance. You find the sensitive parts and start poking." After two years of poking and several widely publicized battles with GM chairman Roger Smith, the EDS-GM partnership dissolved in December 1986 when GM bought out Perot for a reported $700 million.

Eighteen months later, Perot formed his second data-processing company, Perot Systems Corp. In a strange twist of fate, he was hired by IBM to help expand the computer titan's presence in the $5.9 billion systems-management market.

Perot truly made history, however, in January 1992, when during an interview on "Larry King Live," the inquisitive talk-show host asked Perot if there were any scenario in which he would run for president. Perot told a nationwide audience, "If you, the people, will on your own register me in 50 states, I'll promise you this: Between now and the convention, we'll get both parties' heads straight." The phone lines were immediately flooded with calls from people volunteering in droves for Perot's independent presidential campaign. What followed was perhaps the strangest presidential campaign in the history of the United States.

Initially, he seemed eager to pursue the presidency, but as the campaign unfolded, Perot was increasingly painted as an arrogant, paranoid man unwilling to take a stand on any given issue. Perot wasn't used to such public criticism, particularly from the press, and abruptly dropped out of the race on July 16. Urged on by his supporters, however, Perot re-entered the race on October 1, explaining that he had withdrawn his candidacy because he believed that Republican "dirty tricksters" had planned to disrupt his daughter's August wedding. Although Perot didn't carry a single state, he did win 19 percent of the popular vote, more than any third-party candidate since Teddy Roosevelt in 1912.

After his defeat, Perot returned to the helm of Perot Systems, which had begun to flounder in his absence. Through a whirlwind restructuring strategy, Perot brought the company back to profitability and, in April 1999, took it public. After just one day of trading, Perot Systems' worth skyrocketed to $3.6 billion.

A self-made billionaire who proved that the capitalist system works, Ross Perot is something of an American icon. This straight-talking can-do cowboy who's willing to go it alone is a burning example of what one person can accomplish when he or she is determined.

Ron Popeil

Founder of
Ronco
Inventions LLC
Founded: 1951

"My philosophy is, When you snooze, you lose. If you have a great idea, at least take the chance and put your best foot forward."

—Ron Popeil

BUT WAIT—
THERE'S MORE!

Does QVC president Doug Briggs have a shrine to Ron Popeil in his bedroom? Does USA Networks CEO Barry Diller send Popeil a "thank you" card every time his Home Shopping Network racks up another $100 million in sales? If not, they should, because without Popeil, they might not exist. By combining the harried hawking of 19th-century fair barkers with the emerging medium of television, Popeil invented the infomercial and set the wheels in motion for the modern $2.5 million home shopping industry.

Popeil is the Horatio Alger of the television age—a self-made millionaire who started with next to nothing. Born on May 3, 1935, in the Bronx, New York, Popeil's childhood was anything but idyllic. When he was 3, Popeil's parents divorced and abandoned him. Exiled to an upstate New York boarding school, he didn't see them for years.

When Popeil was about 8, his paternal grandparents took him in, but life with them wasn't much better. The couple fought constantly and showed him little affection. It wasn't until they moved from Miami to Chicago—where his father manufactured kitchenware—that Popeil found salvation. When he was 16, he discovered a place where he could break away from his bleak childhood—Chicago's infamous Maxwell Street.

The gritty equivalent of a modern-day flea market, Maxwell Street was a dirty avenue in a bad neighborhood, where a rough-and-tumble collection of street vendors sold clothes, kitchen products and knickknacks and thieves unloaded hubcaps, radios and other stolen merchandise.

When Popeil saw all those people selling products and pocketing cash, the proverbial light bulb went on in his head. "I can do what they're doing," he thought. "But I can do it better." Gathering up some kitchen products from his father's factory, Popeil headed to Maxwell Street to give it a try. "I pushed. I yelled. I hawked. And it worked," he recalls in his autobiography, *The Salesman of the Century*. "I was stuffing money into my pockets, more money than I had ever seen in my life. I didn't have to be poor the rest of my life. Through sales, I could escape from poverty and the miserable existence I had with my grandparents. I had lived for 16 years in homes without love, and now I had finally found a form of affection, and a human connection, through sales."

For the next few years, Popeil would rise before dawn, procure bushels of cabbages, potatoes, radishes and carrots to use for his demonstrations, and set up his table on Maxwell Street and at fairs and shows around Chicago. Barking from atop a Pepsi crate, he sliced and diced while honing his routine. And people bought his gadgets—some weeks he made as much as $500.

Popeil used part of his earnings to enroll in the University of Illinois. But after a year and a half of attending classes, he decided college wasn't for him. Leaving the university behind, Popeil decided to move his act indoors. He cut a deal with the manager of a Chicago Woolworth's to let him push his products in the store for a piece of the action. Popeil hawked a variety of products, most of which he purchased from

Ron's Rules

Popeil credits much of his success to his philosophy that all Ronco products must abide by two rules: 1) The product must be needed by lots of people; and 2) The product has to solve a problem. The philosophy seems to work. Since he began pitching products in the late 1950s, Popeil has had only three flops: the Inside Outside Window Washer (which tends to plummet to the ground), the poorly named Hold-Up (an adhesive that allows you to hang things on the wall without using a nail), and a combination coffee pot/steam iron called the Prescolator.

his father, including shoeshine sprays, plastic plant kits and food slicers. Working six days a week selling products manufactured by his father and other suppliers, the natural-born pitchman was raking in upwards of $1,000 per week at a time when the average monthly salary was $500.

Popeil was still demonstrating products at Woolworth's when he made his first venture into TV marketing. He immediately recognized the tremendous potential of the new medium and began looking for ways to take full advantage of it. His main problem was money. Television commercials were expensive to produce and air, and Popeil simply didn't have the funding. Then, in 1963, a friend told him of a TV station in Tampa that would let him make a commercial for $550. To Popeil, that was just a half-week's pay, and he figured he had nothing to lose. All he needed was a product.

For his TV debut, Popeil wanted an item that was new and different. None of his father's products filled the bill, so he scoured the market for new items. During his search, a friend told Popeil about a high-pressure hose nozzle he felt was the perfect product for a TV pitch. By inserting different tablets (made of detergent, car wax, fertilizer or weed killer) between the hose and the nozzle, you could wash and wax your car, fertilize your lawn and kill weeds. "It was a better mousetrap," Popeil reveals in his autobiography. "It was a great product to begin my TV career with, because everyone could use it."

Popeil bought a small quantity of the product from its Chicago-based manufacturer, named it the Ronco Spray Gun (Ronco is short for Ron's Company—the name he chose for his fledgling venture), and began advertising it on TV stations throughout the Midwest. Popeil wrote, directed and starred in the commercial himself, then aired it during whatever unsold time he could buy cheaply from local TV stations. In so doing, he wrote the first chapter in the history of direct-response television sales.

As Popeil had predicted, the Ronco Spray Gun was a tremendous success. Upon seeing his son's achievement, Popeil's father asked him to sell a revolutionary new food slicer he'd developed called the Chop-O-Matic. Popeil agreed and once again he wrote, directed and starred in his own commercial. Like the Ronco Spray Gun, the Ronco Chop-O-Matic was an immediate hit. The

Chop-O-Matic was the biggest success Popeil's father had ever realized, selling thousands of units. Flush with newfound dollars, the elder Popeil started dreaming up Chop-O-Matic sequels and eventually came up with the product that would make Ronco a household name—the Veg-O-Matic.

Thanks mostly to the Veg-O-Matic, Ronco's annual sales skyrocketed from $200,000 to $8.8 million in just four years. Popeil decided it was time to take his company public and asked investment firm Shearson Hammill to underwrite the initial public offering. Shearson Hammill agreed but suggested that Popeil change the name of his company. "Ronco, they said, didn't really say anything about who we were," Popeil explains in *Salesman of the Century*. "They wanted a name that was descriptive of what we did. So we became Ronco Teleproducts Inc."

When the offering went through in August 1969, Popeil became a multimillionaire overnight, and a direct-response TV marketing dynasty was born. Over the next 20 years, Popeil would introduce late-night TV viewers to a bewildering array of "miracle" products, ranging from the Dial-O-Matic and the Buttoneer to the Pocket Fisherman and Mr. Microphone, many of which he invented or helped design himself. Ronco stock soared up the NYSE, and Popeil, whom, as one reporter quipped, could sell fingernail polish to the Venus De Milo, became a jet-setting millionaire.

Ronco's Greatest Hits

	PRODUCT UNITS SOLD*	TOTAL SALES*
Food Dehydrator	2.10 million	$150 million
Veg-O-Matic	8 million	$80 million
Pasta Machine	0.45 million	$76 million
Pocket Fisherman	1.25 million	$25 million
GLH-9 (spray-on hair)	1 million	$20 million
Mr. Microphone	1 million	$20 million

Source: Ronco Inventions LLC
*Estimated

By the 1980s, Popeil had sold records, choppers, slicers, dicers, hosiery, pottery, candle kits and much more. But dark days lay ahead for the Hemingway of home shopping. In 1984, Ronco (but not Popeil) was forced into bankruptcy when a bank called in a loan unexpectedly and seized the company's inventory. Popeil, demoralized but undaunted, bought back the inventory, rolled up his sleeves and returned to the county-fair circuit. For a time, his blip vanished from the radar screen.

In 1989, Popeil launched his television comeback, blitzing cable stations with infomercials for a product he dreamed up a decade earlier—a food dehydrator. The Einstein of the infomercial proved his genius once again. In one year, he sold more than $150 million worth of dehydrators. Back on top, Popeil followed with GLH-9 (spray-on hair), a pasta maker and a sausage maker.

After 40-odd years of selling everything from tapeless tape measures to bottle and jar cutters to rhinestone-stud setters, Popeil has hawked just about every kind of gadget imaginable. And with sales of his latest project du jour, the Showtime Rotisserie & BBQ, going strong, Popeil promises to remain TV's top salesperson well into the 21st century. In fact, although he has often talked about retiring, Popeil concedes that he probably never will. "You're always going to see Ronco or Popeil in the marketplace," he says. "I'll never stop."

Leonard Riggio

Leonard Riggio Leonard Leonard Leonard Leonard Riggio Riggio Riggio Leonard Riggio Leonard Leonard Riggio Riggio Leonard Riggio Riggio

"Don't look at successful people as aberrations. Excellence is out there for anyone."
—Leonard Riggio

Chairman and CEO of Barnes & Noble Inc.
Bought: 1971

FROM CLERK TO CEO

Leonard Riggio has been called "the Ted Turner of bookstores"—a mercurial maverick whose outsized risks have repeatedly drawn predictions of failure, even while he remade the industry in his image. One of the first book retailers to understand that the store is a stage and that retailing is great theater, Riggio made bookstores fun, turning them into modern village greens where people flock as much for the entertainment value as the huge selection. It is that kind of marketing savvy, combined with a willingness to break the rules, that has helped make Riggio one of the most powerful and controversial figures in the book world.

Riggio began his bookselling career in the early 1960s. Too poor to attend college full time, he took a day job as a clerk at New York University's (NYU) campus bookstore while studying metallurgical engineering at NYU's uptown campus in the evenings. As his interest and experience in retailing grew, Riggio came to the conclusion that he could do a better job than his boss did. So in 1965, at the age of 24, he dropped out of college and, with $5,000 in savings, opened his own college bookstore, SBX (for Student Book Exchange), just around the corner from the NYU bookstore. The store thrived, and Riggio used the profits to open four more campus bookstores throughout New York City. Then in 1971, Riggio convinced bankers to lend him $1.2 million so he could purchase the struggling Barnes & Noble Bookstore on Fifth Avenue and 18th Street.

Until Riggio came along, selling books was a fusty, monkish pursuit. But he would change that. In 1974, he opened the Barnes & Noble Sales Annex across the street from the original Barnes & Noble store. He loaded tables with remaindered books, provided shopping carts, installed wood benches—and gave away free copies of *The New York Times Book Review*. Taking a page from mass merchants like Wal-Mart, Riggio advertised aggressively. His slogan: "If you paid full price, you didn't get it at Barnes & Noble." His genteel competition was appalled, but Riggio knew that retailing was changing. "We feel we're the picture of bookstores to come—there's no question about that," he told a reporter in the late 1970s. "The days of list-price book selling are numbered."

Riggio graduated to the big leagues in 1986, when, using junk bonds for financing, he bought B. Dalton, a chain of 800 mall bookstores. Combined with his 37 Barnes & Noble bookstores plus 142 college bookstores, the purchase made Riggio the biggest book retailer in the country. Over the next few years, he bought one small mall-based bookstore chain after another, including Scribner's, Bookstop and Doubleday Book Stores. But sensing yet another change in retailing, Riggio abruptly abandoned his mall-based strategy in the early 1990s and turned his attention to building superstores.

Envisioning his new stores as gathering places where customers could linger and mingle, Riggio equipped them with comfortable chairs, served Starbucks coffee, and kept the door open until 11 p.m. Riggio's strategy was to sell more than just books—he wanted to build a brand name.

Riggio didn't invent the superstore concept. Borders was the first. But like many entrepreneurs, Riggio took an existing idea and improved on it. "He saw what was going on, bet his company on the concept,

Battling Bookstores

Both Barnes & Noble Inc. and its main competitor, Amazon.com, have claimed to be the largest bookseller in the world. With the aim of appropriating the title, Barnes & Noble initiated a lawsuit in early 1997. Amazon.com countersued. Both suits were dropped in October 1997, with neither party paying or admitting liability, but both agreeing to compete in the marketplace instead of the courtroom.

and it worked,"
recalls Bobby Haft, who was then running Crown
Books. "In the beginning, you had publishing executives who didn't believe [in superstores]. Len went out and built them anyway. And they all said, 'Ah, yes. Of course! That's it!' "

Following this superstore plan, Barnes & Noble Inc.'s total revenue more than doubled, from $1.08 billion in 1992 to $2.4 billion in 1996. By 1998, Barnes & Noble superstores were opening at the rate of 90 per year. But with dominance came controversy. Riggio became the target of criticism from small independent bookstore owners who claimed his superstores were forcing them out of business. They even accused Riggio of coercing publishers into giving him secret and illegal deals. Riggio denied the charges, explaining them away as sour grapes. "The bookstore business was an elitist, stand-offish institution. I liberated it from that."

Indeed, by selling books the way The Home Depot sells two-by-fours, Riggio dragged his industry kicking and screaming into the 1990s. For better or worse, Riggio's superstores changed the book business as profoundly as anything since the advent of the paperback.

Yet Riggio says the revolution has just gotten started...and the Internet will be the battleground. Barnes & Noble is already embroiled in a struggle with online bookstore pioneer Amazon.com for the biggest share of Internet book sales. But Riggio sees the Internet as more than just a place to sell books. Envisioning an online service that will allow shoppers to download and print all or part of a book, Riggio believes the Internet will change the very concept of what constitutes a published work. "The change in the next 10 years," he predicts in a 1998 *Businessweek* article, "will be much more profound than what has happened in the last 10." And if Riggio has his way, Barnes & Noble will write that next chapter in retailing history, too.

Anita Roddick

*"**I**f you think you're too small to have an impact, try going to bed with a mosquito."*

—Anita Roddick

Founder of The Body Shop Ltd.
Founded: 1976

Photo Courtesy: The Body Shop Ltd.

COSMETICS WITH A CONSCIENCE

When Anita Roddick opened her first Body Shop, she didn't expect to get rich. She just hoped to survive. Her plan was disarmingly simple—she would create a line of cosmetics from natural ingredients and, rather than rely on vanity to sell her products, she would appeal to her customers' concern for the environment. Through a combination of low-key marketing, consumer education and social activism, The Body Shop Ltd. rewrote the rulebook for the $16 billion global cosmetics business and made Roddick one of the richest women in England.

Born in 1942, Anita Perella was the third of four children in one of the few Italian immigrant families in Littlehampton, England. Her mother steered her into the teaching profession, but Roddick's craving for adventure was too strong to keep her in the classroom. After a year in Paris in the library of the *International Herald Tribune* and another year in Geneva working for the United Nations, she hit what she calls "the hippie trail," traveling through Europe, the South Pacific and Africa. During her journeys, she became acquainted with the rituals and customs of many Third World cultures, including their forms of health and body care.

When she returned to England, she met Gordon Roddick, a kindred bohemian spirit who wrote poetry and loved to travel as much as she did. The couple married in 1970 and, shortly thereafter, opened a bed-and-breakfast hotel and later started a restaurant. In 1976, Gordon decided to fulfill a long-standing personal goal: to ride a horse from Buenos Aires, Argentina, to New York. Admiring her husband's pluck, Anita agreed to sell their restaurant to finance his trip. "It blissed me out to have a partner who said 'I've got to do this. I've got to be remarkable,' " she explains.

To support herself and her daughters in her husband's absence, Roddick decided to open a small shop where she could peddle some of the back-to-nature cosmetic knowledge she picked up during her travels. With Gordon's help, she obtained a $6,500 loan, contracted with a local herbalist to create her all-natural cosmetics, found a site in the seaside resort of Brighton, and opened her first Body Shop.

Everything was done on a shoestring budget with no concession to aesthetics. She painted the shop green because it hid everything, even the damp spots on the walls. She offered discounted refills to customers who brought back their empty containers, and used minimal packaging to keep costs as low as possible. Customers were allowed to choose from an array of perfume oils to scent their purchases (which were fragrance-free) because it was cheaper than adding expensive perfumes to every bottle of shampoo or lotion. And she eschewed advertising, relying instead on well-placed interviews promoting her social causes and in-store pamphlets to sell products.

The combination of unique products, good public relations, a highly trained staff and a well-defined sense of values quickly generated a buzz. Word spread, and within a year, Roddick's business had grown so large that she opened a second store. When Gordon returned in the spring of 1977, The Body Shop had become so popular that the Roddicks began selling franchises. By the fall of 1982, new Body Shop stores were opening at the rate of two per month.

Controversy = Sales

Early in her career, Anita Roddick displayed a natural talent for garnering free publicity. When the morticians who ran the funeral parlor next door to her first shop complained that her store's name would hurt their business, she leaked a story to the press saying the undertakers were ganging up on a woman shopkeeper just trying to get by. The stunt worked: Curious readers streamed into the store to see what all the hoopla was about.

To capitalize on the massive expansion, the Roddicks took The Body Shop public in 1984. After just one day of trading, the stock doubled in value. It would continue to rise throughout the late 1980s, as hundreds of Body Shop franchises sprung up throughout Europe and the United States.

One of the key ingredients in Roddick's success was her social activism. Her very vocal support for causes such as Greenpeace, Amnesty International, saving the rainforests and banning animal testing not only generated free publicity but also set the company apart from its competitors and generated a loyal customer base. People felt good about buying Body Shop products because they felt good about Roddick's efforts. They wanted to be part of the positive action—and that translated into sales. By the end of 1992, there were more than 700 Body Shop stores generating $231 million in sales.

However, as The Body Shop's profits and name-recognition grew, the Roddicks began paying more attention to social causes than their business, launching an array of environmental projects rather than revamping the company's aging product line. Better-run imitators, such as The Bath & Body Works, ate into The Body Shop's customer base. And critics on the left who were once Body Shop allies suddenly started attacking the company for "hypocritical practices," generating a wave of negative press. As a result, sales fell and profits dulled.

By 1996, it was clear that a change was needed. The Roddicks stepped back from running day-to-day operations and installed managing director Stuart Rose, who promptly restructured the company, bringing in other professional managers, installing tighter inventory control and streamlining processes. At the time, Roddick seemed ambivalent about the new course and railed at the administrative bureaucracy she was forced to adopt. "We've gone through a period of squashing one hell of a lot of the entrepreneurial spirit," she told *Fortune* magazine. "We're having to grow up; we have to get methods and processes in. And the result of that is a hierarchy that comes in—and I think that's antiproductive."

She may have been right. The changes failed to have the desired effect, and sales continued to decline. After a dismal first quarter financial performance in 1998, Roddick ceded her post as CEO to Patrick Gourney, a professional manager from a French food conglomerate, and farmed out her flagging U.S. franchises to the Bellamy Retail Group.

In January 1999, the company announced it was giving up manufacturing to focus on retail and that projections were good. But whether The Body Shop can regain its dominance in the market, only time will tell.

Nevertheless, Anita Roddick's story remains one of the great entrepreneurial, if not cautionary, tales of the late 20th century. She grew a single shop into an international empire and proved that a company can gain loyal customers and succeed by simply providing product information rather than employing high-powered advertising and high-pressure selling.

David Sarnoff

"**N**obody can be a success if they don't love their work."

—David Sarnoff

Chairman of Radio Corp. of America
Founded: 1919

The Father of Broadcasting

David Sarnoff wasn't a scientist, engineer or inventor. Yet he, more than any other individual, was the driving force behind the development of the electronic mass media in the United States. Truly ahead of his time, Sarnoff's vision and ambition fueled some of the greatest technological achievements of the 20th century. His stubborn pursuit of technology turned his employer, Radio Corporation of America (RCA), into a powerhouse in less than a decade. Along the way, he managed to spawn one of America's top three television networks.

Sarnoff's story is a classic American rags-to-riches tale. Born in Uzlian, Russia, in 1891, the young boy and his family traveled steerage to America when he was 9. Knowing no English, Sarnoff entered school but also helped support his family by running errands for a local butcher, selling and delivering newspapers and singing at his synagogue.

When Sarnoff was 15, his father became very sick from tuberculosis, so Sarnoff was forced to quit school and take on the full burden of supporting his family. He bought a telegraph key, taught himself Morse code, and applied for a job at Marconi Wireless Telegraph Co. of America. Although he hoped to be hired as a telegraph operator, he accepted the only job available—office boy. Sarnoff made the most of the opportunity, learning as much as he could about his employer's company by perusing the correspondence and memos it was his job to deliver. He also attached himself to any company executive who could further his career.

His efforts quickly paid off. Within two years he became a full-fledged "wireless" operator, and by 1911, he was managing the 5-kilowatt Marconi station on top of the Wanamaker department store in New York City. In 1915, he submitted a memo outlining an idea for what he called a "radio music box." At the time, radio was mainly used in shipping and by amateur wireless enthusiasts. But Sarnoff boasted that his device would make radio a "household utility," like the phonograph. "The idea," he wrote, "is to bring music into the house by wireless." Marconi management wrote off the concept as a commercial folly.

After World War I, in 1919, General Electric (GE) formed RCA to absorb Marconi's U.S. assets, which included Sarnoff. Figuring the new management might see things his way, Sarnoff again submitted his "radio music box" idea. RCA execs were intrigued but pointed out that in order to sell radios, they had to have programming. But Sarnoff had already conquered that problem. He proposed that RCA, in conjunction with GE and its partners, would produce the radio and underwrite programming at the same time.

To prove his idea would work, on July 2, 1922, Sarnoff broadcast the Jack Dempsey-George Carpentier prizefight. Few people owned radio receivers in those days, so Sarnoff arranged to have receivers connected to large amplifiers

High-Tech Hero

As a member of General Dwight D. Eisenhower's staff during World War II, David Sarnoff spearheaded many of the communications advances that aided the Allies in defeating the Axis forces. Under Sarnoff's direction, RCA developed and produced airborne and ship-borne missiles guided by TV, as well as many other types of equipment, including electronic navigation systems. Sarnoff himself coordinated "D-Day" communications and was later instrumental in restoring communications systems in France.

After the war, as head of RCA, Sarnoff was awarded both the Legion of Merit and the Medal of Merit for the company's contribution to the war effort. He was also named a brigadier general in the U.S. Army, and for the rest of his life he would affectionately be referred to as "The General."

David Sarnoff

Television Revolution

During the first public television broadcast at the 1939 World's Fair, David Sarnoff predicted that television "will become an important factor in American life." But it's doubtful that even he could have imagined how true that statement would be. According to a study conducted by Nielsen Media Research, in 1998, more than 98 million homes—nearly 99 percent of the households in America—had at least one television set, and more than 73.5 million (74 percent) of those households owned two or more sets.

strategically placed
in theaters and auditoriums throughout the eastern
states. The fight was a knockout for both Dempsey and Sarnoff—
the former in the fourth round, and the latter when reports of a
radio audience of some 500,000 people poured in. Within three
years, the radio music box, now called the Radiola (and priced at
a hefty $75) was a success, with sales of $83.5 million. Sarnoff's
career took off.

His next bright idea: RCA could increase its sales of radios by
stringing together hundreds of stations from coast to coast, creating a national broadcasting network. Based on this plan, in 1926,
as general manager of RCA, Sarnoff formed the National
Broadcasting Company (NBC) as a subsidiary of RCA.

With radio clearly a success, Sarnoff turned his attention to
another pet project in which he saw tremendous potential—television. He set up a special NBC station called B2XBS to experiment with the new medium. At the World's Fair in April 1939,
Sarnoff conducted the first public television broadcast. Speaking
from the RCA Pavilion on the fair's Avenue of Progress, Sarnoff
told viewers, "It is with a feeling of humbleness that I come to this
moment of announcing the birth of a new art so important in its
implication that it is bound to affect all society."

Television would have arrived faster if it weren't for the intervention of World War II, during which Sarnoff served as a consultant for General Dwight D. Eisenhower. Upon his return to civilian life, Sarnoff threw himself into making his dream of commercial television a reality. The new medium seemed risky and expensive at the time. But just as Sarnoff had predicted, the postwar TV market boomed, and RCA recouped its $50 million investment in research in just three years. Sarnoff then became obsessed with color television, gambling millions of dollars on its success and nearly losing.

The problem with color TV lay in creating a set that was "compatible"—able to receive both black-and-white and color images. In 1950, the Federal Communications Commission (FCC) approved a noncompatible system developed by NBC's top rival, the Columbia Broadcasting System, but reversed its decision three years later when NBC came up with a compatible system. Sarnoff had spent $150 million to come out ahead, but the investment proved to be worthwhile.

Color television would be Sarnoff's last, and perhaps his greatest, accomplishment. In the summer of 1968, he became ill with a mastoid infection and never fully recovered. In 1970, he retired as chairman of RCA, and he died a year later. At the time of his death, RCA was grossing more than $3 billion annually and had 64 manufacturing plants in the United States and abroad. During his 41-year tenure as head of RCA, Sarnoff had turned the fledgling company into a corporate titan. But his real genius lay in his ability to see further into the future than his contemporaries and, through hard work and determination, bring that future into reality. It was Sarnoff who was primarily responsible for both radio and television and the creation of a truly global village.

Howard Schultz

Howard Schultz

> *"I always wanted to do something to make a difference."*
> —Howard Schultz

Chairman & CEO of Starbucks Corp.
Founded: 1971

Grounds For Success

Everyone knows Starbucks, the ubiquitous retail chain that, in the 1990s, turned coffee drinking into a national pastime. But few know Howard Schultz, the self-effacing chairman, CEO and mastermind behind Starbucks' astonishing growth. By bringing Italy's "coffeehouse culture" to the United States and packaging it for mass consumption, this maverick marketer transformed a little-known four-store chain into the leading retailer of specialty coffee in North America.

Born in 1953, Schultz was raised in the rough and tumble Bay View housing project in Brooklyn, New York. His mother worked as a receptionist, and his father held a variety of jobs, none of which paid much or offered such basic benefits as medical coverage for him and his family. When Schultz was 7, his father lost his job as a diaper-service delivery driver after breaking his ankle. At the time, sick pay or even legally mandated disability assistance were luxuries to those in low-paying jobs, and in the ensuing months, the family was literally too poor to put food on the table. It was a memory that Schultz would carry with him into adulthood.

Determined to build a better life for himself, Schultz channeled his energy into high school sports and earned an athletic scholarship to Northern Michigan University. After graduating with a bachelor's degree in business in 1975, Schultz immediately began working in the sales and marketing division of Xerox Corp. Schultz excelled at Xerox, so much so that he attracted the attention of the Swedish housewares company Perstorp AB, which recruited him at the age of 26 to be vice president and general manager of their American subsidiary, Hammerplast USA.

While at Hammerplast, Schultz noticed that a small Seattle

company named Starbucks (after the first mate in Herman Melville's classic *Moby Dick*) was buying an unusually high number of Hammerplast's espresso machines. Intrigued, he flew to Seattle to investigate and found four Starbucks outlets. Originally founded in 1971 as a single store near Seattle's famed Pike Street Market, Starbucks sold freshly roasted gourmet coffee beans as well as teas, spices and various coffee-making accessories.

Impressed by Schultz's energy and marketing skills, Starbucks owners Gerald Baldwin and Gordon Bowker—who possessed very little business knowledge—asked Schultz to become part of their operation. Enticed by their offer, which included part ownership, Schultz joined Starbucks as head of its marketing and retail operations in 1982.

A year later, during a vacation in Italy, Schultz had what he has described as an "epiphany." While sitting at one of Milan's many espresso bars, he realized that the coffee shop played an integral role in the social life of most Italians. It was a focal point for the neighborhood, where friends met, mingled and lingered at all hours of the day. "Seeing this, I thought to myself, 'Why not open a coffee bar in Seattle?'" Schultz recalls in an interview in *The New York Times*.

To His Benefit

Howard Schultz credits Starbucks Corp.'s benefits policy as one of the keys to his company's dramatic growth. By extending health benefits to all employees, Schultz has created a more dedicated work force and promoted an extremely high level of customer service. He has also achieved a turnover rate that is less than half the average of other fast-food businesses, saving the company countless thousands in training costs and enhancing its ability to attract and retain good employees.

Another benefit that makes Starbucks stand out from its competitors is its stock-option plan. Dubbed "bean stock," unlike most plans, which are only available to top executives, Starbucks gives stock options to everyone in the company. "My aim was to give our employees a vested interest in the company," Schultz says. "And that, I think, has made all the difference."

Cartoons And Coffee

One of the true "good guys" of the business world, Howard Schultz's philanthropic endeavors have extended beyond just helping his employees have better lives. One of his major philanthropic concerns has been helping to improve literacy in America. To this end, in 1998, Starbucks formed an unprecedented partnership with Pulitzer Prize-winning cartoonist Garry Trudeau to create products to benefit local literacy programs across America. The collection marked the first time that a series of licensed "Doonesbury" products had been sold in retail stores. The series featured such "Doonesbury" characters as Duke, Mike, Kim and Zonker on T-shirts, tumblers, ceramic mugs, coffee gift cards and limited-edition lithographs.

Returning to Seattle, Schultz shared his epiphany with his fellow Starbucks owners. Although coffee was brewed in the shops, it was done so only at the request of customers and dispensed as free samples, and Baldwin and Bowker were unwilling to move beyond the stores' core product offerings.

Convinced he had hit upon something big, Schultz left Starbucks in 1986 to open his own espresso bar called Il Giornale (The Daily). The venture was a hit. Schultz wanted to open more shops but didn't have the funding he needed to expand. In a quirky twist of fate, a year later he learned that Baldwin and Bowker wished to sell their outlets, so after rounding up investors from the Seattle area, Schultz purchased the original Starbucks chain for $3.8 million and merged the stores with his own.

Once in charge, Schultz set out to completely overhaul Starbucks according to his vision. In addition to the $1-per-cup "basic" brew, he expanded Starbucks' offerings to include more exotic coffee beverages such as espresso, cappuccino, café latte, iced coffee and café mocha. He also sought to create a more appealing atmosphere for customers—the proverbial "clean, well-lighted place" where they could relax and enjoy coffee in comfort.

But the most radical change Schultz made was to improve the

way his company dealt with its employees. Convinced that friendly, efficient service would boost sales, he instituted a training program designed to groom knowledgeable employees who would enjoy working behind a counter, an occupation considered by many to be menial labor. "Service is a lost art in America … it's not viewed as a professional job to work behind a counter," Schultz says. "We don't believe that. We want to provide our people with dignity and self-esteem, so we offer tangible benefits." Among the benefits Schultz offers is complete health-care coverage to both full- and part-time employees, as well as stock options, practices that are virtually unheard of in corporate America. As a result of Schultz's vision, Starbucks experienced unprecedented growth throughout the 1990s, blossoming from 425 stores in 1994 to more than 2,200 stores in 1998. And the company is on target to break $2 billion in the year 2000.

With annual sales topping $1.7 billion in 1999, Starbucks Corp. reigned as the nation's No. 1 specialty coffee retailer. Quite an impressive achievement for a blue-collar kid from the projects. But despite Starbucks' phenomenal success, what Howard Schultz seems most proud of is not how much he has earned, but the kind of company he has created. "My dad was a blue-collar worker," Schultz explains in an *Inc.* magazine interview. "He didn't have health insurance or benefits, and I saw firsthand the debilitating effect that had on him and on our family. I decided if I was ever in the position to make a contribution to others in that way, I would. My greatest success has been that I got to build the kind of company my father never got to work for."

Charles Schwab

Founder of
Charles Schwab & Co.
Founded: 1971

"I have a passion for the investor. I've always been one myself, and the standard I apply to all our services is: If it's good for me as an investor, you'll see it."

—Charles Schwab

BUDGET BROKER

There's an old marketing adage that goes, "When everyone is headed in one direction, chances are your best opportunities lie in the opposite direction." This is one maxim Charles Schwab takes to heart. By turning his back on stodgy Wall Street conventions, he blazed his own trail and sparked an investing revolution. At a time when most brokers were battling for large institutional clients, Schwab focused his attention on the individual investor. As one of the first brokers to offer low-cost, no-frills trading services, Schwab pioneered the discount brokerage industry and transformed a struggling firm into one of the nation's largest traders.

The son of an upper-middle-class lawyer and a district attorney, Schwab was bitten by the entrepreneurial bug at an early age. While growing up in Woodland, California, a small farm community west of Sacramento, the industrious Schwab found lots of way to make money, from selling magazine subscriptions to raising chickens in his backyard. After graduating from high school, Schwab attended Stanford University, where he earned a bachelor's degree in economics in 1959. While working on his graduate degree at Stanford, Schwab took a job with a local investment advisory service, and upon receiving his MBA, was promoted to vice president of the company. But Schwab had bigger things in mind.

Wanting to be his own boss, Schwab and two friends launched a newsletter for investors in 1962. The company grew quickly and branched out to include a $20 million mutual fund. After the market crashed in 1969, the state of Texas ordered Schwab to stop taking mail orders from Texans because he wasn't registered to do business in the state. He fought the order in court, and the legal fees left him $100,000 in debt. Undaunted, Schwab brokered a land deal for his uncle, who gratefully paid off the rest of his debt and offered him an additional $100,000 to start his own business.

Using the money from his uncle, Schwab opened the first office of Charles Schwab & Co. in San Francisco in 1971. Initially, the company was just one of many struggling young firms in the securities business, with only a dozen employees and 2,000 or so clients. As late as 1974, Schwab was still on the rebound, searching for a niche for his company. Then in 1975, the Securities and Exchange Commission (SEC) discarded the old fixed-rate system for buying and selling securities in favor of negotiated rates. Under the new system, brokers could charge whatever they wanted.

Schwab noticed that most established brokerages were using the new unregulated system to provide lower rates to their large institutional clients while raising the rates for individual investors. Schwab saw his chance and vigorously targeted the small-investor market, offering no-frills service and deep commission discounts that were as much as 50 percent below that of his competition. To afford such discounts and still make money, Schwab did away with the traditional service of offering research, put his staff on salary, and automated order processing via computer (one of the first brokerages to do so).

Industry experts were skeptical. They argued that investors had to be sold stocks by brokers—that people tended not to buy on their own initiative. But Schwab stuck to his guns, and his company quickly emerged as the leading discount brokerage firm. Schwab continued to break new ground by opening branch offices and offering 24-hour order taking, no-fee individual retirement accounts, cash management accounts

The Personal Touch

A major factor in Charles Schwab & Co.'s success has been a unique marketing strategy that features Charles Schwab's photo in most of the company's advertising. Schwab was a reluctant model, but as business grew, the photo provided a personal link between the company and its customers. As one former Schwab executive explains in a 1986 Fortune magazine interview: "We'd interview customers and they'd talk about 'Chuck' or 'Charlie.' [The photo] gave them a human being to relate to."

Stiff Competition

While Charles Schwab may be a hero to individual investors, many of his colleagues were outright hostile toward him when he first ventured into the discount brokerage market. In the early days, Schwab had to fight to get seats on several stock exchanges. He spent hours combating rumors spread by rival firms that his company was going out of business. Banks, influenced by the rumors, refused to lend him money. And he found getting office space particularly difficult as the big brokers apparently told landlords they would move out of buildings if they rented to Schwab. Yet he overcame it all, and in a poetic twist of fate, Schwab's company has outlived many of the competitors that tried to do him in.

(investment accounts that offer subscribers traditional bank services such as personal checks, credit and debit cards as well as financial tracking and management), no-load mutual funds and insurance, all industry firsts.

By 1981, Schwab had branch offices in 40 cities, 600 employees, 220,000 clients and annual revenue of $42 million. But the company's rapid expansion began to cut into profit, and Schwab had trouble raising capital to finance further growth. To remedy this, Schwab agreed to sell his company to Bank of America (B of A) for $57 million worth of B of A stock, making him the bank's largest individual shareholder. However, the deal began to sour almost immediately. While Schwab's group enjoyed healthy profits, B of A suffered heavy losses. As the bank's stock plummeted, Schwab urged his fellow board members to cut overhead and reorganize, but his pleas fell on deaf ears.

After six frustrating years at B of A, Schwab had finally had enough. In an unprecedented move, he repurchased his firm from B of A for $230 million in 1987. A few weeks later, he took the company public to raise capital to pay down its $200 million debt and finance further expansion. With Schwab back in control, the company soon returned to profitability and regained its status as the nation's leading discount brokerage.

Throughout the 1990s, Schwab continued to expand. Anticipating the Internet boom, he began looking into e-commerce in 1995, and by the end of the year, he had opened one of the first online discount brokerages, e.Schwab. By 1998, e.Schwab had become the No. 1 online trader and accounted for more than half the firm's trades.

By following his instincts rather than listening to "the experts," Charles Schwab created a new form of stock brokerage and paved the way for online trading. He took brokering out of the hands of high-powered, high-priced firms; demystified the process of stock trading; and made it easier for individual investors to enjoy the benefits of a wide-open stock market.

Russell Simmons

"*My goal has been to present urban culture in its most true form to the people who love it and the people who live it.*"

—Russell Simmons

Founder of Rush Communications
Founded: 1979

HIP-HOPPRENEUR

Russell Simmons didn't invent rap. But he did play a leading role in the music's astonishing success. Like Motown Records founder Berry Gordy, who brought black soul music into the mainstream (and to whom Simmons is often compared), Simmons is credited for moving rap—or hip-hop, as aficionados call it—from the streets of the inner city into the mainstream of American pop culture.

Yet there's one major difference between Gordy and Simmons. Unlike Gordy, who tried but failed to expand his Motown empire beyond music, Simmons has been able to parlay his success in the music industry into other equally successful businesses. In less than a decade, Simmons' Rush Communications has grown to include publishing, fashion, television, filmmaking, advertising and the Internet—becoming the second-largest black-owned entertainment company in the United States.

Although he made his fame promoting music that celebrates a street-tough lifestyle, Simmons grew up in a comfortable middle-class home in Queens, New York. He first heard rap while he was working on a sociology degree at City College in Harlem, New York. In 1977, he began promoting rap parties in Harlem and Queens with his friend Curtis Walker. Like rock 'n' roll, rap was initially dismissed as a fad. But Simmons knew different. At his parties, he saw a new and lasting subculture emerging. The following year, Walker became a rapper himself, changing his name to Kurtis Blow, and he and Simmons co-wrote a minor hit called "Christmas Rappin'." After this small success with Blow, Simmons left his studies at City College.

In 1979, he formed Rush Communications and began managing other local rap acts. One of the most successful of Simmons' acts was his younger brother, Joey, who went by the name of Run. Putting his brother together with MC Darryl McDaniels and DJ

Jason Mizell, he christened the group Run DMC, dressed them in black leather suits and told them what to record. On a street level, the group's first two records were instant hits.

In 1984, Simmons met Rick Rubin, an NYU student who also wanted to promote rap music. The two scrounged up $8,000 and founded Def Jam. Rubin was a production genius who loved loud, rebellious music. Simmons was a relentlessly enthusiastic and canny businessman. (He has claimed that he learned the basics of business—cash flow, client relations, networking—by selling marijuana on the streets in his youth.)

The combination of Rubin's and Simmons' personalities and talents proved to be a powerful mix. Just two years into their bare-bones operation, Columbia Records approached Def Jam with an offer to promote, market and distribute Def Jam's new rap recordings for a share in their profits. But Def Jam and Run DMC were primarily making black music for black people. The label's next two moves, however, would change that.

First, Def Jam teamed Run DMC with Aerosmith to record a rap version of the rock band's hit "Walk This Way." The song was a smash and landed Run DMC on MTV, which until then had played rap only reluctantly. When the song reached a new white audience, Run DMC and Simmons found themselves with a No. 4 Billboard hit—the first rap song to break the top five. The single also helped the band's third album, "Raising Hell," sell 4 million copies.

A Phat Endorsement

When Run DMC made wearing Adidas sneakers popular after recording the song "My Adidas," Russell Simmons asked the shoe manufacturer to sponsor a concert tour. Adidas executives were skeptical about the marketing potential of the rap band, so Simmons invited them to a Run DMC concert. As the group was performing the song, one of the members yelled out, "Everybody in the house, rock your Adidas," and three thousand pairs of sneakers shot into the air. The Adidas executives couldn't reach for their checkbooks fast enough.

Russell Simmons

Next Def Jam signed the first all-white rap act, the Beastie Boys. The group's bratty lyrics and rock 'n' roll-based riffs brought in an even wider white audience, and the band's first album, "License to Ill," sold 8 million copies. The success of these albums prompted Def Jam to sign additional acts, including Public Enemy, Oran "Juice" Jones, and rap duo D.J. Jazzy Jeff and the Fresh Prince (Will Smith). Amazingly, every record the label released through 1990 went gold.

At the same time Simmons was developing Def Jam with Rubin, he was also becoming involved in other media. In 1985, in cooperation with Warner Brothers, his Def Pictures produced its first film, "Krush Groove," a rap musical based loosely on Simmons' life. The film, which cost only $2.2 million to produce, grossed almost $20 million at the box office. Simmons' second film, "Tougher Than Leather," an action-comedy starring Run D.M.C., achieved similar success. Later Def Picture films would include "The Addiction" (1995) and "The Funeral" (1996)—both directed by Abel Ferrara and starring Christopher Walken—and Eddie Murphy's "The Nutty Professor" (1996).

Rubin left Def Jam in 1988 to form his own company, and Simmons continued to oversee the Def Jam label and Def Pictures as subsidiaries of Rush Communications. Next, Simmons ventured into television with "Def Comedy Jam." Co-produced by Simmons and his TV partners, Bernie Brillstein and Brad Grey, the show, which showcased black stand-up comedians, was an instant sensation.

Simmons further expanded his communications empire in 1992 to include the magazine *Oneworld*, which features articles on music, fashion and hip-hop personalities. In that same year,

Simmons launched a line of clothing called Phat Farm, which by 1998 was grossing almost $22 million a year and is projected to top $100 million in the year 2000. A year later, Simmons started SLBG Entertainment, which serves as an agency for actors and other entertainers.

One of the most recent offshoots of Rush Communications is the Rush Media Company, a marketing and advertising agency that produced award-winning advertisements for Coca-Cola in 1996.

The key to Simmons' success, more than anything, has been his keen sense of promotion. At a time when the record industry was looking for the next one-hit-disco-wonder, Simmons actively sought out artists who could have a career, then promoted them and his label at the same time. In retrospect, Simmons was branding when everyone else was still marketing. As the label took off, Simmons, like another master of promotion, Virgin Group's Richard Branson, looked for other places to use his name and his company's name to sell new products. And there's every indication that Simmons can and will go on to create an expansionistic, diversified conglomerate like Virgin.

Thanks to Simmons, hip-hop is no longer black culture or even urban culture—it's American culture. And no one is counting it out as a fad anymore. "With my first act in '79, people said hip-hop was dead," Simmons has said. "Now look, 20 years later, the culture is so strong we're doing underwear."

Fred Smith

> *"You absolutely, positively have to innovate—if only to survive."*
>
> —Fred Smith

Founder of Federal Express Corp.
Founded: 1971

An Overnight Success

While attending Yale University in the mid-1960s, Fred Smith wrote an economics term paper on the need for reliable overnight delivery in a computerized information age. His professor was less than impressed and responded: "The concept is interesting and well-formed, but in order to earn better than a 'C', the idea must be feasible." Several years later, through a combination of innovative thinking, unbridled charisma and sheer determination, Smith would use this "interesting but unfeasible" concept to found the world's first overnight delivery company and change the transportation industry forever.

Smith was born to a well-to-do family in 1944 in a small suburb outside Memphis, Tennessee. His father, who died when Smith was only 4, became a self-made millionaire after founding the Dixie Greyhound Bus Lines and a chain of restaurants called the Toddle House.

Smith was born with a congenital birth defect—a bone socket hip disorder called Calve-Perthes disease—which caused him to wear braces and walk with the aid of crutches for most of his youth. His mother worked diligently to build his self-esteem and encouraged his participation in all sorts of physical activities. He eventually grew out of the disease, and in prep school, Smith played both basketball and football.

After earning a bachelor's degree in economics from Yale, Smith enlisted in the Marines and was sent to Vietnam, where he received an education of a very different kind. "As a platoon leader in Vietnam, I was in charge of a group of youngsters who had come from very different backgrounds than I had. You know, blue-collar backgrounds: steelworkers, truck drivers, gas station folks," Smith reveals in a 1998 *Fortune* magazine interview. "The experience gave me a very different perspective than most people who end up in senior management positions on what people who wear blue collars think about and the way they react to things, and what you should do to try to be fair to those folks. A great deal of what FedEx has been able to accomplish was built on those lessons I learned in the Marine Corps."

After two tours of duty, Smith left Vietnam weary of destruction and eager to focus his energy on building rather than tearing down. "I wanted to do something productive after blowing so many things up," he remembers. His stepfather, retired Air Force general Fred Hook, had bought a struggling company in Little Rock that modified aircraft and overhauled their engines, and Smith went to Arkansas to help him run it. Difficulty in getting parts brought Smith back to the overnight delivery concept he'd hit upon in college.

Determined to make it work, he came up with a plan for creating an integrated air and ground delivery system in which packages from all over the country would be flown to a central point, or "hub," sorted, and then flown out again along specific routes, or "spokes" to their destinations. Under this "hub and spokes" system, the flying would be done at night, when air lanes were comparatively empty. The airports used would be in sizable cities, and trucks would carry the packages to their final destinations, whether in those cities or smaller communities.

Convinced his idea was feasible, Smith decided to take the plunge with $4 million he'd inherited from his father. At that point, Smith's life became a marathon nonstop journey into the canyons of Wall Street

Head Start

Fred Smith displayed entrepreneurial talents early in life. He learned to fly when he was 15 and took up crop dusting as a part-time hobby. At age 16, he and two friends formed Ardent Record Co., a business that still exists today. The young entrepreneurs operated the firm profitably and even produced a number of hits, including "Rock House" and "Big Satin Mama."

to raise the capital he would need to purchase the fleet of airplanes vital to his plan. "I was a kind of naive about the whole thing," he confesses in a *Nation's Business* magazine interview. "I thought there would be basketfuls of checks right away." There weren't. But Smith kept at it. His charisma and the knowledge he gleaned from several years of studying the air-freight industry (both in the military in Vietnam and later in the United States) impressed investors, and by the end of 1972, he had managed to raise $80 million in loans and equity investments.

Federal Express (FedEx) began operation in April 1971, with 14 Falcon jets servicing 25 cities. Initially business was slow. During its first night, FedEx shipped a mere 186 packages. But volume picked up rapidly, and service was expanded. FedEx was an overnight success. Then the roof caved in. Because of rapidly inflating fuel prices, costs surpassed revenue, and by mid-1974, FedEx was losing more than $1 million a month.

Smith asked his disappointed investors for more money to keep the company afloat, but they refused. Bankruptcy was a distinct possibility. Then fate stepped in. While waiting for a flight home to Memphis from Chicago after being turned down for capital by General Dynamics, Smith impulsively hopped a flight to Las Vegas, where he won $27,000 playing blackjack. "The $27,000 wasn't decisive, but it was an omen that things would get better," Smith says. And indeed they did. Returning to his quest for funds, he raised another $11 million.

Although FedEx had lost nearly $13.4 million in its first two years, Smith never considered giving up. "I was very committed to the people that had signed on with me, and if we were going to go down, we were going to go down with a fight. It wasn't going to be because I checked out and didn't finish," he says.

But FedEx didn't go down. Thanks to an aggressive ad campaign which featured the now famous line, "FedEx—when it absolutely, positively has to be there overnight," the company scored a profit of $3.6 million in 1976. Two years later, FedEx went public, and by 1980, revenue had zoomed to $415.4 million, and profits soared to $38.7 million. From then on, it was smooth sailing for FedEx. By 1999, the company has become the No. 1 overnight shipper in the world, delivering more than 3 million packages to nearly 210 countries each working day.

Fred Smith, now chairman, president and CEO of FDX Corp., FedEx's parent company, compiled a fortune estimated at $700 million by enabling businesses to deliver their goods quickly, anywhere in the world. He was told it couldn't be done. But in the time-honored style of the true innovative visionary, Smith listened to his own counsel, and single-handedly changed the way the world does business.

Martha Stewart

Founder of
Martha Stewart
Living Omnimedia
Founded: 1997

"I think people who have a real entrepreneurial spirit, who can face difficulties and overcome them, should absolutely follow their desires. It makes for a much more interesting life."

—Martha Stewart

AMERICA'S GURU OF GOOD TASTE

Icing gingerbread houses, rolling green grapes in foie gras and boiling quail eggs in champagne vinegar for a living may not seem like the stuff financial empires are built on, but that's exactly how Martha Stewart turned her own good taste into a multimillion-dollar business. Her skill at making a fortune out of fantasy has made her "the Danielle Steel of food authors" and has given her near-cult status among her thousands of devoted followers. As a result, this "driven doyenne of domesticity" has taken homemaking and entertaining to a new level and taught her fans how to add a touch of elegance to their everyday lives.

Martha Kostyra displayed a love of all things domestic early in life. As a child growing up in the working-class neighborhood of Nutley, New Jersey, she would spend hours working in the garden, lending her father a hand "fixing up" around the house, and helping her mother and grandmother prepare exotic dishes. A natural-born hostess, she organized birthday parties for neighborhood children to supplement her baby-sitting income while she was still a grammar-school student.

But while the seeds of her future as a "domestic goddess" had already been sown, Stewart's first career was anything but domestic. In high school, her blond good looks won her modeling assignments in fashionable stores and on television. Yet she was still able to maintain a straight-A average through her senior year of high school and entered Barnard College in New York City. At first she toyed with the idea of becoming a chemist but abandoned that course and concentrated instead on history.

In 1961, while still a sophomore, she married law student Andrew Stewart. To cover tuition and other expenses, she took a number of modeling jobs, appearing in commercials for Clairol,

Lifebuoy soap and Tareyton cigarettes. She graduated from Barnard in 1963 and continued to model until she became pregnant.

Restless and seeking a new career, she contemplated becoming an architect but decided stock brokerage intrigued her more. Shortly after the birth of her daughter in 1965, the 24-year-old Stewart joined the firm of Monness, Williams and Sidel, where she excelled—at one point earning $135,000 a year. But during the 1973 recession, she became "a nervous wreck," and the job lost most of its appeal. "I liked the sales part of it, the human contact," she explains. "But I wanted to sell things that were fun…and stocks weren't anymore." She and her husband left New York and moved to Westport, Connecticut, where they purchased and renovated an 1805 federal-style farmhouse on Turkey Hill Road, "removing the unsightly and replacing it with the beautiful," as Stewart recalls. They also built a Shaker-style barn and planted orchards and vegetable gardens.

Once the renovation was complete, Stewart turned her seemingly boundless energy to another hobby—gourmet cooking. While on a modeling assignment in Europe during the 1960s, she had closely studied Italian, German and French cuisine. Later, as a stockbroker, she had entertained her clients at some of New York City's top restaurants and would often ask chefs to share their secrets. Her efforts to broaden and hone her culinary talents paid off handsomely in 1973, when Stewart started a catering business. After placing an ad in the local newspaper, she almost immediately found herself, in her words, "preparing blindly for a wedding for 300."

Getting "The Dirt"

One of the reasons Martha Stewart's books have been so successful is that she spends a tremendous amount of time researching them and then writes from personal experience. In preparation for writing Martha Stewart's Gardening, Month by Month, she frequently gardened 12 hours per day for weeks at a stretch.

Working out of a kitchen (which she had designed) in the basement of her Turkey Hill home, Stewart and her staff cooked gourmet meals for as many as 1,500 people at a time, using many ingredients grown in her own garden. Within a decade, Stewart's enterprise had mushroomed into a $1 million business, and her clients included prestigious corporations, museums and celebrities. She also contributed articles to *The New York Times* and served as the newspaper's food and entertainment editor.

Then in 1980, an event happened that would establish Stewart as America's most closely watched hostess and arbiter of good taste. While attending a party she'd catered at the Cooper-Hewitt Museum, the president of Crown Publishers asked Stewart to write a book for the company's lifestyle imprint, Clarkson Potter. Oversized, beautifully photographed and packed with suggestions for 35 different parties as well as decorating and presentation tips, *Martha Stewart's Entertaining* was an immediate hit, selling more than 625,000 copies. It was followed with a series of equally successful sequels, including *Martha Stewart's Quick Cook Menus*, *The Wedding Planner* and *Martha Stewart's Christmas*. She also began marketing how-to videos and CDs.

But Stewart's success didn't come without a price. Regularly putting in 18- to 20-hour days took its toll on her marriage, and she and Andrew were divorced in 1990. Martha refocused on her business ventures and shifted her entrepreneurial skills into high gear. She signed a deal with Kmart to act as its national spokeswoman and promote a line of linens and tableware she designed for the chain. She also set her sites on another form of publishing. In 1991, with financing from Time-Warner, she introduced the bimonthly magazine *Martha Stewart's Living*, which had a circulation of 2.3 million by the time Stewart took over ownership of the magazine from Time Inc. in 1997. During that time, she also increased her TV presence, appearing on a variety of talk shows and producing several specials that eventually led Stewart to her own syndicated television show. Her most recent ventures have included a Web site tie-in to her TV show and an interactive online version of her popular "Ask Martha" newspaper column.

Stewart's success in her many different roles is a tribute to her unique entrepreneurial skills in marketing—not so much a product, but herself and her sense of taste. In essence, she turned her own life into a business empire and left an indelible mark on the way America views cooking, home decoration, gardening and entertaining. "My books are 'dream' books to look at, but they're very practical," Stewart says, summing up her influence on the American public. "People can take the recipes, the ideas, and use them every day, because what I'm giving them is not a fantasy, but a reality that looks like a fantasy."

Ted Turner

*Founder of
Turner Broadcasting
System Inc.
Founded: 1969*

*"**Y**ou'll hardly ever find a superachiever
anywhere who isn't motivated at least
partially by a sense of insecurity."*

—Ted Turner

CAPTAIN OUTRAGEOUS

Intense, arrogant, full of braggadocio, combative for the sheer hell of it—Ted Turner has been called a genius, a flake, a fruitcake, a maniac and a visionary. Derided as "the Mouth of the South" because of his over-the-top public behavior, he has often been seriously underestimated. But behind the outrageous facade is a shrewd innovator who transformed the television industry.

Born in 1938 in Cincinnati, Robert Edward (Ted) Turner III was the oldest child of Ed and Florence Turner. When Turner was 9, his father, a native Southerner, moved the family to Savannah, Georgia, where he formed the outdoor advertising venture Turner Advertising Co. A "problem child," Turner spent much of his youth in military schools in Georgia and Tennessee. He wanted to go to the Naval Academy but instead enrolled at Brown University at his father's insistence. He was eventually expelled from Brown when he was caught with a woman in his room—a flagrant violation of school policy.

In 1960, after a stint in the Coast Guard, Turner joined the family business. It turned out he had a flair for sales, and his father watched proudly as he quickly outdistanced the company's best salesperson. His father rewarded Turner with a manager's position in their Macon, Georgia, operation. But in 1963, Turner was shocked to learn that his father, deeply in debt and fearful the business was overextended, had initiated plans to sell the company. Turner accused him of quitting. But in truth, the self-made millionaire was suffering a nervous breakdown, and on March 5, 1963, he committed suicide.

So at the age of 24, Turner inherited his father's company and immediately set out to stop the deal his father had set into motion before ending his life. The buyer agreed to void the sale, and under Turner's management, the company thrived. But it wasn't long before Turner became bored with billboards. Deciding to diversify, in 1970, he bought the near-bankrupt Atlanta TV station Channel 17. He renamed the station WTCG (for Turner Communications Group) and plastered unleased billboards with prominent advertisements for the new Channel 17.

By showing primarily reruns of sitcoms such as "Gilligan's Island" and "Leave It to Beaver" and old black-and-white movies, Turner had the station turning a profit within three years. But he knew that eventually he would have to run original programming if he wanted sizable growth. Sports seemed to be just the ticket. His first success came with wrestling. Turner built a full-sized wrestling ring in his tiny headquarters building and broadcast live professional wrestling matches. Ratings soared, but his biggest coup was winning the rights to broadcast Atlanta Braves games. The station became so dependent on the Braves that Turner purchased the team in 1976, ensuring a regular and marketable source of programming.

That same year, he took the gamble that would transform his backwater UHF station into a national broadcast phenomenon. In 1975, RCA had launched a communications satellite capable of sending television signals nationally.

Colorful Controversy

Ted Turner's career may seem like an unending string of beating the odds, but he has had his setbacks and made his fair share of mistakes. One of his major gaffes was when he began colorizing classic movies to give them greater mass appeal. While it was an ingenious and profitable business move (the first 12 films he colorized grossed an average of $900,000 for one-year syndication rights), it antagonized a very vocal segment of the film industry. Woody Allen, Martin Scorcese, Steven Spielberg and other Hollywood heavyweights went so far as to testify before Congress in an attempt to prevent further colorization of the MGM library. As for Turner, he replied in classic Turneresque style: "I wanted to do it, and they're mine."

Bucking The Odds

Few industry experts thought CNN would succeed. But as has often been the case with Ted Turner, they couldn't have been more wrong. When it signed on in 1980, CNN had 1.7 million subscribers. By 1999, it was being carried in 80 million households and had a total of 32 bureaus and more than 600 national and international affiliates.

Realizing that he could significantly increase the number of viewers by broadcasting via satellite, Turner built a $750,000 transmission tower and began beaming a signal which could be received and rebroadcast by cable operators across the nation. The move created the country's first "superstation," WTBS. By 1978, Turner's station was reaching 2 million homes, more than double the number it had previously been capable of reaching.

His superstation a success, Turner looked for other ways to exploit satellite technology and proposed launching a 24-hour live-news network. Turner was not the first to think of an all-news channel. Other media heavyweights had long thought about doing it but were leery after very costly failed attempts. Turner's gut told him it was a good move. Risking everything he owned, he started the Cable News Network (CNN) in 1980, and once again, the gamble paid off. According to many experts, by providing live coverage of breaking events, CNN transformed the way news was reported. "The definition of news was rewritten—from something that has happened to something that is happening at the very moment you are hearing it," *Time* magazine editors explain.

Regarding himself as an underdog battling the media giants, Turner desired a foothold among the networks. After a failed attempt to take over CBS in 1985, Turner purchased MGM for $1.6 billion in order to gain control of the MGM/UA film library. At the time, many investors felt Turner had overpaid for the library. In later years, however, the transaction would be regarded as a steal. By purchasing some 3,300 MGM/UA movies, including such classics as "Gone With the Wind," "Casablanca" and

"Citizen Kane," Turner had essentially acquired a library of films whose value would not depreciate in the future. To capitalize on this vast library, Turner started two more networks—Turner Network Television (TNT) in 1988 and Turner Classic Movies (TCM) in 1994.

But the biggest deal of Turner's mercurial career would come in 1996, when he agreed to sell Turner Broadcasting to Time Warner for $7.5 billion. Turner became Time Warner's largest shareholder and was given the job of overseeing Time Warner's cable networks division as its vice chairman. One of the major reasons Turner agreed to the merger, which at the time created the largest media conglomerate in the world, was that he gained the use of Time Warner's library of films and cartoons, thereby significantly increasing his own cable channels' range of programming. In addition, Time Warner was the second-largest cable systems operator in the nation, and the merger gave Turner easier access to limited cable channel space.

By the end of the 1990s, Turner was worth nearly $7 billion, but a new Ted Turner was emerging. Although still outspoken, Turner set his sights on philanthropy, and in 1997, pledged to donate $1 billion to the United Nations in hopes of inspiring others to be as generous. Explaining his actions, Turner told *Time* magazine, "I'm not going to rest until all the world's problems are solved." Pundits may poke fun at this lofty goal, but considering what Turner has already accomplished in his stellar career, he just might be able to pull it off. Stay tuned.

Lillian Vernon

Vernon Lillian Lillian
Lillian Vernon Verno
Lillian Vernon
Vernon Lillian
lian Lillian Verno
Lillian Vernon Lillian
Vernon Vernon Lillian
Vernon Vernon

*"I never let my
mistakes defeat
or distract me, but I
learn from them and
move forward in a
positive way."*
—Lillian Vernon

Founder of Lillian Vernon Corp.
Founded: 1951

CATALOG QUEEN

Lillian Vernon is one of the catalog industry's most accomplished and well-known leaders. A true pioneer who blazed the trail for women in a field once dominated by men, her achievements rank with those of such mail order giants as Richard Sears and A. Montgomery Ward. Realizing that vanity is a powerful magnet, she was the first catalog entrepreneur to personalize products, and in the process, she turned a mom-and-pop start-up operation into the leading gift catalog in the world.

In 1951, while pregnant with the first of her two sons, Vernon began to worry that her husband's $75-per-week salary would not be enough to support a growing family. She wanted to help, but her options seemed limited. "It was very unfashionable for women to work in those days," she writes in her autobiography, *An Eye for Winners.* "So I thought mail order was a wonderful thing. I could do it from the house, stay home, change diapers, the whole thing."

From the very beginning, Vernon showed a natural talent for marketing and product selection. While walking through her father's leather-goods plant in Manhattan, New York, she came to the conclusion that she should sell handbags. "I knew about those," she writes. "Why not sell them and belts to match? Didn't every teenage girl strolling along the street anywhere in the United States sport a handbag and belt?"

Working from her kitchen table in Mount Vernon, New York, and using for seed money cash she received as wedding gifts, Vernon placed a $495 sixth-of-a-page ad in *Seventeen* magazine offering a monogrammed leather handbag and matching monogrammed belt for $7. "I knew with absolute certainty that teenagers would go for items that made them feel unique," she explains. What she didn't know was that she'd hit upon an idea that would become her company's trademark—monogramming.

Within three months of placing the first ad, Vernon received $32,000 worth of orders. Inspired by her success, she officially formed Lillian Vernon Corp. Plowing her profits back into the business, she expanded her product line to include combs, blazer buttons and cuff links, and took out larger ads in a half-dozen fashion magazines. As before, she offered personalization free with any purchase. "Monogrammed items make such nice gifts," she remarked in a 1987 *Nation's Business* interview. "You simply can't rush out to a store and buy a present that's instantly monogrammed. It takes planning and thought. That makes the gift all the more special to the recipient."

In the early days, Vernon handled virtually the entire operation by herself—selecting and designing the products, writing the copy, opening the mail and shipping the orders. But by 1954, Vernon's business had outgrown her kitchen, so she rented three buildings in downtown Mount Vernon to serve as a warehouse, a shipping department and a monogramming workshop.

Despite Vernon's success, some suppliers refused to do business with a woman. She had difficulty getting credit, and when she did find suppliers who would work with her, she was often dissatisfied with the quality of their products. To get around these obstacles, Vernon set up her own light manufacturing plant to produce such items as charm bracelets, signet rings and bobby pin holders. By the end of the 1950s, her plant was accepting orders from big-name cosmetic companies such as

"I Know My Customer Because I Am My Customer"

One of the key ingredients in Lillian Vernon's success is her knack for picking winning products. Surprisingly, she avoids using traditional marketing techniques, such as focus groups, relying instead on her own keen intuition, which she refers to as her "Golden Gut." Her selection philosophy is simple: She only offers products that are interesting and that she herself would use.

Revlon, Elizabeth Arden, Max Factor and Avon for customized lipstick containers and makeup cases.

As her business grew, Vernon decided that she could reach more customers more effectively through catalogs than magazine ads. In 1956, she put together a 16-page black-and-white catalog featuring dozens of inexpensive gifts, knickknacks and household items and mailed it to 125,000 customers. "We sold a $1 sterling silver monogrammed ring and got thousands and thousands of orders," she told one interviewer. Response to the catalog was, in Vernon's words, "fabulous," and raised her annual revenue to $150,000 by 1956.

In 1965, Vernon officially assumed the titles of chairman of the board and CEO. She continued to experience tremendous success, but it didn't come without a price. The long hours she regularly put in took their toll on her marriage, and Lillian and her first husband divorced in 1969. He took over the manufacturing business while she kept the catalog, which by then was pulling in nearly $1 million per year in sales.

During the 1970s, Vernon's company experienced explosive growth, spurred in part by the legions of American women entering the work force. With a newly found discretionary income but little time to waste strolling through malls, working women became Lillian's best customers. At the same time, the energy crisis made casual station-wagon expeditions positively un-American and prompted a boom in catalog sales across the board.

In 1987, with annual sales at $112 million, Vernon decided to take her company public, selling 35 percent of the stock and keeping the rest for herself. The sale yielded $28 million, $12 million of which was reportedly split between Vernon and her children. The remainder was used to help finance a $25 million computerized national distribution center in Virginia Beach, Virginia, which opened the following year.

Not content to rest on her laurels, Vernon branched out into the specialty mail order market in 1989 with the debut of her *Neat Ideas* catalog, which featured merchandise for bath, bedroom and kitchen, with an emphasis on "organizers" such as dish racks and drawer dividers. The catalog was an instant hit, yielding an average order of $80—more than double the flagship catalog's average sale for the same year.

Despite difficulties caused by a sharp increase in paper and postage costs in the early 1990s, Vernon's company continued to prosper, and by 1998, it boasted revenue of $255 million.

Vernon's awesome success is a tribute to her talent for working overtime in bringing unique products to customers wanting personalized service. While the catalog industry has become pervasive, with new catalogs emerging monthly, none have been able to dislodge Vernon from her dominant position at the top of the industry. A self-confessed workaholic, Lillian Vernon stands poised and ready to guide her company into the next century. "Toughness is a good thing," she says. "Yet it is considered good only in men. When a woman is tough, men can't stand it. I like being tough. Tough…and smart."

Madam C. J. Walker

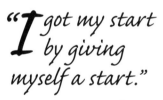

*"**I** got my start by giving myself a start."*
—Madam
C.J. Walker

Founder of Madam C.J. Walker Manufacturing Co.
Founded: 1905

FROM POVERTY TO PROSPERITY

Many of the 20th century's most influential entrepreneurs overcame tremendous odds in their quests for success. But none faced greater obstacles than Madam C.J. Walker. The daughter of former slaves, she was orphaned at the age of 7, married at 14, a mother at 17, and a widow at 20. Yet she was determined to build a better life for herself and her daughter. Starting with a meager investment of only $1.50, she built one of the most successful black-owned businesses of the early 20th century and became the nation's first woman self-made millionaire.

Walker was born Sarah Breedlove on December 23, 1867. Her parents were sharecroppers on the sprawling Burney cotton plantation in Delta, Louisiana, and like most children of her time, Sarah went to work in the cotton fields at an early age. After her parents died, Sarah moved to Vicksburg, Mississippi, to live with her sister, Louvenia. But the arrangement proved to be less than ideal. According to Sarah, Louvenia's husband was "a cruel and contemptuous scoundrel" who treated her terribly. To escape his tyranny, Sarah married a Vicksburg laborer named Moses McWilliams when she was only 14.

On June 6, 1885, Sarah gave birth to a daughter named Lelia. She believed that if she worked hard enough, she could provide her daughter with a better life than she had. Tragically, shortly after Lelia's second birthday, Moses died. At age 20, now a widow and a single mother, Sarah moved to St. Louis, where she worked as a laundress for $1.50 per day for the next 18 years. She scrimped and saved until she had enough money to send Lelia to Knoxville College.

By the time she was in her late 30s, Sarah's hair had started falling out, due to a combination of stress and years of using damaging hair-care products. She was not alone. In fact, most black women of the time experienced the same problem, but there were no hair-care products on the market to correct it. Sarah tried everything that was available but met with little success, so she started experimenting with her own hair-care products.

Her big break came in 1905, when, as she would later tell a reporter, "I had a dream, and in that dream a big black man appeared to me and told me what to mix up for my hair. Some of the remedy was grown in Africa, but I sent for it, mixed it, put it on my scalp, and in a few weeks my hair was coming in faster than it had ever fallen out. I tried it on my friends; it helped them. I made up my mind I would begin to sell it."

Starting with a few dollars' worth of medicinal ingredients, Sarah mixed batches of her products in her washtub and began selling them door to door to friends and neighbors. A natural marketer, Sarah pushed her products by giving free demonstrations. This technique worked, and black women throughout St. Louis began buying her wares with enthusiasm. It was about this time that Sarah received word that her sister-in-law had been left a widow with four daughters to care for. She decided to move to Denver to help out. There, she continued selling her products door to door with tremendous success.

Shortly after she arrived in Denver, Sarah married newspaperman C.J. Walker and adopted Madam C.J. Walker as her professional name. With help from her husband, she began running advertisements in black newspapers and quickly developed a thriving mail order business.

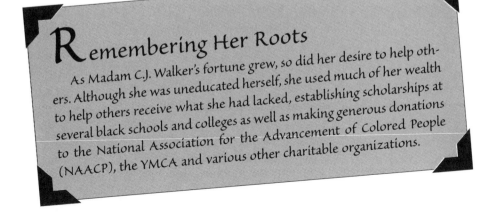

Remembering Her Roots

As Madam C.J. Walker's fortune grew, so did her desire to help others. Although she was uneducated herself, she used much of her wealth to help others receive what she had lacked, establishing scholarships at several black schools and colleges as well as making generous donations to the National Association for the Advancement of Colored People (NAACP), the YMCA and various other charitable organizations.

Madam C.J. Walker

Cosmetics Crusader

Madam C.J. Walker saw her innovative line of beauty products and techniques as more than just a way to make money—she saw it as a way to help other black women achieve their full potential. By training and recruiting scores of "Walker Agents" to sell her products, she enabled literally thousands of black women to go into business for themselves at a time when the best most could hope for were menial jobs for low pay.

Lelia left college and moved to Denver to help with the family venture, and before long, the Walkers were bringing in $10 per week—which was quite a lot of money at that time. C.J. decided that the business had reached its full potential. His wife disagreed. She believed that black women across the country would be interested in her products, if only they knew about them. Leaving Lelia in charge of the mail order buisness, Walker embarked on an extended sales tour throughout the southern United States. Within a few months, she was making weekly sales of $35—more than twice the salary of the average white American male worker and 20 times that of the average black woman worker.

Realizing that she could only do so much selling herself, Walker recruited and trained a team of door-to-door saleswomen to demonstrate and take orders for her products—much like Avon and Mary Kay Cosmetics would do decades later. With a team of trained saleswomen crisscrossing the country, Walker's company grew rapidly. In 1908, she expanded into the East, establishing a business office in Pittsburgh. Two years later, she built a large manufacturing plant in Indianapolis.

By 1917, the Madam C.J. Walker Manufacturing Co. had become black America's most successful business, boasting a combined 3,000 employees and "Walker Agents." Madam C.J. Walker was America's first self-made woman millionaire. To celebrate her success, she commissioned black architect Vertner Tandy to design and build a lavish mansion for her on the Hudson River in

Irvington, New York. Sadly, she was unable to enjoy her new home for long. For several years, Walker had been experiencing problems with high blood pressure. Her doctors advised her to take it easy, but Walker could not—or would not—slow down her hectic pace. Long years of traveling and hard work finally took their toll. On May 25, 1919, Walker died of kidney failure resulting from hypertension.

A woman of extraordinary courage and vision, Madam C.J. Walker blazed the trail for the generations of women entrepreneurs that would follow her. The grit and determination that carried her from a cotton field to a mansion, from abject poverty to riches, remain a burning inspiration for Americans of all races who yearn to realize their dream of achieving a better life.

Sam Walton

Founder of
Wal-Mart Stores Inc.
Founded: 1962

*"There is only one boss—the customer.
And he can fire everybody in the
company from the chairman on down,
simply by spending his money somewhere else."*

—Sam Walton

BARGAIN BASEMENT BILLIONAIRE

Part P.T. Barnum, part Billy Graham, Sam Walton single-handedly built Wal-Mart into the biggest retailer in the world, transforming the way America shopped and making himself one of the world's richest men in the process. Thanks to his "aw, shucks" demeanor and his strategy of targeting rural areas, retailing giants like Kmart, Sears and Woolworth's never saw the scrappy, pickup-driving country boy coming. And when they did, it was too late to stop him.

Walton began what would be a lifelong career in the retail business in 1940, when he took a job as a sales trainee at a J.C. Penney store in Des Moines, Iowa. Walton was enthusiastic about his job, but he was never one of Penney's most thorough employees. He hated to make customers wait while he fussed with paperwork, so his books were a mess. His boss even threatened to fire him, saying he was not cut out for retail work. Walton was saved by his ability as a salesman, and he added about $25 per month in commissions to his beginner's salary.

Drafted into the United States Army in 1942, Walton served stateside as a communications officer in the Army Intelligence Corps for the duration of World War II. By the time he was released from the military in 1945, Walton had a wife and child to support, so he decided to strike out on his own. Putting up $5,000 of his own money and $20,000 that he borrowed from his father-in-law, at the age of 27, Walton purchased a Ben Franklin variety store in Newport, Arkansas.

Through hard work and a policy of pricing products well below what other retailers charged, Walton soon tripled his business, and by 1950, he owned the leading Ben Franklin store in a six-state region. The store's success wasn't lost on Walton's landlord, who decided to acquire the business for his son. Sam had no intention of selling, so the landlord simply refused to renew his lease.

The experience would have caused most people to give up. But not Sam Walton. He searched the rural towns of Arkansas for a new place to do business and found it in the tiny community of Bentonville. There he set up shop in a store on the town square, this time insisting on a 99-year lease.

Walton opened Walton's Five & Dime in the summer of 1950. There were two other variety stores in town, but neither offered the consistently low prices that Walton did. As a result, the new enterprise quickly achieved the same success of his previous venture, prompting Walton to look for other such opportunities. "Maybe it was just my itch to do more business," he would later muse, "And maybe, too, I didn't want all my eggs in one basket."

Throughout the 1950s, using borrowed money and the profits from stores he already owned, Walton acquired one variety store after another. By 1960, he was the proud owner of 15 stores. But he wasn't seeing the profits he'd expected and thought he ought to be making more money for the kind of effort he was putting in. He decided to adopt a new strategy—discounting—dramatically cutting prices in hopes of

Sam Walton's 10 Commandments

1. Commit to your business.
2. Share your profits with your associates and treat them like your partners.
3. Energize your colleagues.
4. Communicate everything you possibly can to your partners.
5. Appreciate everything your associates do for the business.
6. Celebrate your success.
7. Listen to everyone in your company.
8. Exceed your customers' expectations.
9. Control your expenses better than your competition.
10. Blaze your own path.

undercutting his competition and making up the difference in price through a higher volume of sales. The practice wasn't exactly new, but at the time, discount stores tended to be small, to be located in cities, and to only discount specialty items. Walton's idea was to build big stores that discounted everything they stocked and to place them in small towns.

Initially, he approached the company that franchised Ben Franklin stores with his idea. But the company directors loudly refused to back him when Walton explained that they would have to cut their standard wholesale margin in half to accommodate the low prices he intended to charge. So Walton decided to take the gamble himself. Mortgaging his home and borrowing to the hilt, he opened his first Wal-Mart (short for Walton Mart) in 1962 in Rogers, Arkansas—not far from Bentonville.

Walton wasn't alone in his venture into discounting. That same year, S.S. Kresge launched Kmart and Woolworth's started Woolco, both of which could have easily crushed Wal-Mart. But Walton was too far off the beaten path to attract the attention of these retail giants.

Thrilled that big-city discounting had come to small-town America, rural customers flocked to Walton's stores, and sales soared. This early success provided funding for further expansion, and by 1969, there were 18 Wal-Marts throughout Arkansas and Missouri. Until that time, Walton had funded expansion from profits and borrowing, but in 1970, he decided to take the company public. The initial offering generated nearly $5 million, and although Walton and his family retained 61 percent ownership of the stock, the proceeds allowed him to pay off the company's debts and move forward with his ambitious expansion plans.

In the first year after going public, Wal-Mart added six stores, followed by 13 stores in each of the next two years, then 14, then 26. By the end of 1980, Walton had 276 stores and would soon be opening stores at the rate of about 100 per year. In 1983, Walton launched the first of his Sam's Wholesale Clubs, which were aimed at small-business owners and others who wished to buy merchandise in bulk. Once again, Walton had struck gold. In 1985, *Forbes* magazine pronounced him the richest man in America, with an estimated worth of $2.8 billion. By 1987, Wal-Mart had become the third-largest retailer in the United States, trailing only Sears and Kmart. His retail success in the bag, Walton announced in 1988 that he was handing over the duties of CEO to Wal-Mart executive David Glass but said he would continue to serve as chairman of the company.

Two years later, Walton was diagnosed with an aggressive strain of bone cancer. But even this dire pronouncement could not dampen his competitive spirit. At Wal-Mart's annual meeting in June 1990, Walton predicted that the company's revenue would quintuple to $125 billion within the next decade. Over the next two years, Wal-Mart soared past Kmart and Sears to become the nation's largest retailer.

On March 17, 1992, President George Bush presented Walton with the Medal of Freedom for his entrepreneurial spirit and his concern for his employees and community. It would be his last, greatest achievement. A few days later, Walton checked into the University of Arkansas Hospital and passed away on April 5, 1992, six days after his 74th birthday. At the time of his death, he had a net worth of nearly $25 billion.

Sam Walton didn't invent retailing, just like Henry Ford didn't invent the automobile. But just as Ford's assembly line revolutionized American

What Do The Pentagon And Wal-Mart Have In Common?

An essential ingredient in Wal-Mart's success was its rapid adoption of the latest technology. Almost from the beginning, Sam Walton recognized that the key to keeping costs down and profits up was tight inventory control—ordering just the right items in just the right amounts. Too much inventory meant undue expense; too little meant lost sales. Finding a way to keep track of what was selling, what was in the stores, what was on order and what was on backorder became one of Walton's obsessions. As a result, Wal-Mart was one of the first major retail chains to install electronic scanners at cash registers linked to a central inventory-control computer. Today, Wal-Mart's computer database is second only to the Pentagon's in capacity.

industry, Walton's dogged pursuit of discounting revolutionized America's service economy. Walton didn't merely alter the way America shopped—he changed the philosophy of the American retail business establishment, instigating the shift of power from manufacturer to consumer that has become prevalent in industry after industry. His pioneering concepts paved the way for a new breed of "category killer" retailer—the Home Depots, Barnes & Nobles and Blockbusters of the world—and forever changed the face of retailing.

Thomas Watson Jr.

*"**F**ear of failure was the most powerful force in my life."*

—Thomas Watson Jr.

Chairman of IBM Corp.
Founded: 1924

MAINFRAME MOGUL

When Thomas Watson Jr. assumed control of IBM from his father, he had some pretty big shoes to fill. After all, the senior Watson had built IBM from an obscure time-clock maker and punch-card tabulator company into a corporate titan. Dogged by self-doubt, the would-be successor to the IBM throne once wailed to his mother, "I can't do it. I can't go to work for IBM." Yet Watson not only succeeded his father, he eventually surpassed him. He boldly carried IBM—and the world—into the computer age, and in the process, created a company whose awesome sales and service savvy and dark-suit culture stood for everything good…and bad…about corporate America.

Thomas Watson Jr. was born in 1914, the same year his father was appointed manager of Computing-Tabulating-Recording Co. (CTR). In 1924, Watson Sr. became CEO and renamed the company International Business Machines (IBM). Because of his father's position, Thomas Jr. had a very privileged upbringing, attending private schools, traveling the world and enjoying the benefits of considerable wealth. But this would prove to be more of a handicap than an advantage for the troubled young man.

Watson Sr. was curt and unforgiving and had unreasonably high expectations for his son—expectations Watson Jr. often felt he could never live up to. Indeed, early on it seemed clear that he might not be the equal of his father, nor a competent successor. A perpetually failing student, "Terrible Tom," as his classmates and instructors called him, vented his frustration by pulling pranks and tangling with authority. It took him six years and three schools to get through high school, and college wasn't much better. At Brown University, he spent most of his time fooling around and only graduated through the intervention of a sympathetic dean.

After college, Watson enrolled in IBM sales school but didn't fare much better. "My three years as a salesman were a time of sickening self-doubt," he writes in his autobiography, *Father, Son & Co.: My Life at IBM and Beyond*. And Watson had good reason to feel that way. He could never be sure what he'd accomplished on his own and what had been arranged to curry favor with his father, as when the head of his sales-training class fixed it so he'd be elected its president. "Unfortunately for me," Watson recalls, "I lacked the force of character to say 'I won't have this.' "

But World War II would change that. As aide and pilot for Major General Follett Bradley, the Army Air Forces' inspector general, Watson flew throughout Asia, Africa and the Pacific, displaying raw nerve, visionary foresight and shrewd planning skills. As a result of his experiences, he returned from the war confident and thinking for the first time that he might be capable of running IBM.

His father, however, was not as confident. Watson Jr. had been so unimpressive before the war that it was hard for the senior Watson to accept that he had changed. Yet not only had he changed, but he had also returned to IBM with a new perspective. He quickly realized that IBM's future lay in computers, not in outdated technology like tabulators, which were the company's stock and trade. Many people, his father included, refused to believe that the company's core products would soon become obsolete.

Nevertheless, when Watson became president of IBM in 1952, he followed his vision, recruiting electronics experts and luminaries, such as computer pioneer John von Neumann, who were responsible for creating IBM's first successful computers, the 700 series and the 650 series. By 1963, IBM had grabbed an 8-to-1 lead in revenue over Sperry Rand,

Aviation Pioneer?

Not only did Thomas Watson Jr. spark a computer revolution, but he also broke new ground in aviation. While serving in the Army Air Forces during World War II, Watson trailblazed the Alaska-Siberia ferry route, which the United States used to ship planes to the Soviet Union.

Thomas Watson Jr.

its closest competitor and maker of Univac—the first large commercial computer.

With IBM clearly on top, Watson took the biggest gamble of his career. He proposed spending more than $5 billion to develop a new line of computers that would make the company's existing machines obsolete. His vision was to replace specialized units with a family of compatible computers named System/360 that could fill every data-processing need and would allow customers to start with small computers and move up as their needs increased, without having to discard their existing software.

It was a bold strategy that nearly failed when software problems created delivery delays. In a "hail Mary" play, Watson assigned 2,000 engineers to work on solving the software problems. Although the first machines were slow, they became better as more were built. By 1966, the long-delayed software programs were delivered, and System/360, which would ultimately revolutionize the computer industry, proved to be a phenomenal success. IBM's installed base of computers skyrocketed from 11,000 in 1964 to 35,000 in 1970, and its revenues more than doubled to $7.5 billion.

In 1971, years of overexertion and stress caught up with Watson, and he suffered a near-fatal heart attack. While recuperating, he decided to retire. "I wanted to live more than I wanted to run IBM," he explains in *Father, Son & Co.* "It was a choice my father never would have made, but I think he would have respected it." After his retirement, Watson pursued his interests in sailing and flying and even served as ambassador to the USSR under President Jimmy Carter. In December 1993, the man *Fortune* magazine praised as "the greatest capitalist who ever lived," died of complications following a stroke.

Under Thomas Watson Jr., IBM so thoroughly dominated the computer industry that it left even powerful competitors such as Sperry Rand flailing in its wake. And although newcomers like Compaq and Microsoft nearly brought the company to its knees in the 1980s, as the new millennium begins, the colossus that Watson inherited and reinvigorated in the 1950s and 1960s stands strong as the sixth-largest company in the United States.

Leslie Wexner

Founder of
The Limited Inc.
Founded: 1963

"*You have to understand that no one has to buy anything…everybody has enough clothing in their closets to last them 100 years. So the issue is to create a demand to stimulate people to buy.*"

—Leslie Wexner

TURNING "RAGS" INTO RICHES

He knows Victoria's Secret. Pushed the limits with The Limited. Rode the Express to fashion fame. A true pioneer of specialty clothing stores, the dozens of retail concepts Leslie Wexner has whipped up over the past 40 years have not only made him a very wealthy man but also helped create a new marketing niche that blazed the path for such brand-oriented ventures as Talbot's, The Gap, J Crew and countless others.

Wexner seemed to be destined for a career in the "rag trade." After emigrating from Russia, Wexner's parents worked in a variety of garment-industry positions before opening their own women's clothing store in Columbus, Ohio, in 1951. They named the store Leslie's after their son.

Initially, Wexner didn't aspire to a career in retailing. One of his earliest ambitions was to become an architect. Yet as he grew older, at least partly as a result of pressure from his father, Wexner became increasingly interested in running his own business. After graduating from The Ohio State University with a degree in business administration, he began helping his parents run the family store. At the time, Leslie's was a moderately successful operation that sold all types of women's clothing. But Wexner believed the store could be more profitable if it specialized only in sportswear. "Although I didn't understand fashion, I understood that [sportswear] was what all my female friends wore," Wexner explains. "[Sportswear] was our most profitable line, and my feeling was that if you made money in chocolate ice cream, why sell other flavors?"

After several unsuccessful attempts to talk his father into stocking just sportswear, Wexner decided to strike out on his own. With a $5,000 loan from his aunt, he opened his own shop in

Columbus in 1963, dubbing it "The Limited" because he limited his stock to women's sportswear. Determined to make his new venture a success, Wexner followed a grueling work schedule—often arriving at the store at 7 a.m. and leaving after midnight.

It wasn't long before Wexner's hard work and unique retailing strategy began to pay off. In its first year, The Limited's sales topped $160,000, and by the end of the second year, Wexner had opened two more stores. In 1965, Milton Petrie, chairman of a large chain of women's specialty stores, was so impressed with Wexner's operation that he offered to buy 49.5 percent of the operation. But Wexner wanted to run his own business, and promptly turned Petrie down. Still, Wexner credits Petrie with helping him overcome his "shopkeeper's mentality" and to think like an entrepreneur in terms of building a multistore chain.

Throughout the 1960s, The Limited continued to grow. Looking to extend his operations beyond Ohio, Wexner took The Limited public in 1969 to raise money for further expansion. Around that time, he struck up a friendship with Alfred A. Taubman, a real-estate developer who specialized in malls, who would prove to be a key element in Wexner's success. Taubman taught Wexner the importance of attractive store design and finding the right locations for his stores. Thanks to Taubman's help and advice, by the 1980s, Wexner's stores were recognized as the industry leader in store presentation.

Victoria's Real Secret

Despite the perception of aristocratic roots and Victorian-era imagery, Victoria's Secret is as American as apple pie. Originally a small, five-store chain in San Francisco, there was little difference between Victoria's Secret and other lingerie retailers when Leslie Wexner took it over in 1982. But, as he had done with The Limited and The Limited Express, Wexner quickly went to work making over the stores to make them unique. By decorating them with Victorian furnishings and sensuously displaying silk and lace lingerie on padded hangings, Wexner helped make the chain synonymous with genteel sexiness.

As times and tastes changed, Wexner's ability to keep abreast of and meet the evolving needs of his customers enabled him to stay one step ahead of the competition. In the 1980s, many of the teenage baby boomers whose penchant for sportswear had inspired Wexner's first stores had begun climbing the corporate ladder. They still wanted comfortable clothes at reasonable prices, but they also wanted clothes of higher quality and of a style that reflected their new level of sophistication. To meet this new demand, Wexner signed on several top designers to produce exclusive collections for his company.

Realizing the importance of bringing these designs to market as quickly as possible, Wexner purchased Mast Industries to produce his fashion line and instituted a computerized distribution network that enabled The Limited to manufacture its own garments and have them on the racks within a matter of weeks. As a result, The Limited could ship new designs to its stores every few weeks rather than on a seasonal basis, as was then the industry standard.

With The Limited's soaring success, Wexner turned his attention to other avenues of retailing. In 1982, he purchased and expanded both the Lane Bryant and Victoria's Secret chains; started a chain of stores in 1983 called Express and aimed at younger buyers; took over the near-bankrupt 796-store Lerner chain and the Henry Bendel stores in 1985; opened Bath & Body Works in 1985 to compete with Anita Roddick's The Body Shop; launched The Limited Too to sell children's clothes and the menswear chain Structure in 1987; and purchased Ambercrombie & Fitch in 1988.

At the end of the 1980s, Wexner seemed virtually unstoppable. But there were storm clouds gathering. The recessionary 1990s caused sales to flatten. Even worse, while his core businesses began to deteriorate, Wexner became distracted by outside pursuits ranging from real estate to interior design. Stock prices plummeted, and investors placed the blame firmly as Wexner's feet.

Realizing that he had overextended himself, Wexner began spinning off noncore ventures to concentrate on women's apparel, and he embarked on a series of stock buybacks in order to increase its value. By 1999, these strategies began to bear fruit. In June of that year, The Limited Inc. was named one of the fastest-growing firms in Ohio by *The Plain Dealer* newspaper, and by August, stock prices had risen by 11 percent.

Whether Wexner and The Limited can return to their former glory remains to be seen. But the fact remains—Wexner has greatly influenced the fashion industry and shown the corporate world how success can be obtained by paying attention to market factors and by understanding what drives buyers to purchase products. One of the first to recognize the appeal of smart-looking sportswear, Leslie Wexner helped create the stylish, affordable casual clothing that now dominates the fashion market.

Oprah Winfrey

Founder of
Harpo Productions Inc.
Founded: 1986

"I don't think of myself as a poor, deprived ghetto girl who made good. I think of myself as somebody who from an early age knew she was responsible for herself—and I had to make good."

—Oprah Winfrey

The Queen
Of Talk

Oprah Winfrey is living proof that the American dream is alive and well. The illegitimate daughter of a Mississippi sharecropper, she overcame poverty, parental neglect, sexual abuse and racism to become one of the richest and most powerful women in the entertainment industry. Through sheer force of her personality and by simply being herself, she reinvented the talk show and still reigns as the undisputed champ of daytime television.

Winfrey was born in 1954 on a farm in Kosciusko, Mississippi. Her unmarried parents drifted apart and moved elsewhere shortly after her birth, leaving her in the care of her maternal grandmother, a harsh but loving disciplinarian whom Winfrey credits with fostering her outgoing personality and precociousness. Under her grandmother's tutelage, she learned to read by the age of 2, and by the time she was 3, her speaking talents had already begun to emerge. She was often invited to recite poetry at social clubs and church teas, where they referred to her as "the little speaker."

At age 6, Winfrey moved to Milwaukee, Wisconsin, to live with her mother, who was working as a domestic. Adjusting to life in the urban ghetto after enjoying the peace of a Mississippi farm proved to be a difficult challenge for Winfrey. To make matters worse, her mother was so preoccupied with her own problems that she had little time for Winfrey. This lack of parental supervision left her vulnerable, and beginning when she was 9 and continuing for several years thereafter, Winfrey was sexually abused by several different men, including a teenage cousin and her mother's boyfriend. (Years later, during a show she was doing on incest, Winfrey burst into tears and shared with her audience the story of her ordeal.)

Confused, ashamed, guilt-ridden and afraid to tell anyone what was being done to her, Winfrey began to act out. Her increasing belligerence and delinquency proved too much for her mother to handle. She tried to put Winfrey in a detention center, but the institution didn't have enough beds, so instead she sent her to live with her father in Nashville, Tennessee. A strict disciplinarian, Winfrey's father changed the course of her life. "My father turned my life around by insisting that I be more than I was and by believing I could be more," Winfrey told *Good Housekeeping* magazine. "His love of learning showed me the way."

Under her father's guidance, Winfrey became an honor student and rediscovered her flair for public speaking, emerging as a standout orator. Her speaking skills earned her a scholarship to Tennessee State University, where she majored in speech and drama. In 1973, while only a sophomore, the 19-year-old Winfrey was offered a job as a news co-anchor at Nashville's CBS affiliate, WTVF-TV, and became not only Nashville's first female co-anchor but the first black co-anchor as well.

Inspired by her success at WTVF-TV, Oprah left college during her senior year to accept a position in Baltimore with WJZ-TV as co-anchor of the evening news. But she soon found that hard news wasn't truly her forte. Deeply empathetic, she had difficulty distancing herself from her work, often having to fight back tears while reporting stories that touched her. Unable to get past this emotional connection to her subjects, she was fired.

Fortunately, a new manager at the station saw a way to make a virtue of Winfrey's reporting shortcomings. Phil Donahue's nationally syndicated talk show had won a large following in Baltimore, and the manager

Comic Relief

To polish her instinctive flair for entertainment and improve her spontaneity, Oprah Winfrey once studied improvisation with Chicago's Second City comedy troupe, whose alums include such famous comedians as Dan Aykroyd, John Belushi and John Candy.

A Really Bad Hair Day

While Oprah Winfrey was co-anchoring the evening news in Baltimore, an assistant news director decided that her hair was "too thick" and sent her to an expensive New York City salon for a makeover—with disastrous results. A botched permanent left her completely but temporarily bald, and she was forced to cover her scalp with a scarf. Although she cried "constantly," she found in the ordeal an opportunity for self-discovery, admitting in a Ms. magazine interview, "You learn a lot about yourself when you're bald."

wanted to tap the market with a local version. In 1977, "People Are Talking" aired with Winfrey as co-host. Oprah had found her niche. Her uncommon ability to connect intellectually and emotionally with a wide variety of topics made the show an instant success. "I came off the air," she says of her first show, "and said to myself, 'This is what I should be doing. It's like breathing.' "

"People Are Talking" rocketed up the ratings chart, eventually becoming the top show of its genre in the Baltimore market. Winfrey's success attracted the attention of Chicago-based WLS-TV, which offered her a chance to anchor the station's floundering talk show "AM Chicago." Winfrey's earthy, down-home, comfortable style captivated audiences, and the show became an instant smash hit. It bested even hometown-boy Phil Donahue in the ratings and was quickly syndicated in 120 cities.

But Winfrey's biggest break came in 1985, when producer Quincy Jones offered her a role in the screen adaptation of Alice Walker's *The Color Purple*. Winfrey's acting debut garnered rave reviews, won her nominations for both a Golden Globe and an Academy Award, and catapulted her to national stardom. Riding this wave of publicity, "The Oprah Winfrey Show" made its national debut in 1986, and within five months became the third-highest rated show in syndication and the No. 1 talk show, reaching upwards of 10 million people daily in 192 cities.

To further capitalize on her success, in 1986, Oprah formed

Harpo ("Oprah" spelled backward) Productions Inc. In 1988, she purchased a state-of-the-art production studio in Chicago and took over ownership and production of "The Oprah Winfrey Show." The move made Winfrey only the third woman in history—behind Mary Pickford and Lucille Ball—to own and produce her own show as well as the first African-American, male or female, to own her own entertainment production company.

During the 1990s, the airwaves became flooded with talk shows, but Winfrey's ratings continued to soar despite the increased competition. Part of the reason for her success is that she has avoided the tabloid "nuts and sluts" approach many of her competitors adopted. Choosing to take the high road, she empathized with people in trouble and emphasized solutions to the problems her show revealed, instead of wallowing in the mire of sensationalism. Even more so, she went beyond being merely a talk-show host to become a shaper of American culture. The books she likes invariably become bestsellers. The records of musicians she invites on her show shoot up the charts. And diets concocted by her personal cook have influenced the eating habits of millions.

But Oprah isn't about to stop there. In January 2000, she cut a deal with *Hearst* Magazines (the world's largest publisher of monthly titles) to publish *O, The Oprah Magazine*. Launched in April 2000, the monthly magazine focuses on beauty and fashion, health and fitness, spirituality and other topics Oprah regularly explores on her show. And with more than 22 million weekly viewers who can't seem to get enough of this talk show diva, *O* seems destined to be a publishing phenomenon.

As the 21st century opens, it would appear that the sky's the limit for Oprah. Her $415 million talk empire has made her the wealthiest woman in show business and one of the most powerful figures in the television industry. Yet, her recipe for success is simple: "Follow your instincts," she says in a *Ladies Home Journal* magazine article. "That's where true wisdom manifests itself."

INDEX

M

Madam C.J. Walker
  Manufacturing Co., 411, 414
Maidenform, 49, 51-53
Marcus, Bernie, 61-65
Marriott, J. Willard, 291-295
Marriott International Inc.,
  291, 295
Mary Kay Cosmetics, 15-20,
  414
Mattel, 171-175
Mayer, Louis B., 297, 299-301
McDonald's, 249, 251-253
McGowan, William, 303-307
MCI Communications,
  303-307
Metro-Goldwyn-Mayer
  MGM), 297-301
Microsoft, 117, 135, 137-139,
  142, 145-146, 223, 334, 427
Monaghan, Tom, 309-313
Moore, Gordon, 159-164
Morita, Akio, 315-319
Motown Records, 153, 154,
  155-157, 382

N

Netscape Communications, 1,
  4-7, 118
Nidetch, Jean, 321-325
Nike, 243, 244, 245-247
Noyce, Robert, 160-162

O

Ogilvy, David, 327-331
Ogilvy & Mather, 327, 329-331
Omidyar, Pierre, 333-337

P

Packard, David, 201-206

Perot, Ross, 339-343
Perot Systems Corp., 339,
  341-342
Playboy Enterprises, 183-188
Popeil, Ron, 345-350

R

RCA (Radio Corp. of America),
  363, 364, 365-367, 401
Riggio, Leonard, 351-355
Robbins, Irvine, 27-32
Roddick, Anita, 357-361, 433
Ronco Inventions LLC, 345,
  347, 348-350
Rosenthal, Ida, 49-51, 53
Rosenthal, William, 49-51
Rush Communications,
  381-385

S

Sarnoff, David, 363-367
Schultz, Howard, 369-373
Schwab, Charles, 375-379
Seagram (Joseph E.) & Sons,
  73, 76-78
Simmons, Russell, 381-385
Smith, Fred, 387-391
Sony, 315-319
Starbucks, 369-373
Stewart, Martha, 393-397

T

Time, 285-289
Toys "R" Us, 267-271
Turner, Ted, 399-403
Turner Broadcasting System,
  399, 401-403

V

Vernon, Lillian, 405-409
Virgin Group, 67-72, 385

ABOUT ENTREPRENEUR

Entrepreneur Media Inc., founded in 1973, is the nation's leading authority on small and entrepreneurial businesses. Anchored by *Entrepreneur* magazine, which is read by more than 2 million people monthly, Entrepreneur Media boasts a stable of magazines, including *Entrepreneur's Business Start-ups*, *Entrepreneur International*, *Entrepreneur's Be Your Own Boss*, *Entrepreneur's Home Office* e-zine, and *Entrepreneur Mexico*.

But Entrepreneur Media is more than just magazines. Entrepreneur.com is the world's largest Web site devoted to small business and features smallbizsearch.com, a search engine targeting small-business topics. Entrepreneur Media also sponsors a series of small-business expos across the country and launched a nationwide seminar series in 2000.

Entrepreneur Press, started in 1998, publishes books to inspire and inform readers. For information about a customized version of this book, contact Christie Barnes Stafford at (949) 261-2325 or e-mail her at cstafford@entrepreneurmag.com.

About the Author

Thaddeus Wawro is an award-winning advertising copywriter, direct marketing consultant and author. He lives in Los Angeles, California.

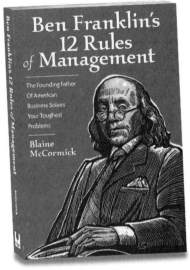

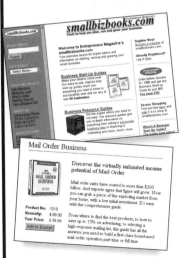

get in the KNOW

Plus a fREE ISSUE + SAVE 72%

Please enter my subscription to BUSINESS START-UPS for one year. I will receive 12 issues for only $9.99. That's a savings of 72% off the newsstand price. <u>The free issue is mine to keep, even if I choose not to subscribe.</u>

Name ☐ Mr. ☐ Mrs. _____
(please print)

Address _____

City_____ State _____ Zip_____

[ ] bILL me   [ ] pAymeNt encLOseD

Guaranteed. Or your money back. Every subscription to Business Start-Ups comes with a 100% satisfaction guarantee: your money back whenever you like, for whatever reason, on all unmailed issues! Offer good in U.S. and possessions only. Please allow 4–6 weeks for mailing of first issue. Canadian and foreign: $34.97. U.S. funds only.

Mail this coupon to: 5HBK2
B.S.U., P.O. Box 50368, Boulder, CO 80321-0368

Entrepreneur's **Business Start-Ups** — 5 simple ways to make over your Web site..

the Truth

VENTURE CAPITAL You can get it. We show you how!

YOUNG MILLIONAIRES DISH THE DIRT What's it really like to run your own business?

DIARY OF A START-UP

MILLION DOLLAR secrets

Exercise your right to make it BIG Get into the small business authority now at 80% off the newsstand price

YES! Start my 1 year subscription & bill me for just $9.99. I get a full year of ENTREPRENEUR & save 80% off the newsstand rate. If I choose not to subscribe, the free issue is mine to keep.

Name ☐ Mr. ☐ Mrs._____
(please print)

Address _____

City_____ State _____ Zip _____

[ ] bILL me   [ ] pAymeNt encLOseD

Guaranteed. Or your money back. Every subscription to Entrepreneur comes with a 100% satisfaction guarantee: your money back whenever you like, for whatever reason, on all unmailed issues! Offer good in U.S. and possessions only. Please allow 4–6 weeks for mailing of first issue. Canadian & foreign: $39.97. U.S. funds only.

Mail this coupon to: 5G9J9
Entrepreneur MAGAZINE P.O. Box 50368, Boulder, CO 80321-0368

50 Top New Franchises — NEWSSTAND ONLY! SPECIAL START-UP GUIDE!

Entrepreneur THE SMALL BUSINESS AUTHORITY

Cash In ON THE NET
(No, It's Not Too Late)

How Your Dot.Com ... Partner With The Big Boys

plus FREE issue!